Writing Global Trade Governance

Writing Global Trade Governance operationalizes a key post-structuralist methodology in order to expand understanding on the institution at the heart of the global political economy. Despite the World Trade Organization's (WTO) centrality and the growing popularity of methods utilizing discourse theory, no other text has yet demonstrated how these two topics can be productively combined. The book seeks to move beyond existing literatures that assume the WTO to be a structure, institution or normative framework, in order to enquire into the discursive processes of identity formation that make the WTO both possible and contested.

The book criticizes conventional approaches that treat critical civil society as distinct to the WTO, arguing instead that it is only through including such social practices within the field of relations making that we can properly understand what makes the WTO work. This book presents an empirical analysis of the discursive character of the present-day WTO (including its formation and operation) and then moves on to evaluate how it is subject to change within a broader social context. The final stage of the book seeks to discuss the impact of the findings on future research, both on the WTO and other institutions.

This work is a significant intervention in the literature on the World Trade Organization and the politics of global trade and social movements, and will be of great interest to students and scholars of global governance, discourse theory and international organizations.

Michael Strange is a senior lecturer in the Department of Global Political Studies, Malmö University, Sweden.

Interventions

Edited by:
Jenny Edkins, *Aberystwyth University* and Nick Vaughan-Williams, *University of Warwick*

As Michel Foucault has famously stated, "knowledge is not made for understanding; it is made for cutting." In this spirit the Edkins–Vaughan-Williams Interventions series solicits cutting edge, critical works that challenge mainstream understandings in international relations. It is the best place to contribute post disciplinary works that think rather than merely recognize and affirm the world recycled in IR's traditional geopolitical imaginary.

> Michael J. Shapiro, University of Hawai'i at Mãnoa, USA

The series aims to advance understanding of the key areas in which scholars working within broad critical poststructural and postcolonial traditions have chosen to make their interventions, and to present innovative analyses of important topics.

Titles in the series engage with critical thinkers in philosophy, sociology, politics and other disciplines and provide situated historical, empirical and textual studies in international politics.

Writing Global Trade Governance

Michael Strange

Routledge
Taylor & Francis Group

LONDON AND NEW YORK

First published 2014
by Routledge
2 Park Square, Milton Park, Abingdon, Oxon OX14 4RN

Simultaneously published in the USA and Canada
by Routledge
711 Third Avenue, New York, NY 10017

Routledge is an imprint of the Taylor & Francis Group, an informa business

British Library Cataloguing in Publication Data
A catalogue record for this book is available from the British Library

Library of Congress Cataloging in Publication Data
Strange, Michael.
  Writing global trade governance / Michael Strange. – 1 Edition.
    p. cm. – (Interventions)
  Includes bibliographical references and index.
  1. World Trade Organization. 2. International cooperation.
3. International organizations. I. Title.
  JZ1310.S77 2013
  382'.92–dc23
            2013006157

ISBN: 978-0-415-68507-8 (hbk)
ISBN: 978-0-203-79723-5 (ebk)

Typeset in Times New Roman
by Taylor & Francis Books

MIX
Paper from
responsible sources
FSC
www.fsc.org   FSC® C013604

Printed and bound in Great Britain by
CPI Group (UK) Ltd, Croydon, CR0 4YY

To Toby, Ravnhild and Samuel.

Contents

Illustrations

Acknowledgements

This book has one author stated on the cover but owes its existence to a collective who have helped steer it to completion. Academic writing is, thankfully, far from a solitary process, as it depends so much on input from others. I 'grew up' as a graduate student within the dimly lit corridors of the Department of Government at Essex University, where both discourse theory and non-discourse theory (or 'Non-Disco theory' as those unaffiliated liked to call it) friends and colleagues contributed greatly. In particular, I owe a special debt of thanks to Aletta Norval and Hugh Ward (my co-supervisors), David Howarth, Albert Weale and Vicki Squire. In life beyond Essex, the project has received help from conversations with many excellent scholars, including Vivien Schmidt (with whom I've been able to use the research in teaching PhD students), Ian Manners, Lene Hansen, Len Seabrooke, Jan Aart Scholte, Mark Blyth, Rob Walker, and everyone within the vibrant research communities at Roskilde and Malmö.

Colleagues whose names I missed but provided insightful and rigorous critique at conferences, workshops and guest talks – including at MMU, BISA, ISA, as well as the North-South Institute in Ottawa – have provided a continual drive as the project moved from PhD research into a later post-doc and then, now, its current form. Each of these stages has also largely only been possible due to the generosity of research funding from both the Department of Government at Essex and the Danish Social Science Research Council.

Much of the material presented in this book has required the assistance of numerous activists and campaigners from groups based all over the world, as well as members of the World Trade Organization Secretariat, international trade legal firms and the International Centre for Trade and Sustainable Development, and to them I am especially thankful, since without giving me access to meetings as well as their time for often extremely long interviews, I could not have acquired such data.

I am enormously grateful to the editors of Interventions – Nick Vaughan-Williams and Jenny Edkins – for encouraging me to write for what is one of the best book series in International Relations today. The two anonymous reviewers provided excellent feedback and gave me belief in the value of this project. At Routledge, Nicola Parkin, Pete Harris, Dominic Corti and Alison Neale have helped to answer my every query, however minor, and kept me calm whenever hitting trouble.

On a personal note, this book has taken longer than expected. The last years have seen many changes. Some have been fantastically welcome – my two agents of chaos: Toby and Ravnhild; achieving tenure at Malmö. Others have been less so, but throughout my partner Signe has, as always, kept me sane.

Michael Strange
Copenhagen
February 2013

Abbreviations

ATTAC	Association for the Taxation of Financial Transaction for the Aid of Citizens
AUT NZ	Association of University Teachers, New Zealand
AUT UK	Association of University Teachers, United Kingdom
CAFOD	Catholic Agency for Overseas Development
CCPA	Canadian Centre for Policy Alternatives
CEO	Corporate Europe Observatory
CG-18	Consultative Group of Eighteen
CIIR	Catholic Institute for International Relations
CIN	Consumer Information Network
CofC	Council of Canadians
CoTD	GATT Committee on Trade and Development
CSI	US Coalition of Services Industries
CUSFTA	Canadian-United States Free Trade Agreement
DDA	Doha Development Agenda
DFID	Department for International Development (UK)
DSB	WTO Dispute Settlement Body
DSU	WTO Dispute Settlement Understanding
ECOSOC	United Nations Economic and Social Council
EDM	Early Day Motion (UK Parliament)
EECOD	European Ecumenical Organization for Development
EI	Education International
ESF	European Services Forum
EU	European Union
EUROSTEP	European Solidarity Towards Equal Participation of People
FAT	Frente Auténtico del Trabajo
FoE	Friends of the Earth
FoEE	Friends of the Earth Europe
FoEI	Friends of the Earth International
FoE UK	Friends of the Earth, United Kingdom
G7	Group of 7
G8	Group of 8

G20	Group of 20
G21	Group of 21
G77	Group of 77
G90	Group of 90
GATS	General Agreement on Trade in Services
GATS 2000	Negotiations starting in 2000 to expand the GATS
GATT 1947	General Agreement on Tariffs and Trade established 1947 to be part of the ITO
GATT 1994	General Agreement on Tariffs and Trade revised in 1994 to be part of the WTO
GPE	Global Political Economy
GSP	General System of Preferences
ICDA	International Coalition for Development Action
ICFTU	International Confederation of Free Trade Unions
ICITO	Interim Commission for the International Trade Organization
ICTSD	International Centre for Trade and Sustainable Development
IFG	International Forum on Globalization
IGTN	International Gender and Trade Network
ILO	International Labour Organization
IMF	International Monetary Fund
INGOs	international non-governmental organizations
IOs	international organizations
IPC	Integrated Program for Commodities (part of the NIEO)
IPE	International Political Economy
ITO	International Trade Organization
JITAP	Joint Integrated Technical Assistance Programme
KPSU	Korean Federation of Transportation, Public and Social Services Workers' Unions
LOTIS	UK Liberalisation of Trade in Services Committee
MAI	Multilateral Agreement on Investment
MEP	Member of European Parliament
MFN	Most-Favoured Nation principle
MTN	Multilateral Trade Negotiation, the GATT Tokyo Round, 1974–79
MTO	Multilateral Trade Organization
NAFTA	North American Free Trade Agreement
NDP	New Democratic Party, Canada
NGO	non-governmental organization
NIEO	New International Economic Order
NUS	National Union of Students, UK
OECD	Organisation of Economic Co-operation and Development
OPEC	Organization of the Petroleum Exporting Countries
OTC	Organization for Trade Cooperation
OWINFS	Our World Is Not For Sale network
P&P	People and Planet

PSI	Public Services International
RTAA	US Reciprocal Trade Agreements Act 1934
S2B	Seattle to Brussels network
SAMWU	South African Municipal Workers Union
StC	Save the Children
TJM	Trade Justice Movement
TMB	Textiles Monitoring Body
TNC	WTO Trade Negotiations Committee
TNC	transnational corporation
TNI	Transnational Institute
TPRB	WTO Trade Policy Review Body
TRIMS	Trade-Related Investment Measures
TRIPS	Trade-Related Aspects of Intellectual Property Rights
TWN	Third World Network
TWNA	Third World Network Africa
UK	United Kingdom
UKTN	United Kingdom Trade Network
UN	United Nations
UNCTAD	UN Conference on Trade and Development
US(A)	United States (of America)
USBIC	US Business and Industrial Council
USTR	US Trade Representative
WDM	World Development Movement
WIDE	Women in Development Europe
WTO	World Trade Organization
WWF	World Wide Fund for Nature

1 Introduction

Embedding the World Trade Organization

Headquartered in Geneva, the World Trade Organization (WTO) has become one of the most high-profile international organizations in existence today, equipped with not just a broad array of legislative agreements but also its own quasi-court system able to give those rules teeth. It is a landmark achievement in the history of not only global economic governance but also inter-governmental negotiations. The continually expanding notion of what is 'trade' has seen its jurisdiction expand considerably with huge social significance at all levels. Nothing else like it exists. Appropriately enough, the WTO has attracted substantial attention – both critical and supportive – from national politicians, the media, various publics and academia. With only a few years away from the organization's twentieth anniversary, in 2015, the field of WTO studies has grown exponentially.

There is significant disagreement over how to understand the WTO in both academia and wider public debates. For some, the WTO is an apolitical legalistic means to escape or at least lessen the impact of old school state-to-state trade politics. For others, however, the WTO is an imperialistic project led by realpolitik concerns that sweep unheedingly over the needs of individual societies. Both poles of this debate suffer, as this book argues, from a basic fallacy: that is, they treat the WTO as abstract from the historical or social environment in which it operates. This is because at each end of this spectrum, the WTO institution is rarefied as alien to the very social interactions through which it is made possible and continues to change. Too little attention is given to how the WTO is itself imbued with power relations linking multiple political identities within the production of contemporary global trade governance. The task undertaken here is to analyse the WTO as embedded within a particular context, constituted via a series of specific social relations and practices. The analysis works to unpick those constitutive social practices, looking under the bonnet, and the primary tool utilized in this endeavour is a discourse theoretical methodology developed from the work of Ernesto Laclau and Chantal Mouffe (2001).

The WTO cannot be limited to a formal political structure or any fixed set of actors, but consists of a much more complex and diffuse process. A discursive approach is shown to advance social science on the WTO by incorporating both ideational and material explanations. Demonstrated in the book, the salience and value of this perspective can be evidenced within new empirical research into the formation, operation and transformation of the WTO in which the category of agency and its political arena – including its governance domain – is subject to change. Such an approach is critical within WTO studies, where otherwise key categories like 'Member states' and the institution of the WTO are taken as given facts without examining their discursive character. The task of the book is then to unpick this institution and show its discursive character within a series of social practices stretching far beyond any institutional walls. In particular, interviews and observation with civil society activists demonstrate how new political identities continue to emerge as part of the political arena in which the WTO is constituted.

This book can be read as both a critical intervention within WTO studies, but also as part of the family of new approaches to international (or global) political economy (IPE) and international organizations studies that re-embed the technocratic architecture of global governance within particular social contexts (e.g. Watson 2005; Gammon 2008; Hobson and Seabrooke 2007; Antoniades 2010). In so doing, the point is better to understand how that architecture comes to exist, be maintained and is subject to change. Wider literature along this vein has focused on new actors and changed concepts of the political arena.

The first section of this introductory chapter reviews current studies on the WTO. Within this literature, there is contestation over two key questions: how to define their object of study; and how they map agency. Second, the chapter outlines the problem of defining agency in the WTO with specific reference to the discursive construction of the 'Member states' identity that more mainstream approaches in WTO studies have taken to be a clear designator of actorness but that covers over the important question of who or what is able to act in the WTO. In this light, the third section makes the argument that the WTO is a *sedimented discursive formation* – a series of social practices linked within an historically contingent relational sequence that exceeds any fixed or finite borders. As will be explained further on, social practices are all those practices through which individuals interact – either directly or indirectly – with one another. This situates the approach within the growing body of IPE literature that seeks to highlight the social processes constituting global economic transactions (Watson 2005; Gammon 2008; de Goede 2005; Antoniades 2010). In this respect, and with particular reference to the work of Matthew Watson, a discursive approach to the WTO contributes to Karl Polanyi's project to exhibit the social embeddedness of the market, but here, with focus on the technocratic institutional basis of that market (Watson 2005: 141–58). The fifth and final section summarizes the book's research strategy by outlining how the WTO comes to appear within its approach. It shows that treating the WTO as a sedimented discursive formation allows research better to understand the organic character of its central object of study and the interplay between both order and uncertainty that exceeds its legal-institutional borders and provides the conditions for an ongoing process of change.

The book makes apparent that the approach advocated in this chapter, and developed throughout the proceeding empirical chapters, reinvigorates WTO studies by repositioning the organization at the centre of a dynamic discursive context. It is in this context that the concept of 'trade' and its governance, as well as who or what constitutes an 'actor' within its political arena, is subject to a continual process of change whether the relationship between the constitutive social practices is rearticulated. The reader is presented with a provocative intervention that challenges existing studies on both the politics and the institutional identity of the WTO. As such, the book develops an analytical approach equipped to appreciate how both the material and ideational factors overlap so as to make the WTO possible, and explain change within the governance of global trade.

The WTO as the 'rule of law' or as 'power politics'

The literature on the WTO has grown to fill a decently sized library and yet can be summarized as falling somewhere between viewing the WTO as either the *rule of law* or the product of *power politics*. Variance is found along a spectrum based on the extent to which institutional rules/norms may be argued to ameliorate capability (e.g. economic, military) differentials outside the institution. Consequently, some studies consider the legal-institutional design paramount – the ideational (e.g. Jackson 2009, 2000; Hoekman and Kostecki 2009; Matsushita *et al.* 2003). Others stress the weakness of formal norms of decision making against the strength of realpolitik considerations – the material (e.g. Kwa 2003).

The field of WTO studies is dominated by research on the WTO institution itself, the series of legal texts it hosts, and the possibility that it represents the beginnings of a world polity. First, much literature exists to provide a general overview of the formal institution understood as the 'WTO' (Hoekman and Kostecki 2001, 2009; Jackson 1998a, 1998b, 2000; Matsushita *et al.* 2003; Adamantopoulos 1997). Second, there is more specialist focus upon the trade agreements held under its banner, such as the General Agreement on Trade in Services (GATS) (Sauvé and Stern 2000). Third, research has focused extensively on both the use of legal mechanisms, with particular attention on the Dispute Settlement Body (Bronckers 2000; Cameron and Campbell 1998), but also the role of the WTO as a constitution at the centre of a global trade polity (Cass 2005). Fourth, the ideational literature includes publications debating future reform of the institutional arrangement (Jones 2010; Barfield 2001; van der Borght *et al.* 2003).

Research that concentrates on the role of material forces driving the WTO has emphasized the highly politicized character of global trade governance (Lanoszka 2009; Wilkinson 2006; Kim 2010). This includes work on WTO negotiating practice and decision making (Steinberg 2002; Schott and Watal

2000; Hoda 2001); disparities in the influence exercised by different Member states in the WTO (Dunkley 2000; Kwa 2003); the relatively weak position of developing countries in the WTO (Narlikar 2001; Blackhurst *et al.* 1999; Meléndez-Ortiz and Shaffer 2010); human rights impact of WTO rules (Joseph 2011); the role of non-state actors (e.g. 'non-governmental organizations') (Wilkinson 2005; Scholte 2004); and the implementation of WTO agreements (Blackhurst 1998).

Whilst neither literature is mutually exclusive – nor, indeed, are scholars permanently wedded to either one or the other of the ideational and materialist camps – there is a gap in understanding between how material and ideational explanatory factors interact to make the WTO possible. The relevance of this gap becomes clearer when considering the problem of defining agency in the WTO.

The problem of defining agency in the WTO

The puzzle of two WTOs – one ideational and the other material – is illustrated in the difficulty of defining who or what constitutes an actor in the WTO. The emergence of actors as subjects able to alter their political environment forms a key question for discourse theory, as will be shown when discussing the book's research strategy. However, for now it helps first to outline exactly why there is uncertainty over how to define agency in the WTO.

Formally, there are at least two categories of 'actor' utilized in the literature. First, there are the 'Member states'.[1] These are nation-states that have applied and been accepted as Members of the WTO. Second, WTO negotiations and the monitoring of domestic trade policy within Member states are facilitated by a Secretariat with a staff of approximately 550, and a headquarters office in Geneva (WTO Secretariat 2008: 2). Incorporating the formal structure, the informal practices and the two categories of actor as modelled in the literature, the WTO appears as in Figure 1.1.

The use of a Venn diagram is not meant to represent the actual political operation of the WTO but the intersection of variables taken into account within how the WTO is defined as a research object.

The first category of actor includes the professional trade diplomats representing their national governments (or the European Union, in the case of EU member countries), as well as trade ministers and civil servants. Several studies have focused on the composition of these delegations (e.g. Blackhurst *et al.* 1999: 20), which vary greatly depending on how a Member prioritizes specific negotiations, as well as the resources determining their capability to provide technically qualified personnel to attend negotiations.

The two-stage flow model by which much of the literature understands how 'business interests' and 'non-governmental organizations' are to influence the formation of WTO agreements further evidences the significance of how one defines a Member. This is argued by one of the most influential texts within the field of WTO studies (Hoekman and Kostecki 2009), and takes the form

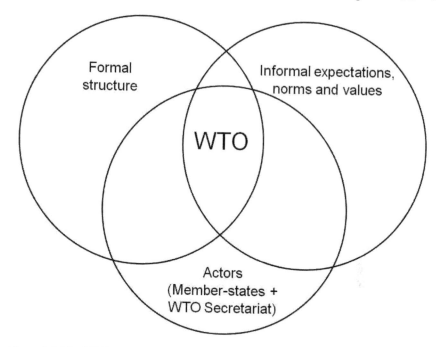

Figure 1.1 The WTO as modelled in the literature

of a pluralist model in which the national level consists of competing 'interests' spread across different identities such as 'businesses', 'trade unions', 'issue-groups' (e.g. environmental), and so on. Within this model, it should be noted that 'business' does not constitute a unified position because sub-identities such as 'exporters' or 'importers' will presumably possess diametrically opposed 'interest-positions'. Additionally, 'trade unions' includes representatives of workers in both import/export industries and might therefore be expected to be similarly heterogeneous.

The contestation between these 'interests' is understood to occur at the national level, so that the negotiating position of that country's trade delegation to the WTO is the product of that contestation. Business, trade unions and non-governmental actors have no formal direct access to the WTO and so this is seen to imply that Member states effectively act as the gatekeepers to the WTO through their ownership of the franchise over decision making (Hoekman and Kostecki 2009: 159–61).

The WTO is thus understood as the product of nation-states balancing domestic 'interests', and can be simply modelled as in Figure 1.2.

The model can be multiplied to reflect the number of Member states, with the WTO at the centre and each Member acting as gatekeeper against its own plurality of competing domestic 'interests'. The perspective taken by Hoekman and Kostecki positions the various 'actors' in their respective fields of

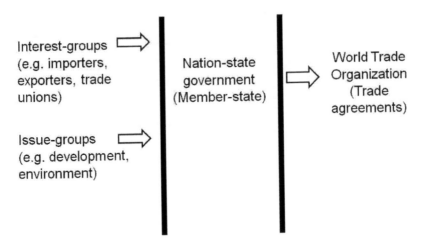

Figure 1.2 Member states as the gatekeepers to the WTO

influence, so that, for example, 'businesses', 'trade unions' and 'environmentalists' operate as 'lobbyists' at the 'national' level. However, despite stating that non-state actors are not able to 'lobby' the WTO directly, Hoekman and Kostecki do briefly note the role played by, in particular, financial corporations such as American Express and Citibank in the Uruguay Round which provided the negotiations, and thus the initial sedimentation, of the series of practices that would become the formal institutional structure and trade agreements that emerged as the 'WTO' in 1995 (Hoekman and Kostecki 2009: 159). They note that large businesses have been important in providing the 'force' by which various trade agreements have been first created as well as then implemented (ibid.:159).

The literature traces the rise in political support for 'open markets' with the emergence of new industries such as consumer electronics and aviation, which have the most to gain from reduced trade restrictions, according to such accounts (Dunkley 2000: 23). Understood thus, the history of multilateral trade negotiations might be traced as a product of a balance between competing 'interests', where the present is indicative of the ascendency of such global businesses as Citibank.

In this respect, Hoekman and Kostecki (2009: 62) suggest that the WTO is a 'network', with the WTO Secretariat at the centre. The WTO includes 'official representatives of members based in Geneva, civil servants based in capitals, and national business and nongovernmental groups that seek to have their governments push for their interests at the multilateral level' (Hoekman and Kostecki 2001: 53). This suggests a model in which the 'WTO' exists, then, as the sedimentation of the practices of a multiplicity of 'actors'.

However, the anatomy of politics at play in the WTO becomes increasingly complex if one acknowledges the transnationalization (or 'globalization') of 'businesses' and 'non-governmental organizations', so that the flow of influence or force exceeds the 'nation-state' as gatekeeper to the WTO, and moves to the supranational level so as to be able to affect multiple nation-states and thus play one off against the other (Hoogvelt 2001). Though the Member remains as gatekeeper to the WTO, Hoekman and Kostecki's multi-level model of WTO policy formation appears increasingly untenable as the nation-state is shown to be not a distinct and isolated identity, as such, but part of a network of 'influence' that exceeds (and supersedes) national boundaries. Hoekman and Kostecki (2001: 121) themselves argue that the WTO is 'incomprehensible without an understanding of the forces that brought an issue to the table'. These 'forces' remain hard to pin down if one remains within a two-level flow model. The problem of identifying agency in the WTO is clearly shown in a problematization of the WTO as 'Member-led', as will be done next.

Problematizing the WTO as Member-led

When discussing the balance of 'influences' – or 'power' – within the WTO, the literature typically highlights the formal status of the WTO as Member-led.[2] As a minimum, the WTO is seen to facilitate negotiation between its Members on matters definable as 'trade-related' (Matsushita *et al.* 2003: 9). However, as those lobbying nation-state governments move beyond national borders, what is meant by a 'Member' becomes increasingly less clear. This is reflected in the literature, where much research has attempted to illustrate and explain gross inequalities in the ability of different Members to influence WTO negotiations.[3]

The influence a particular Member state has within the WTO is seen as more than a simple matter of 'wealth', or percentage of overall trade, but is also affected by the 'stake' a Member has in the particular matter under discussion. Curzon and Curzon (1973: 330) discuss this with regard to the history of the GATT process. However, much of the literature emphasizes the role played by material resources. Weaker Members are seen as lacking the sufficient resources necessary to achieve an influential presence in WTO bodies. Dunkley argues that richer Members are better able to provide a sufficiently large body of personnel to sustain strong representation in all WTO bodies (Dunkley 2000: 217). This view is repeated throughout much of the literature so as to explain the dominance of WTO negotiations by the industrialized countries, and the USA, EU, Japan and Canada in particular (Blackhurst *et al.* 1999; Narlikar 2001; Kwa 2003).

The literature is faced with a contradiction in the question of whether there is equality between Members in the WTO. Despite provisions in which some countries may be given 'special a differential' treatment in order to allow them more time to meet the terms of various WTO trade agreements, such agreements are formed on the principle of the 'single undertaking' (or 'single package') approach, meaning that all Members possess collective responsibility for ensuring their eventual implementation. Additionally, the

WTO saw the sedimentation of consensus that had been carried over from the GATT. This potentially means that even the weakest Member, as long as they are present in a meeting, has effective veto over decisions utilizing the consensus norm and influence radically disproportionate to its current stake in world trade. Though there are some exceptions, participation in the majority of everyday decision making within the WTO is formally open to the entire membership.

The literature has responded by emphasizing the role that informal negotiations play within the WTO, and how they are facilitated by the formal decision-making mechanisms, so as to favour 'material power' (Footer 1997: 667; Qureshi 1996: 6; Kwa 2003). Steinberg (2002) has borrowed Krasner's concept of 'organizational hypocrisy' – in which the norm of 'sovereignty' is both supported and broken within global politics – and applied it to the WTO to argue that such a contradiction is constitutive of the WTO. The current international political economy (IPE) requires both a claim to 'sovereign equality' between all Members and an actual praxis that facilitates expression of 'power asymmetry' between those Members (Steinberg 2002).

Whether one explains differences between Members as related to different 'interests', disparities in 'material resources', or as structured by the (formal/informal) institutional arrangement of the WTO, what constitutes a 'Member' is clearly important. A 'Member' might be defined as a 'nation-state that has applied and been accepted for entry to the WTO', for example, though this by no means acknowledges the gross differences between those 'Members'.

First, nation-states are very differently represented as 'Members' within the WTO, so that certain Members have many more times the number of delegates than others. This determines not only that Member's spread over the various trade meetings, but the extent to which it is understood by other Members to be both informed and capable of offering side payments. Second, the composition of a 'Member' may vary greatly in terms of quality, not only with regard to the economic or legal expertise of the individual delegates but also their own identities as government officials, or representatives of 'business' or 'nongovernmental organizations'. The composition of Member delegations will often contain more than government officials (Barfield 2001: 143). Consequently, such variance questions the universality of the identity 'WTO Member'.

The social construction of the Member state identity

Ford's (2003) analysis of the WTO, in which she applies social constructivist explanation, argues that the 'Member state' identity has come to exceed the identity of the respective 'nation-states'. The analysis is social constructivist through its understanding of 'power' as formed within a specific social setting. That is, the WTO as an institution is seen to constitute an alternative social environment, as opposed to the wider international political economy, which affects the distribution of influence between the respective actors. That environment has facilitated a gradual shift in which, Ford contends, the creation of nation-states as Member states has altered the previous interaction between those nation-states. She argues that through the practice of the organization, a 'new collective identity' has emerged between those participating nation-states (ibid.: 133). The WTO represents a cultural change which, for Ford, has formed a 'Self of multilateral traders', in which national politicians have altered their perceptions so as to realize their nations' combined 'interests' as 'multilateral traders' (Ford 2003: 135). In Ford's analysis, the collective identity produced via the WTO has overcome disparities in material capabilities (e.g. economic) so that developing countries have more influence over the shape of global trade through their identity as 'Members' (ibid.: 135).

The norm of a 'collective identity' has, according to the study, been actively promoted (constructed) by developing country Member states in order to tie the more materially capable developed country Member states closer to a rule-based system than they would have accepted otherwise (Ford 2003: 135). Legalization as well as the norms of trade liberalization were 'taught' by the developing countries in order to obtain influence not achievable materially, according to Ford's (2003: 134–35) study. To support this argument, Ford contrasts the WTO to the European Union and the North American Free Trade Agreement (NAFTA), arguing that whereas the latter two include environmental and labour standards, the WTO does not (ibid.: 135). This, Ford claims, is because the particular culture of a 'collective identity' has empowered developing countries and made it possible for them to prevent the inclusion of these standards that they deemed to bias against their 'national interests' (ibid.: 135).

For Ford, then, whilst there are gross material disparities between nation-states that may be attributed to factors within the wider international political economy, these relations alter once a nation-state becomes a WTO 'Member', or at least in as much as those are relations with other Members (Ford 2003: 135). In other words, the effect of disparities in material capabilities is constrained by social norms within the institutional structure. Change in relationships occurs due to active effort to alter the social norms through which they are structured. In Ford's model, such agency is possessed by the Members. Though identity formation is seen to affect relations, in Ford's study it remains unclear what creates the identity of a Member state in the first place. If the institutional norms are capable of not only ameliorating material disparities but also shifting actors' interests within that material environment external to the institution, this accords the WTO institution with a significant ability to alter state-to-state relations. However, if one questions the construction of 'interests', what space is left for the actor? For example, if one further develops the constructivist logic it means questioning earlier actor identities, such as nation-state, and so on, so that ultimately all power appears to be no more than a product of social construction rather than enacted with agency.

In Ford's model, disparities in the material resources of nation-states are assumed to be altered via an ideational shift so that they are understood via a collective identity of 'multilateral traders' (Ford 2003: 135). Yet, it remains unclear what role there is for agency in this scenario. As said, it might be argued that the political actor is capable of constructing her/his world as they choose, yet experience tells us that never can such a scenario exist, devoid of constraints. In addition to it being unclear what constraints exist, it remains unclear how a political actor is formed.

In actively promoting social norms that alter the balance of power in their favour, are developing country Member states themselves free of the constraints they construct in order to constrain 'material power'? Additionally, if one can (de)construct the identity of 'developing country Member state', how is one to understand agency and the constitution of the political actor? If political actors are understood as social constructions, is the only essence with which we are left *construction* itself? This question is put by Stavrakakis, who develops the point to then ask, if everything is constructed, 'what stimulates the production of new social constructions?' (Stavrakakis 1999: 67).

This is the paradox faced if one remains within social constructivism: how to explain political change if the political world is constructed by actors who are themselves no more than the product of construction? In contradistinction to this position, the WTO needs to be reconceptualized as a sedimented discursive formation, as will be done next.

The WTO as a sedimented discursive formation

Despite a formal institutional structure, the precise borders of the WTO as a political object are uncertain. There is no 'end of history' at which one can say *this is the WTO*. It is argued here that treating the WTO as a sedimented discursive formation enables research better to understand this uncertainty and, in turn, the formation, operation and transformation of the WTO.

Since Laclau and Mouffe (2001) first introduced their ontology, there has been a burgeoning of research applying their theoretical presuppositions to all forms of politics.[4] In the following, the chapter will outline the core components of discourse theory relevant to studying the WTO – and other institutions of global governance – and how it provides a distinct perspective on stability and change within global politics that both challenges and advances already existing literature on the WTO, including Ford's social constructivist perspective which already acknowledges the role of identity. The value of this research strategy is demonstrated in the remaining chapters, which present new empirical research on the WTO, informed by discourse theory.

As will be argued here, discourse theory has utility for studies of the WTO – and other institutions of global governance – because it theorizes the link between the order embodied in the formal institution and the wider series of practices through which it is constituted and which provide the conditions for its transformation. To construct this argument, the chapter will develop three core propositions that frame the book. These are: 1) political institutions are formed through the *sedimentation of a series of social practices into a particular relational sequence*; 2) moments of collective action involve the *linking of otherwise distinct identities within a common identity*; and, 3) this *process is not relative but is instead historically embedded* within the wider series of relations constituting the context of its emergence, with the consequence that all political institutions embody an *ineradicable tension between both autonomy as distinct systems and overdetermination* where their constitutive social practices exceed any formal institutional borders. The salience of these three propositions will now be made clear.

Sedimentation of a series of social practices into a particular relational sequence

This first point directs research to unpick the basic social mechanisms – or practices – shaping the various interactions collectively constituting the WTO. If, as is argued above, what is signified by the name 'WTO' cannot be taken for granted but is subject to contestation then the importance of identifying the social practices making up what we mean by the 'WTO' when using this name is paramount.

Within discourse theory, social practices are understood in the broadest possible sense to refer to all mechanisms through which social actors interact with one another both directly and indirectly (including across spatial-temporal dimensions). Social practices thus include both the ideational (e.g. institutions, rules, texts, speech) as well as those aspects otherwise categorized as distinct – the material (e.g. military/trade capabilities, such as tanks and consumer electronics). This demands a much more holistic view of what constitutes a practice relevant to the WTO than that utilized in traditional definitions of international regimes (e.g. Young 1986) and institutions (e.g. Peters 1999). For discourse theory, there is no distinction between linguistic and extra-linguistic social practices (Laclau and Mouffe 2001: 107). Every social practice is understood to be discursive, though this does not mean that post-structuralist discourse theory is idealist (Laclau and Mouffe 2001: 108). Rather, it has to do with the core argument of this approach, that is: social practices *cannot* constitute themselves as objects within the human world 'outside any discursive condition of emergence' (Laclau and Mouffe 2001: 108). Following on from this, Laclau and Mouffe assert the *material* nature of discourse (ibid.: 108), so that the material co-exists alongside the ideational within discourse.

Here, one must distinguish between *existence* and *being*. Everyday practices within the human world are based upon a series of interactions, in which the practices (e.g. 'trade', 'money') we utilize and are confronted with are inscribed with particular meaning. Thus, practices are 'always given to us within dis-cursive articulations' (Laclau and Mouffe 1990: 103). Acutely put by Laclau and Mouffe, 'outside of any discursive context ... [practices] do not have *being*; they have only *existence*' (ibid.: 104, emphasis added). A person does *exist* outside of discourse, but s/he can only have *being* – and so be understood by other persons – as a 'Head of a Member state delegation' within a certain sedimented series of social practices defined here as discourse. In other words, social practices are constituted – have *being* – within the context of other social practices.

To frame the WTO as a research object with discourse theory, then, requires not only that we must identify its constitutive social practices but equally how those practices are related to one another. This brings the discussion to its next point on the formation of collective identities central to moments of collective action.

Linking distinct identities within a common identity

All forms of collective action involve a bringing together of distinct political demands – however similar – such that they may be at least temporarily represented as a whole within the moment of their joint venture. The moment of collective action – or moments, as the WTO involves multiple forms of collective action between its member states – embodied within the WTO requires a claim of representation where the collective moment can stand in place of the individual member states. The advantage of discourse theory here is that by highlighting the role of representation inherent to collective action, research is better able to appreciate the transformative function this plays. Representation without transformation is unattainable because, as Laclau (1996: 97–98) writes, of the 'very logic inherent in the process of representation'. Representation implies that identity formation is not fully complete at the level of the represented, because the role of the representative in providing that fullness. For example, the identity 'WTO Member state' is incomplete if not represented outside its national borders at the WTO. This is the incompleteness of identity, described by Laclau:

> So far as the represented is concerned, if he or she needs to be represented at all, this is the result of the fact that his or her basic identity is constituted in a place *A* and that decisions that can affect this identity will be taken in a place *B*. But in that case his or her identity is an incomplete identity, and the relation of representation – far from referring to full-fledged identity – is a *supplement* necessary for the constitution of that identity ... [Thus] it is an entirely *new* addition, in which case, the identity of the represented is transformed and enlarged through the process of representation.
>
> (Laclau 1996: 98)

The growth in regional and international institutions – such as the WTO – affecting policy issues traditionally administered within the domain of the nation-state, such as trade tariffs or fishery regulations, means that the role of representation increases as 'there is a proliferation of the points in society from which decisions affecting ... [representeds'] lives will be taken' (Laclau 1996: 99). Indeed, for Laclau and Mouffe, the very act of being able to point to the historical contingency of our world is itself historically contingent: 'It is only in the contemporary world, when technological change and the dislocating rhythm of capitalist transformation constantly alter the discursive sequences which construct the reality of objects, that the merely historical character of being becomes fully visible. In this sense, contemporary thought as a whole is, to a large extent, an attempt to cope with this increasing realization, and the consequent moving away from essentialism' (Laclau and Mouffe 1990: 119).

Linking distinct identities within a common identity is modelled in discourse theory as the building of equivalential relations between the differential identities under a general collective identity which itself becomes temporarily empty for the duration that it has to stand for the collective. Understood thus, the WTO as a name becomes what Laclau calls the 'empty signifier' (Laclau 1996: 43). An empty signifier is that which represents the absent 'fullness of the community' (Laclau 2004: 280). The 'World Trade Organization' (or 'WTO') is an absent fullness to the extent that it has no specific content in itself, yet represents a chain of differences that equivalentially form the 'WTO'. In a basic form, this process may be modelled as in Figure 1.3.

The example by no means covers the full discursive formation of the WTO, though in this form it serves to illustrate that whilst each of the various practices is in itself different, they may only form a chain of equivalence with one another under a certain banner, or the empty signifier, which has no fixed content in itself yet comes to represent the illusion of fixity for the whole system. As argued, the name 'World Trade Organization' serves as the empty signifier holding together that totality.

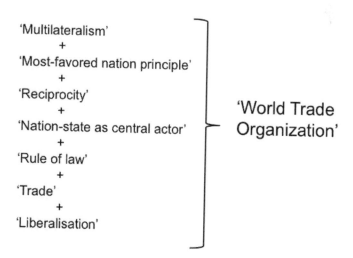

Figure 1.3 The WTO as an equivalential sequence

However, this model does not make clear how the WTO may be alternative discursive formations, such as one in which trade is to be negotiated between nation-states on a 'multilateral' basis, or as where trade between nation-states is to be 'liberalized'. The equivalential chain constituting the WTO might be modelled quite differently and thus be a different discursive formation. That said, if these practices are equivalential under the WTO, how is it possible to argue that there could ever be a multiplicity of discursive formations titled the WTO, where some leant towards 'multilateralism', whilst others towards 'liberalization'? The empty signifier is only empty within the context of the particular system of meaning at play in the equivalential chain, so that it can be re-described as the *tendentially* empty signifier (Laclau 2004: 281). Just as the totality can never be fixed, nor can such emptiness. Articulation means that there is always an attempt to fill that void, so that it can never be truly empty, just as it can never be truly full. As a tendentially empty signifier, 'World Trade Organization' possesses a certain content. That content is provided by one of the practices (or signifiers) within the equivalential chain, which for historically contingent reasons has been articulated so as to be able to 'stand in for and represent the chain as a whole' (Thomassen 2005: 292). Acknowledging this tendential emptiness requires re-modelling the discursive formation, as in Figure 1.4.

'Multilateralism' in this model serves the filling role, itself becoming the tendentially empty signifier that represents the whole chain whilst remaining one part among the others (Thomassen 2005: 294). The original title for an international trade regime debated during the Uruguay Round that would lead to the WTO was, in fact, the 'Multilateral Trade Organization' (MTO), illustrating the process by which the regime faced competing attempts to fill its constitutive lack from the very beginning (Jackson 1998a: 5). Alternative

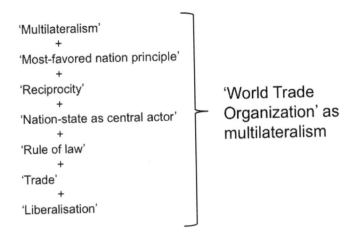

Figure 1.4 The WTO as 'multilateralism' as an equivalential sequence

labels such as 'liberalization' could serve this role, as could any of the others, including 'rule of law'. As Laclau (1996: 44) writes, '[t]o hegemonize something is exactly to carry out this filling function'. Additionally, though the social practices are tendentially equivalential to one another in that specific moment of collective action that is politics, they are not equal. The articulatory process sees a hegemonic struggle between social practices, providing both the empty signifier and the complex discursive formation in which those demands operate together.

Understanding collective action as affecting the identities of those actors involved accords with Ford's (2003) social constructivist analysis of the WTO, described above, to the extent that there is a shared concern with how the moment of collective action transforms the identities – including interests – of those actors involved. However, where discourse theory advances further is its ability to model the wider sphere of relations constitutive of that process. This leads into the third point in which the political being of the WTO is argued to exceed its formal institutional borders.

The WTO beyond its institutional borders

Representation means that the WTO cannot be understood as self-defined, atemporal or complete but rather as inherently lacking that which is supplemented externally to the WTO itself. An obvious lack provided by the relations that exceed the WTO's institution are the social practices in which 'trade' is understood and performed. The WTO can only achieve the appearance of being a coherent institution within these relations that exceed it – what Laclau and Mouffe (2001: 111) term the 'field of discursivity'. This means not only viewing the WTO as constructed within a particular social context, but treating the practices constituting that social context as part of the WTO's political being. In other words, examining how something like 'trade' can be articulated – and rearticulated – should be viewed as part of WTO studies.

Laclau and Mouffe's (2001: 98–104) concept of 'overdetermination' explains the logic of this argument. Overdetermination is used to acknowledge that social practices overlap one another so that there are never any clear boundaries with which permanently to fix their identity (Laclau and Mouffe 2001: 98–104). No one social practice can ever be fixed to one single meaning, as it will always be overdetermined by the incompleteness of its identity. For example, the 'WTO' can be said to *exist* to the extent that one can point to a formation of bricks in Geneva and a group of people sat round various tables and talking to one another. However, the 'WTO' only achieves *being* within a certain discourse, where it might be determined as 'a forum for conducting the reduction of barriers to trade between nation-states', or as a 'rich man's club'. It is open to multiple determinations which exceed the 'WTO' itself. As an example this is of course simplistic, but it needs to be stated that overdetermination means that one can neither derive meaning from the object outside of discourse or later fix a specific meaning ad infinitum. Constituted by a system of relationality between different social practices which are themselves discourses, any one discourse will be forever subject to the contingency upon which it is constituted (see Torfing 2005: 14).

Overdetermination is helpful here not only because it embeds the WTO within its historical-social context and, in so doing, stresses the importance of those social practices that are constitutive although outside its institutional structure. By colouring in the fuller story in which the WTO is made possible, research is also better equipped to explain transformation within that story. Discourse theory explains change in political phenomena via shifts in the discursive formations through which they are made possible. The possibility of change is founded upon the ultimate contingency of such discursive formations. Contrary to structuralism, discourse theory accords agency to the 'actor' – or *subject*, via distinguishing between *subject positions* and *political subjectivity* (Howarth 2000: 108).

Subject positions are the identities by which individuals – or groups of individuals – exist as 'actors' and, because any individual – or group of individuals – may be involved within more than one set of social practices, they may possess multiple subject positions, such as 'United States of America', 'WTO member state', 'developed country', 'free trader', 'protectionist', 'land of opportunity', 'rich market', 'bully', 'war-monger', 'multicultural', 'Christian', 'multi-faith', and so on. The point of the example is that as well as being articulated within a multiplicity of subject positions, those positions do not need to be mutually consistent. Whereas subject positions are structured within discourse, political subjectivity is made possible via the contingency of discourse (Howarth 2000: 109).

Political subjectivity emerges as a product of what is termed *dislocation*. Dislocation is the 'process by which the contingency of discursive structures is made visible' (Howarth and Stavrakakis 2000: 13). Making visible that contingency alters the relational structure through which discourse is formed, shattering the subject positions by which individuals obtain identity, and consequently inducing an 'identity crisis' for the individual – or group of individuals (ibid.: 13). This is a regular process by which actors realize the contingency of the social. In the process of realizing contingency, agency is made possible, which in turn leads to an:

> Accelerated tempo of social transformation and … continual rearticulatory interventions … [which] lead to a higher awareness of historicity. Without a realm of extra-discursivity, the conditions for realising contingency are themselves discursive. Dislocation is not a rare event but a regular occurrence constituted by the impossibility of closure. This, as discussed, is overdetermination – where discursive formations overlap. It is in this moment of overlap, where the contradictions of discursive formations are made visible, that contingency is made visible and dislocation is threatened. The rapid change in discursive sequences organizing and constituting

objects leads to a clearer awareness of the constitutive contingency of those discourses.

(Laclau 1990: 39)

It is this crisis of identity in the subject that allows the individual agency, through being forced to re-identify with new political projects and the discourses they articulate (Howarth and Stavrakakis 2000: 14).

Thus, post-structuralist discourse theory both theorizes how political subjects are positioned, and where they achieve agency as political 'actors'. It should be noted, also, that this therefore questions the possibility of 'objective interests' outside of discourse. As Laclau and Mouffe (1990: 118) state, '[t]o construct an "interest" is a slow historical process, which takes place through complex ideological, discursive and institutional practices'. The very notion of 'interests', as calculated and negotiated, requires engagement within a collective totality and, therefore, an act of construction (or representation) (Laclau and Mouffe 1990: 118). For 'interests' to be objective and pre-given would be to argue that they can exist outside of such collective totalities (or discourse). Interests do exist, but they are 'historical products which are always subjected to processes of dissolution and redefinition' (Laclau and Mouffe 1990: 118).

Overdetermination means that the WTO as a discursive formation cannot be said simply to mirror its formal institutional boundaries. As the 'network' model of the WTO discussed earlier makes clear, these borders do not reflect the actual political operation of the WTO. For example, if the WTO is understood to be a discursive formation in which economic relations (as far as they are defined as 'trade') between nation-states are to be 'liberalized', the frontiers of the WTO would be the point at which economic policy was unresponsive to such a demand. The limits of the WTO would thus be that which is *anti-liberalizing*. This is very clearly illustrated where, currently, such WTO 'Members' as the USA and the EU retain high agricultural subsidies, which is understood to be 'anti-liberalizing' and is seen to suggest the weakness of the WTO. Alternatively, if the WTO is understood to be a discursive formation in which trade is to be negotiated between nation-states on a 'multilateral' basis, the presence of bilateral trade agreements would present a limit to the WTO. Whenever negotiations have stalled within the WTO, bilateral trade agreements are highlighted as examples that the organization is under threat and about to collapse.

A remaining question to be addressed is the degree to which one might argue that the 'WTO' is autonomous. For example, if understood discursively, how does the 'WTO' constitute a polity in which a certain process of decision making takes place? This brings us back to *sedimentation*. Earlier it was argued that the 'WTO' can be described as a sedimented discursive formation. That is to say that it is constituted within discourse, and consists of a series of practices that have for historically contingent reasons become sedimented into a particular system. For Howarth, post-structuralist discourse theory views institutions as '"sedimented" discourses, which despite their political origins as products of hegemonic practices have become relatively permanent and durable' (Howarth 2000: 120). The terms 'relatively permanent and durable' need to be qualified, since institutions remain embedded within discourse and are thus open to contestation. This book also avoids describing the WTO itself as a discourse, because of the potential confusion in seeing 'discourse' as both an infrastructure of being and a singular object. Rather, it makes logical sense to argue that the WTO is a formation within discourse, and thus a discursive formation.

The above development of discourse theory has been applied within ongoing empirical research into the WTO, which will be summarized next in order to illustrate the significance and value of reconceptualizing the WTO as a sedimented discursive formation.

A new research strategy: the WTO in this book

This first chapter to the book began by making two arguments: first, the WTO cannot be understood via a formal organization or regime alone but consists of a much more complex and diffuse political process; and second, current literature understands the WTO via an interplay between material- and ideational-based explanations. Developing the former whilst problematizing the latter, the chapter has responded with a research methodology that it argues to be capable of providing the analytical tools necessary to trace such complexity.

Current studies suggest that the WTO cannot be limited to a specific legal-institutional arrangement. A complex network of actors can be identified from the various civil servants, interest- and issue-group lobbyists working to affect the shape of the WTO's trade governance regime. This network is shown to exceed a two-step flow model in which nation-states are gatekeepers to the WTO, suggesting a much more complex and diffuse process shaping the WTO. This is important as it means that the WTO cannot be understood via focusing on the formal actors alone – the Member states (*qua* nation-states), but demands a more nuanced analytical approach.

This book shows that the WTO is neither purely material nor purely ideational. The WTO is an ideational construction – consisting of specific regime practices – yet the policies it helps to implement are felt in a very material sense and the organization clearly has a material Secretariat staff and a material headquarters. In addition, the series of interactions that comprise the WTO are structured by a mixture of material and ideational factors. For example, the categorization of 'trade' – central to the WTO's issue domain – is both an historically contingent ideational construction and yet refers to the exchange of items such as grain or computers – things that appear to be material.[5] Whilst some studies (Ford 2003) have attempted better to theorize the ideational construction of the WTO, this has been at the expense of material explanation and has resulted in the constructivist fallacy: if the essence of everything is construction, what stimulates new constructions? The material-ideational problem remains – theory is stuck at the abstract level debating to what extent the material and ideational affect one another without concretely theorizing how they co-exist within discursive practice.

In response to this problematization, an innovative methodology approach has been introduced, based on post-structuralist discourse theory. Through the concepts of articulation, sedimentation and dislocation, the approach is argued to theorize rigorously how the ideational and material co-exist as both discursive objects within what is termed *being*. The material cannot exist without the ideational, and vice-versa. The emphasis in discourse theory on articulatory processes facilitates appreciation of how an object such as a 'trade agreement' may be created in what appears to be a material world as an ideational product with material effects. The concept of 'discourse' utilized here, as argued, is consequently much wider than the linguistic, characterized as much by its materiality as it is by its ideational qualities. Post-structuralist discourse theory is, crucially, not a relativistic or ideational perspective, but theoretically bridges the ideational-material distinction.

Discourse theory's sensitivity to political change makes it particularly suitable for analysing the complex and diffuse political process evident in the WTO. By theorizing the co-existence of the ideational and the material, a whole new research agenda not previously possible in WTO studies is opened up. For instance, attention must be given to the processes through which identities, with which individuals collectively identify, are formed and, hence, to how 'actors' are constituted within the WTO. This means that the primacy of nation-states cannot be taken as given. The WTO, as the book demonstrates, is at the centre of a diffuse political process, exceeding not only any formal political structure but also a fixed set of actors. What holds for the actors constitutive of the WTO also holds for actors interacting with, but critical of, the WTO. These sorts of critical activities, as will be shown, form a constitutive part of its political operation. Though challenging, the advantage of the perspective developed in this book is that by adopting a more nuanced concept of 'actors' – and the process of articulation – it is better equipped to appreciate change in the politics of the WTO.

Chapter plan

Bearing this in mind, the book's empirical investigation begins in Chapter 2 by first identifying the contestability of the founding concepts underlying the WTO, with specific attention given to the changing rationalities for multilateral trade governance. While conventional history focuses on human agency and the material world (e.g. resources), the discourse theoretical analysis looks at the social practices underlying political action. From this analysis it becomes clear that the category of 'trade' is not static. To the contrary, it is subject to repeated rearticulations. The significance of such rearticulation, understood within a discourse theoretical perspective, highlights how changing conditions of possibility shape political action.

Since the 1934 US Reciprocal Trade Agreements Act (US-RTAA), the concept of 'trade' and its governance has gone through multiple and overlapping rearticulations, including 'national security', 'peaceful cooperation', 'Cold War weapon', 'development tool' and 'anti-terrorist'. Each articulation has been at the centre of quite alternative political projects. The emergence of 'development' demands – centred in the 'developing-country' identity and contextualized by the emergence of new nation-states (post-independence) – forced further dislocation and rearticulation of 'trade' governance, and provided the discursive context in which the Uruguay Round and the WTO itself would eventually appear. Rearticulation has occurred in moments of 'crisis', whereby the former discursive formation is shown to be contingent. This is most evident in the Uruguay Round, where the feared 'collapse' of 'multilateralism' facilitated a significant expansion of the 'trade' category to include many new spheres of social activity, including those equivalentially linked under the new category of 'trade in services'. The current so-called 'crisis' facing the Doha Round may, on this basis, lead to a further rearticulation of 'trade' governance.

The 'crisis' that conditioned the Uruguay Round and the formation of the WTO – a largely unintended consequence – can be seen as a rearticulation in the wake of a series of dislocations in the discourse of global politics that took place in the 1970s. Rather than just seeing alternate moments of multilateral trade governance as shaped by their historical context, they can be seen as intimately constituted within the contingent series of social practices native to their temporal being which they, as social practices themselves, affect in a mutually constitutive relationship. It is in the tensions between these practices that political subjectivities emerged and provided the agency driving change. In contrast to those accounts that limit 'trade' to the technical-apolitical sphere, it becomes clear that it is subject to multiple articulations, each facilitating an alternative form of relational practices such that it remains an inherently political object subject to transformation.

Exhibiting the contingency within the social practices most central to multilateral trade governance, the fluidity of the WTO as a sedimented discursive formation becomes apparent. The articulatory process is immensely complex and diffuse. Much of the articulatory process has taken place in formal and informal forums external to the regime. In the case of 'trade in services' – which went from a highly marginalized articulation of trade to become a central tenet of the WTO's understanding of 'trade' within its governance – much has relied upon a vast network of actors (or subject positions) far exceeding those defined by the formal legal-institutional arrangement of the WTO. In the same process, new actors have emerged, including the agency of the GATT (General Agreement on Tariffs and Trade) and, now, WTO Secretariat, as well as transnational corporations and non-governmental organizations. The emergence of new actors within the wider articulation of multilateral trade governance in the WTO is further evidenced when tracing the continual development of the WTO since its birth in 1995, during which time it has increasingly incorporated a 'democratic' claim within its identity. Formal rules and procedures and informal norms provide a means by which to trace the discursive formation. However, in so doing, they also make clear that the WTO cannot be understood as limited to any finite set of practices but consists of a much less certain and diffuse process.

Taking this as its point of departure, Chapter 3 argues that the boundaries of the WTO are, as constituted within discourse, inherently uncertain. This uncertainty is reflected in the rearticulation of the WTO post-1995, as reflected in rhetoric produced by the WTO Secretariat in response to a changing dis-cursive context. The primacy of informal mechanisms has been used by critics to suggest that the WTO is no more than the product of 'power politics' – reflecting the ideational-material problem at the heart of this book. However, as has been argued, discourse theory has great utility here because by theo-rizing the ideational and material as co-existent the informal and formal mechanisms appear as part of the same political process. Where formal or informal, all political mechanisms rely on the articulatory process as they are part of discourse. This demands further research into the shifting articulation of the WTO post-1995, where the WTO Secretariat has attempted to present the WTO as 'development-friendly' or as 'democratic'. Whilst the articulatory process cannot be limited to public relations, such carefully formed rhetoric does give a useful impression of the wider discursive process in which the WTO operates and the forces through which it is shaped.

The emergence and formalization of non-governmental organizations as a new category of actor recognized by the WTO is utilized in Chapter 4 to map the relationship between the organization and its wider discursive context. An 'NGO' identity has emerged in the WTO not as a result of individual or group agency, but through a series of dislocations in which a narrow articulation of 'trade' has been rearticulated to include many identities not previously con-nected to 'trade' as a governance field. This has been a slow and gradual process in which equivalential links have been formed between identities, bringing more and more into the field of multilateral trade governance embodied in the WTO. Who or what constitutes an actor in the WTO is subject to contingency. Through tracing the formalization process of a non-governmental organizations (or 'NGO') identity, it becomes apparent that the emergence of an NGO identity in the WTO cannot be understood as a development within the WTO alone.

Rather, it reflects a much wider and more diffuse process in which a 'trade' demand has appeared within the remit of an ever-growing series of actors previously not attentive to multilateral trade governance. This diffuse process includes both the emergence of new actors within multilateral trade govern-ance, and a series of overlapping issues. For example, environmental groups as national-level public-interest lobbyists find their identities destabilized by the intrusion of the WTO decisions overriding domestic regulations framed as protecting the environment. The group identity is shown to be contingent in two ways: first, the inability to define the 'national level' as an autonomous political sphere; and second, the inability to define the 'environment' as a separate policy sphere. The environmental identity is shown to be overlapping with trade. The effect is that both environment and trade are rearticulated to include new demands.

This has clearly radical implications for defining the WTO as a research object. Focusing on the articulatory processes constitutive of the WTO rather than on its formal structure provides a much deeper-level insight than otherwise possible. In addition, it demands that attention be given to many areas previously seen as external to the WTO, e.g. issue groups contesting WTO policies. The activities of such groups cannot be separately categorized as 'social movements' or 'civil society'. Instead, they are to be treated as constitutive parts of the political operation of the WTO. This clearly has much wider implications for political science, as it suggests so-called 'low' politics (e.g. gender, identity, social movements) cannot be separated from 'high' politics (e.g. international political economy, military conflict) but are part of the same (much more complex) political process.

The emergence of new political subjectivities within the discursive formation of the WTO has been further traced through interviews and first-person observation at key events marking the formation of collective action critical of negotiations to expand the WTO's General Agreement on Trade in Services (GATS) in the early-to-mid 2000s, in Chapter 5. Understanding such moments of contestation is of great importance because: 1 they map how previously unconnected social practices become linked into a particular relational sequence such that they emerge within the political operation of the WTO; 2 they indicate a series of mutually constitutive relationships in which the WTO both shapes, and is shaped by, its historical context; and, 3 it helps to trace out the complexity inherent in contemporary forms of global governance such as embodied in the WTO, and which exceed any institutional borders. The discursive context of this emergence consists of a relational network of social practices, with different degrees of sedimentation and subject to constant rearticulation. These practices coalesce around certain nodal points, such as individual figures, groups and networks. It is at these points that collective action (such as critical research, lobbying governments, group petitions) takes place, leading to further sedimentation of identities around the WTO.

The final and concluding chapter, Chapter 6, will both summarize the book's overall enquiry and address what implications its approach to the WTO has for the future study of global governance. Principally, acknowledging the articulatory process creates potential problems for research design because it demands that attention be given to practice previously abstracted out of research strategies focused on such entities as the WTO, e.g. issue group campaign formation. Whilst the first chapter of the book has introduced the theoretical basis for its research strategy, it is in the final chapter that the discussion considers what implications the approach formulated in these pages has for further research on global governance.

What is the 'WTO'?

Claims that the WTO is based on the 'rule of law' or the 'balance of power politics' both have validity to the extent that they embody particular discursive formations coalescing around the name 'WTO'. Though apparently contradictory, the presence of the two articulations suggests that they are both somehow important to making the WTO possible as a political object. The tension between the two positions does not equate to an ideational/material dichotomy, since such a distinction is untenable in post-structuralist discourse theory. 'WTO' = 'balance of power politics' is as much a product of discourse as is 'WTO' = 'rule of law'. Of interest in this book is how those different articulations represent aspects of the wider discursive formation of the WTO. For example, they reflect a certain articulation of who/what constitutes an 'actor'.

Overall, the book utilizes a mixture of primary and secondary sources through which to understand the formal institution of the WTO, whilst incorporating innovative analysis of new empirical data through which to understand the much more complex and diffuse political processes that exceed the legal-institutional arrangement. The book is important to understanding both the WTO and global governance because they are characterized by complexity, change and the apparent interplay between material and ideational factors. Post-structuralist discourse theory, as the book evidences, is well placed to study the WTO. As such, the argument outlined in these chapters should be of interest to students and researchers of not only the WTO and new actors within global governance, but also those intent on developing discourse theory into a coherent research strategy by which better to understand global politics.

Notes

1 'Member states' are capitalized here to acknowledge that this is a formal title given within the Marrakech Agreement establishing the WTO.
2 For example: 'Only officials from member governments can deal with the important routine tasks of the organization: accession of new members; initiation of disputes or complaints; interpretation of WTO rules; judgements on waivers of obligations; or working parties on free trade areas' (Winham and Lanoszka 2000: 28).
3 See Jackson 1998a: 45; and Jackson 1998b: 73; Hoekman and Kostecki 2001: 58; Kwa 2003; and Dunkley 2000.
4 For example: Hansen 2006; Campbell 1998; de Goede 2006; Griggs and Howarth 2000; Howarth and Torfing 2005; Epstein n.d., forthcoming; Dunn 2009.
5 This remains so even in the case of less tangible traded items – such as management consultancy – because it may be quantified (e.g. hours purchased).

2 Contesting global trade governance
A genealogy of the WTO

Introduction

> What it is possible to do in politics is generally limited by what it is possible to legitimise.
>
> Quentin Skinner[1]

To begin a discourse theoretical investigation of any political object it is essential first to evidence its discursive origins – that is, to underline the inherent contingency of things otherwise taken as given facts. This chapter is an exposition of the contingency of the present-day World Trade Organization, exhibiting the multiple articulations underlying the formulation of global trade governance. The WTO represents a particular articulation framing the conduct of global trade governance. For the WTO to be approached as a discursive formation, it is essential that it be understood as embedded within a particular social process and not an asocial entity driven by economic necessity. Literature debating the relative merits of the WTO's design allows consideration of how best to govern global trade rationally but, in so doing, further abstracts the WTO from the society in which it functions by positioning the WTO as the result of an economistic calculation of necessity. That is because they fail to underline the inherent contingency of the global trade governance as embodied in the WTO, limiting it to a politicized but still rationalistic argument of what works best for different policy goals. What is lacking within this perspective, as shown in the previous chapter, is a focus on the social origins of those particular rationalizations. By highlighting the contingency of present-day global trade governance, the discursive character of the WTO is made evident. In so doing, the political character of that enterprise becomes apparent, expanding debate beyond questions of what the economy necessitates to what type of societies one wishes to foster.

This chapter incorporates a Foucaultian genealogical approach within its broader discourse theoretical analysis, enabling the book to begin re-embedding the WTO within wider social practices. Utilizing a mixture of secondary historical texts and primary sources, the genealogical lens makes available a unique perspective that would otherwise be obscured within a traditional historical reading. While conventional history focuses on human agency and the material world (e.g. resources), a genealogy looks at the logics underlying political action. From this analysis it becomes clear that the discourse around global trade governance is not static. To the contrary, it is subject to repeated rearticulations. The significance of such rearticulation, understood within a discourse theoretical perspective, highlights how changing conditions of possibility shape political action. In other words, the genealogy makes visible the process through which, at different moments, global trade governance is made possible. Discussion of the Uruguay Round forms the last section of the chapter, showing how the GATT was articulated to be in 'crisis' and in 'need' of a new political configuration: the WTO. This is particularly significant with respect to contextualizing and better understanding the current 'crisis' facing the WTO – the stalling of the so-called Doha Round.

The rationalization of global trade governance is central to the WTO and yet, as this chapter makes clear, it is historically contingent and subject to a continuing process of change. Despite contingency, the present-day articulation of the WTO is based on the pretence of stability tracing the WTO along a line of continuity. For example, speeches are made during WTO meetings, where the present is claimed to have direct lineage to the creation of the General Agreement on Tariffs and Trade (GATT) in 1948, characterizing the present regime as a fixed, stable entity with a linear history. For example, at the 2005 WTO Ministerial Conference, Director-General Pascal Lamy stated to the trade ministers present that:

> You are the heirs of almost 60 years of tradition in trade negotiations, of a remarkable set of rules and decisions, and an impressive body of legal interpretations. You have also inherited a well-oiled machine that oversees and ensures the implementation of a balanced system of rights and obligations. You have every reason to be proud of the past achievements of your collective enterprise.[2]

Genealogy

While conventional historical accounts focus on human agency and the material world (e.g. economic resources),[3] a genealogy looks at the social logics underlying political action. Genealogical analysis is important to the discourse theoretical approach developed in this book because it helps draw out the underlying articulatory processes through which discursive formations are made possible. The genealogical lens is used in this chapter to trace out alternate articulations of global trade governance, where it has been at the centre of quite divergent political logics. From this analysis it becomes clear that the articulation of global trade governance is not static. On the contrary, it is subject to repeated rearticulations. The significance of such rearticulation highlights how changing conditions of possibility shape political action. In other words, the genealogy makes visible the process through which, at different moments, global trade governance is made possible.

The genealogy outlines a series of historical moments showing alternate articulations of global trade governance pre-dating the formal emergence of the WTO organization and regime in 1995, including the Uruguay Round from which it unexpectedly emerged. The use of a linear narrative allows the chapter to trace the iteration of certain concepts (e.g. 'development'), mapping out the rearticulation of such concepts in relation to different political projects.

Post-structuralist discourse theory differs from Foucault to the extent that he maintained a distinction between the discursive and extra-discursive (Laclau and Mouffe 2001: 107). However, this does not mean that parts of Foucault's project cannot help inform a discourse theoretical enquiry. The genealogical methodology that Foucault developed is particularly well suited for tracing the sedimentation and contestation characteristic of articulation, as will be discussed here.

For Foucault – as with Laclau and Mouffe – power is not a possession, nor a capacity (Sarup 1993: 73). It is more complex than a one-way relationship of domination (Dreyfus and Rabinow 1983: 186); better characterized as a relational network (Sarup 1993: 74). Relationships of domination and sub-ordination, within power, demand a network of reciprocation so that both parties are constrained by their mutuality (Rouse 1994: 107). Foucault, therefore, can point to no one group as in control of power. He writes:

> Power is not an institution, and not a structure; neither is it a certain strength we are endowed with; it is the name that one attributes to a complex strategical situation in a particular society.
>
> (Foucault, quoted in Nilson 1998: 64)

The subject is neither autonomous nor responsible for this situation, as Foucault sees it (Sarup 1993: 75); the subject is a product of the situation.

Agency and genealogy

Denying any explicit intentionality, Foucault 'finds force relations working themselves out in particular events, historical movements, and history' (Dreyfus and Rabinow 1983: 109). Here, then, is the process of what Laclau and Mouffe call *subject positioning* (Howarth 2000: 108–9), whereby identities are formed, as discussed in the previous chapter. This helps to elucidate how to understand moments where 'nation-states' appear as actors in the history of the multilateral trade regime. Statements such as the 'USA did this … ' refer not to any specific set of individuals but the particular discursive formation articulated as, for example, the 'USA' at that moment under discussion. Rather than suggesting agency from a unitary actor, such statements become indica-tive of the articulatory process through which certain logics operate. For the individuals operating within those identities, the subject position of the 'USA' will, at different times, facilitate quite alternate political projects than, for example, 'China'.

Contingency of the present

Foucault problematizes how certain ideals and concepts have been articulated at different historical moments.[4] This is not a concern with the past, but with the contingency of the present. A genealogy utilizes past events in order to trace out how a particular object has been differently articulated at various historical moments. Rather than drawing out any linear lines of causation, a genealogy is focused on the historical context of articulation. Whereas historical accounts of the GATT/WTO might trace its origins back to the 1929 Wall Street Crash, a genealogy is specifically interested in the articulatory moment, and would therefore approach 1929 as a point of dislocation facilitating the emergence of new identities and political action, rather than necessarily proving the validity of any system over another. As Foucault wrote, 'What is found at the historical beginning of things is not the inviolable identity of their origin; it is the dissension of other things. It is disparity' (Foucault 1991: 79). By examining discursive formations as historically emergent, a genealogy poses thought for what might otherwise have been, and aids a discourse theoretical project by highlighting that which has been 'excluded by the exercise of power and systems of domination' (Howarth 2000: 49). Such an approach is interested in discontinuity, rather than a narrative of causal chains. It is not meant to be a description of the past, but to use historical moments in order to, first, expose the contingency of the present, so that, second, one may begin to understand its construction.

Though certain social objects may reappear throughout history, apparent continuity cannot be taken for granted. As illustrated below, global trade governance signifies a plurality of distinct meanings. A social practice, which achieves being within discourse, is both repeatable and alterable – and, thus, *iterable* – so that the process of articulation is never permanently fixed (Howarth 2000: 41).[5] There is a trace of continuity just as much as there is discontinuity, with the consequence that social practices may reappear though their actual discursive form – their *being* – may have altered.

A genealogy's concern with discontinuity is thus equipped to draw out alternate historical articulations of global trade governance, so as to exhibit its contestatory nature in the present. This helps to mark out the series of sedimentation and dislocations underlying any discursive formation.

History of the present

Foucault (1991: 88) distances himself from any form of history that attempts to achieve self-discovery. There is no ultimate truth to discover. If history is to be 'effective', as he terms it, then it must:

Introduce discontinuity into our very being – as it divides our emotions, dramatises our instincts, multiplies our body and sets it against itself. 'Effective' history deprives the self of the reassuring stability of life and nature, and it will not permit itself to be transported by a voiceless obstinacy toward a millennial ending.

(Foucault 1991: 88)

Foucault avoids finalism, or presentism, stating clearly that his historical accounts are not intended to offer any form of understanding that might suggest that the past still animates the present (Foucault 1991: 80). Foucault's history is, quite differently, an unashamed history of the present.

Incorporating post-structuralist discourse theory terminology introduced in the previous chapter, the genealogy here utilizes a mixture of primary and secondary historical texts, tracing out the particular sedimentations and dislocatory moments at play within the articulation of global trade governance embodied in the GATT/WTO.

Domestic political representatives are currently able to influence the outcome of WTO negotiations in as much as those negotiating the various texts know that the finished product will eventually have to survive those representatives if it is to achieve ratification. The WTO rests upon this simplification of the political space, so that rather than submitting a large number of policy decisions as individual issues for separate contestation, they are effectively lumped together into packages called 'agreements' or 'rounds'. The discursive move at play here will become clearer in what follows.

Foucault's own use of genealogy was for what he called *problematization* (Schwartz 1998: 19). As said, Foucault was not concerned with ever writing a history of the past, nor of the meaning of ideas. Instead, he was interested in analysing problematization, which he defined as:

How and why certain things (behavior, phenomena, processes) became a problem. Why, for example, certain forms of behavior were characterized and classified as 'madness' while other similar forms were completely neglected at a given historical moment; the same thing for crime and delinquency, the same question of problematization for sexuality.

(Foucault 1983)

For Foucault, a particular problematization 'defines objects, rules of action, modes of relation to oneself' (Foucault 1984b). Schwartz (1998: 19) suggests that Foucault goes as far as to conceive it impossible for the human mind to think of its own existence without there first being a problematization with which to respond. Though an abstraction, problematization has concrete roots. Any problematization can only ever be understood, Foucault (1983: 66) thought, 'as a reply to some concrete and specific aspect of the world'. He continues, 'There is the relation of thought and reality in the process of problematization. And that is the reason why I think that it is possible to give an answer – the original, specific, and singular answer of thought – to a certain situation' (Foucault 1983: 66). Thus, narratives of 'crisis' can be found at the heart of political projects, where there is a 'need' for an answer. In this chapter, such moments are common, marking the continuing interplay between sedimentation and contestation that is constitutive of the articulatory process.

As evident in the account that follows, emphasizing discontinuity over continuity means that a genealogical method draws out the contingency through which one becomes aware of particular discourses. Genealogy helps achieve discourse theory's goal to denaturalize that which is taken as given. Additionally, by re-presenting those articulations that have fallen aside in the path of history, the contestatory process is made vivid. Thus, rearticulation can be seen as a constant process, in which discourse shifts. It is the high-lighting of these shifts that gives genealogy its utility within a discourse theoretical perspective.

Multiple articulations of global trade governance

Intended as a genealogy, this chapter should be read as outlining the multiple and divergent articulations through which global trade governance – as insti-tutionalized in the GATT/WTO – has been made possible. The basic question considered is: how is global trade governance rationalized? This query is put to a series of key periods in the history of the GATT/WTO regime. The con-cept of trade itself stretches back to a much earlier period and there are numerous alternative histories of its development, function and the inter-state treaties intended to govern it within human society. The analysis conducted here has a narrower scope, tracing out the hegemonic formations in the immediate history of the GATT/WTO regime rather than looking back to antiquity, since it amply demonstrates the discursive character of global trade governance.

Where a particular concept is mentioned when discussing an historical moment, this is because it is argued to be constitutive within the discursive formation that has made it possible to view trade governance as a policy problem at the global level – exceeding the identity of the nation-state. Certain concepts reappear as if constant in an historical process, but, as will be argued, they are not the same but altered depending on the particular discursive formation operating at that historical moment. The account given here is not a descriptive history, but is instead intent on understanding the articulatory process – and all its inherent tensions – through which the present being of the WTO is made possible. In the process, the purpose of looking back is to see the contingency of the present and its discursive underpinnings.

National security

The account begins in 1930s USA, mapping out the dislocatory process in which the governance of international trade was increasingly articulated as outside the sphere of the nation-state identity. The period and geographical location witnessed a shift away from the norm of reciprocity in international trade negotiations as retaliation against nation-states preventing access to their markets. A changing historical situation in which there was a growth of new high-technology companies in the USA seeking new consumers, and thus export, played an increasing role in this shift by dislocating then dominant understandings of the identity industry. Further dislocation was to be facilitated in the problematization that followed the Great Depression. In this context, a series of new identities emerged in which global trade governance as an act confined to the nation-state appeared as 'irresponsible/dangerous' and 'anti-progress'. Reciprocity was rearticulated to mean 'positive-sum bargaining'. Trade was being rearticulated as good for national security. This is not to say that the USA, or any other country, in this period was managing trade in a manner non-responsive to its perceived domestic 'interests', but that the articulatory process at this point marked a significant move towards global trade governance as 'multilateral' that involved a definite shift, particularly with respect to the USA.

The US Reciprocal Trade Agreements Act (RTAA), passed by Congress in 1934, authorized the US Executive a three-year (renewable) mandate to negotiate trade agreements with other states with no further need for Congressional consideration (Goldstein 1993: 209). This transference of authority from Congress to the Executive tied tariff-setting policy to US foreign policy like never before, as well as, argued by Hart, altering the built-in bias of US trade policy from protectionism (with high tariff rates on foreign imports) to liberalism (and lower tariff rates) (Hart 1995a: 127). At the foundation of the RTAA's legal justification was the 'Most-Favoured Nation' (MFN) principle. Although the agreements to be signed under the RTAA were bilateral, the MFN principle radically changed their nature so that, in the aggregate, these bilateral agreements came to provide the bedrock for the development of a much more multilateral approach to trade negotiation. In effect, trade was abstracted from the domain of domestic governance – subject to domestic political representatives – to the executive of the nation-state and negotiation with other nation-states.

The MFN principle was able to provide this hardcore for multilateralism because of the twin concepts of *reciprocity* and *equality* (or non-discrimination) contained within its operating logic. Bilateral trade negotiation, however weighted, incurs a certain degree of reciprocity between the present partners. If the partners grant MFN status to one another, it is agreed that each will accord to the other any trade concessions granted to a third party in future negotiations in which the other is not present. The MFN clause sediments a body of trade agreements to which more than two states are party and, as Snyder states, 'embodies the principle of *equality* of treatment in international economic relations' amongst those granted MFN status (Snyder 1940: 77, emphasis added). In effect, MFN provides for the formation of a regime.[6]

MFN was not unique in the USA. What made the RTAA significant, however, was the unconditional nature of its MFN clause. Goldstein (1993: 206) argues that this radically changed the meaning of reciprocity within US foreign trade policy. MFN had, within the USA, depended upon a high degree of conditionality, so that no concession would be extended to any state without receiving concessions in return. Without further country-by-country negotiation, the MFN meant relatively little, refusing tariff reductions for certain states' produce and, thus, was discriminatory (Goldstein 1993: 206). Reciprocity was, without unconditionality, available as much as a tool for retaliatory discrimination as it was for reduction of tariff barriers. The addition of unconditionality was a significant rearticulation, changing the political operation of the MFN principle.

Certainly pre-1934 it might have seemed that if any multilateral trade organization was to develop with the intent to reduce tariffs, as the GATT would later do, it would emerge from within Europe. The Most-Favoured Nation principle had existed since the seventeenth century, but it was in nineteenth-century Europe that it came to impact upon trade between nations (Fisher 1967: 841). The Cobden-Chevalier treaty, signed between Britain and France in 1860, has been described by Fisher (1967: 841) as the most important early commercial treaty to include the MFN clause. According to Boltho (1996: 250), Napoleon III signed the treaty to pacify the British, and from then on inserted the clause within numerous treaties signed by the French with other powers throughout Europe so that for a decade tariffs reduced throughout the continent. As that decade drew to a close, the 1870s ushered in a decline in the proliferation of unconditional MFN, so that the later nineteenth century witnessed a return to nationalism and protectionist trade policies (Fisher 1967: 842). This took place in the context of economic recession and a rise in competition from foreign produce (Boltho 1996: 252). European trade was also negatively affected by the eruption of the Franco–Prussian war (Fisher 1967: 842). To facilitate trade between nation-states, the period from 1890 onwards witnessed a succession of international forums held to discuss global economic relations and the flow of international commerce.[7]

In the USA, which had a history of utilizing an approach to foreign trade relations in which trade was viewed as the policy domain of domestic political representatives, the House of Representatives was approached with the plan for a multilateral trade organization (Goldstein 1993: 214). The idea was presented in the midst of the 1914–18 Great War, and came from Cordell Hull – an individual who became an important nodal point for the emerging discourse of 'trade liberalization'. At this point, however, the proposal was dismissed.

The USA had traditionally conducted its trade relations with foreign states on a bilateral basis of reciprocation, country by country. In 1923, a then little-noticed procedural change to US legislation effectively introduced the MFN clause into US trade treaties via non-conditionality. The Tariff Act of 1922 was articulated as a means to increase the flexibility of US tariffs to ease the country's ability to reciprocate high tariffs imposed by foreign states on US imports.[8] It was an Act set up to facilitate tariff control as *retaliation*, and championed by one of the leading advocates for tariff rates as national protection, Senator Reed Smoot. However, when passed, the interpretation of the ruling was queried in a letter to the US Secretary of State, sent by a proponent of the MFN clause and trade liberalization. The query stated that it was unclear if the increased flexibility facilitated by the Act might require the USA to raise tariff controls against the produce of all states that had signed a tariff agreement to which the USA was not party. The letter's author, William Culbertson, then argued that such an interpretation, as possible as it was from the act as it stood, would run opposite to the intention of Congress. In order to avoid such a reading, Culbertson suggested that the USA should ensure that all treaties it signed were unconditional. According to Goldstein, this communiqué was passed onto President Harding, 'who with little thought, approved this new policy'.[9] The consequence was an announcement that the USA would, from then on, adopt an unconditional MFN clause in all future trade treaties. Despite this formal policy change, however, it appears that the discursive shift only became apparent later.

The Act had been articulated to ease the ability of the USA to raise tariffs in retaliation against foreign states. However, a re-interpretation of the Act created a ruling in which the principle of flexible reciprocity was retained, but now included the addition of non-conditionality. Non-conditionality was adopted by the USA in order to avoid being obliged to raise tariffs, but in freeing its tariff controls from those of foreign states, the USA rearticulated the concept of 'reciprocity'. The adoption of non-conditionality meant that those countries granted MFN status by the USA could legitimately demand the same trade concessions granted to third parties. As such, all bilateral trade negotiations now carried significant secondary effects for states beyond those immediately present. The effect of this shift remained, however, unclear because in the 1920s there was still no mandate to reduce tariffs. There was little appetite for reducing tariffs, and all trade agreements remained under the authority of Congress, meaning that the re-interpretation seemed relatively unimportant. Consequently, the re-interpretation met little contestation, left as a small procedural change with minimal political significance (Goldstein 1993: 206). This event, though apparently of little notice at the time, illustrates that articulation is potentially an extremely slow process. The effect would not be felt at this point.

In 1927, the World Economic Conference produced the Geneva Convention on Import and Export Prohibitions and Restrictions, the most ambitious attempt so far to reduce the perceived rise in 'protectionism' via, arguably, multilateral means (Beane 2000: 53). However, the convention failed to receive ratification due to disagreement over agriculture, in particular, and the 18 countries required to provide their signatures, one by one, withdrew their support. The immediate period preceding 1930 was therefore marked by a period of rising 'self-interest'[10] in the foreign trade policies of the leading states and unsuccessful attempts at multilateral management of global trade.

However, the norm of the unconditional MFN clause was now recognized within the trade treaty making apparatus of the hegemon-in-ascent, the USA, due to a relatively unnoticed rearticulation of the 'reciprocity' norm so that it was now twinned with the concept of 'non-conditionality'.

The dominance of 'economic nationalism' was interrupted in the early 1930s following the crisis marked by the Great Depression and growing hostilities in Europe, framed by the history of the Great War. This event represented a dislocatory moment in which the hegemonic formation was exposed as contingent, the concept of 'reciprocity' as 'retaliation' appearing no longer central to 'national security' in the context of such instability. Those who perceived 'liberalization' of international trade to be in their favour articulated their arguments for lowering tariffs and other barriers to free-flowing global commerce as a last-ditch attempt to stave off yet further sorrow and bloodshed (Trebilcock and Howse 1999: 20). The story of a world overtaken by out-of-control economic nationalism was easily epitomized by the Smoot-Hawley tariff act of 1930. This act instigated unilateral raising of US tariffs and was blamed for being the spark that lit the taper to retaliatory tariff rises throughout Europe and Japan.[11] The revulsion evoked by the Smoot-Hawley tariff opened the ground for changes that would not have been possible had it not been for this moment of crisis. When the Democrats came to the presidency in 1933 with Franklin D. Roosevelt, a potent moral economy existed in which there was a general desire for change, to push against the 'old' ways. In this environment, 'protectionism' was susceptible to the charge of being 'old' (Goldstein 1989: 69). Present at this moment is the articulation of a dichotomy between 'liberalization' and 'protectionism'. Each acts effectively as an empty signifier, so that 'liberalization' = 'progress' + 'internationalism' + 'export-led economics' + 'new industry'; and, 'protectionism' = 'anti-progress' + 'nationalism' + 'self-sufficient economics' + 'old industry' (see Figure 2.1).

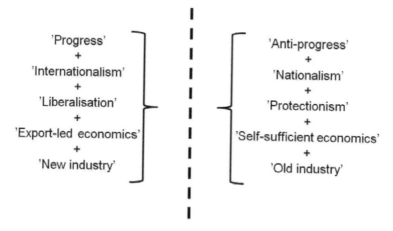

Figure 2.1 Articulation of 'liberalization' vs 'protectionism' under F.D. Roosevelt

Roosevelt's 'New Deal' and the space for rearticulation

At Roosevelt's side as Secretary of State was Cordell Hull, who had long and ardently advocated the USA take an active approach to the 'liberalization' of international trade. Despite this, Roosevelt's 'New Deal' of reform by no means suggested the new president to be fully enamoured by 'open trade'.[12] This was exemplified in legislation to provide state intervention to protect agriculture and labour from foreign imports articulated as 'external threats' (Haggard 1988: 102; Goldstein 1993: 210–11). Trade was thus understood as protecting agriculture and labour, defined within national borders. Traditionally contained under the same approach to trade policy as agriculture, in the 1930s US industry took a steadily divergent position, with coalitions of US merchants and new companies (including General Electric and IBM), all keen to find new export markets, lobbying for trade liberalization.[13] US economic planners were uncertain as to the future of US agriculture, recommending price supports and subsidization programmes with state intervention (Goldstein 1989: 50–68). However, US manufacturing was understood to advocate that in order to succeed, it required new export markets (Goldstein 1989: 32). The combined force of this particular brand of economic thinking and industry lobbying found resonance in a Democrat Administration which, unlike the former Republican Administration of President Hoover, was less dependent upon the more traditional economic sectors that were most threatened by the risk of increased foreign competition. Here, then, the identity of the 'USA' was being rearticulated. 'Trade liberalization' was a way of ensuring that the new industries developing in the USA were able to open up Europe as a market for lucrative expansion, especially at a time when the European industries would have been preoccupied by growing tensions between their countries (Sen 2003: 117).

In this discursive context, Cordell Hull's demands persuaded Roosevelt to allow him to create an interdepartmental Committee on Commercial Policy, chaired by his State Department, to suggest reform of US foreign trade policy (Haggard 1988: 110). The committee called for the strengthening of the unconditional MFN principle (Haggard 1988: 111). The group drew up a secret list of sectors in which the USA had definite 'comparative advantage' over other nations, to support future negotiations geared towards finding the export markets necessary to support the 'economic recovery' of post-depression USA, key to Roosevelt's presidency (Haggard 1988: 111).

The figure of Hull stands out as a nodal point at the centre of the developments that would lead to the GATT/WTO regime. The contest over trade policy was frequently articulated in terms of 'ideology', advocates of protectionism and trade liberalization accusing the other of blind faith in the divinity of their perspective (Wolman 1992: 27). In order to ensure the success of his own particular outlook, Hull surrounded himself in the State Department with a close entourage of fellow thinkers, schooled in an economic perspective that favoured his brand of trade liberalization, based as it was in Wilsonian internationalism (Haggard 1988: 100). He, and those around him, were instrumental in ensuring that the USA played an assertive role in the management of global trade relations.[14] To achieve this end, Hull set about the centralization of foreign economic policy, attempting to remove it from the legislative control of an inward-looking Congress.[15] In referring to Hull, the intention is not to suggest that the individual should be taken as an explanatory variable, but that he represents – through the discursively constructed identity in which he is positioned – a much wider discursive shift in which the ideas he advocated were formed, and found resonance.

The Reciprocal Trade Agreements Act (RTAA) was passed by the US Congress in 1934, despite controversy, as an 'emergency' act intended to provide the president with special temporary powers to negotiate the trade agreements which, it was argued, would reinvigorate the US economy (Haggard 1988: 111). The RTAA's centralization of trade-negotiating authority within the US Executive was opposed by Republicans on the grounds that it was 'unconstitutional', providing the president with the power to make decisions that had the potential to dictate the fate of different economic sectors without accountability to either those sectors or Congress (Haggard 1988: 112). Despite objections, the RTAA was passed on the proviso that it would run for only three years, with renewal subject to Congress's approval, and that it incorporate an institutional mechanism by which different economic sectors might express their views on trade negotiations (Haggard 1988: 113). The Administration opposed any form of public hearing that might open trade negotiations to the pressures from which the RTAA was intended to free the USA (Haggard 1988: 113). Articulated thus, trade became increasingly sedimented as an issue for a more 'internationally aware' (or 'liberalist') identity, than the 'nationalist' identity of 'old industry'.

To overcome the requirement that different economic sectors be provided a say in US trade negotiations, the 'Committee for Reciprocity Information' was created as an obstacle, narrowing down the field of contestation open to those lobbying against 'trade liberalization' (Haggard 1988: 115–16). Those attempting to influence any pending negotiation met a committee of 'experts' rather than members of a legislature, in an institutional structure designed to make politics as invisible as possible (Haggard 1988: 115–16). The RTAA's technocratization of foreign trade policy took tariff policy away from the high politics of the last few decades so that it appeared to become a matter to concern only trade 'experts' rather than the wider public (Haggard 1988: 94).

The above depoliticization of foreign trade policy occurred in the context of a joint strategy in which multilateral trade management and liberalization were articulated as efforts to reverse the growing tension in Europe. Cordell Hull managed to create an equivalential logic between protectionism, nationalism and international conflict, in the minds of the American people (Haggard 1988: 104). As an example of the presentation of Hull's argument, a similarly minded colleague within the US State Department stated in 1939 that:

The world today is in too perilous a state to risk further conflict. It is for peace-loving America, with its incomparable natural resources, its intelligent population, and its economic strength, to lead the way in a program of economic liberalization and deliverance; and upon no other policy than that of equality of treatment can such a liberalizing program be based. America could not be true to her traditions and follow any other cause.

(Sayre 1939: 423)

Hull's RTAA sedimented the concept that setting tariffs based upon either unilateralism or bilateral retaliation had a negative effect upon not only national trade but also national security (Beane 2000: 54). Critics of the RTAA argued that the unconditional MFN principle effectively risked 'unilateral economic disarmament' by forfeiting the right to use retaliatory tariff measures (Haggard 1988: 115). To such arguments, Hull replied that the unconditional MFN clause did not prevent the USA from launching retaliatory measures against a state that raised tariff barriers to US industry to which it had signed under the MFN clause of the RTAA. Whether disingenuous or mistaken, the legal meaning of the MFN clause present in the RTAA did, in fact, prevent such retaliatory action against a state party to an agreement signed under the Act (Goldstein 1993: 208).

In terms of its immediate physical impact upon US trade relations, the RTAA was limited, with only two of the trade agreements signed under its remit having been made with large countries. These were Canada and Britain. The remaining agreements were made with economically minor countries (Haggard 1988: 92). The RTAA also contained 'escape clauses', leaving it responsive to its environment, and thus meaning that it has been described as 'embedded liberalism' (Haggard 1988: 102).[16] Such inconsistencies point to the role of discourse. It would also be misleading to suggest that the RTAA removed all authority over trade agreements from the US Congress. Congress still retained ultimate legislative control, but only once an overall package had been discussed by the Executive, meaning that the actual management of trade negotiations was now the prerogative of the president, leaving the Administration with the ability to pre-shape the field of contestation at the domestic level (Sen 2003: 125).

The 1930s witnessed a sedimentation of the juxtaposition between particular articulations of the concepts of 'reciprocity' and 'non-conditionality' in the foreign trade policy of the USA. This articulation was the product of a series of dislocatory moments, and reflected a battle between different sectors of capitalism within the USA, as well as labour for the articulation of the identity of the 'USA'. Those companies that saw exports as necessary for profit maximization, and viewed themselves as capable of protection against the threat of imports, were the capital-intensive high-technology firms. They fitted into an emerging discursive formation in which they were constructed as 'progressive', and representative of the trade that would improve national security. These concepts were shaped in terms of a project in which American policy makers sought to rebuild their national economy after the devastation of the late 1920s/early 1930s via aggressively expanding their modern manufacturing sector into European markets. In this context, Haggard has described the RTAA as a tool of 'hegemonic predation', in which the USA took advantage of its status as a hegemon in ascent to open up new export markets (Haggard 1988: 93). However, within this project, legitimized by the need to rebuild the US economy and reverse tensions for which 'economic nationalism' was blamed, the concept of equal treatment was sedimented at the centre of international trade relations by a USA that was being sedimented as 'global hegemon/leader', and the ground was set for the developments of the 1940s, into which the GATT/WTO regime would emerge.

Peaceful cooperation

The discursive formation in which trade was articulated as equivalential with peaceful cooperation took a new turn in the 1940s, which would see a further sedimentation of global trade governance as beyond the preserve of the nation-state. The management of trade was sedimented as a 'multilateral' issue. This was made possible in the context of a series of dislocatory moments in which former colonial relations were weakened, as there was a dramatic shift in the identity of European nation-states, which moved from the virility of Empire to the weakness of decline. This movement was emphasized by the 1947 US Marshall Plan. Although several European nation-states tried to revive the concept of trade governance as the preserve of the nation-state, the USA – in which the concept had already been sedimented – was able to prevent this through its own sedimented identity as 'global hegemon'.

The 'multilateral' dimension of Cordell Hull's liberal trade philosophy gained new resonance with the onset of the Second World War, 'multilateralism' argued by Roosevelt to be important to the allied cause (Zeiler 1999: 9). The belief that unilateral tariff measures and economic nationalism exacerbate international conflict came to shape much of the planning for the post-war world, which had already begun as early as 1941 in earnest in the Atlantic Charter signed between Roosevelt and British Premier Churchill (Beane 2000: 57). Hull's earlier calls for a multilateral trade organization were matched by Britain's James Meade, who advocated the creation of a commercial union to facilitate the management of global trade (Hart 1995a: 138–39). Although the concept of a regulatory institution for trade between nations was discussed at the 1944 Bretton Woods summit, all negotiating energy was absorbed in the creation of the International Monetary Fund (IMF) and the International Bank for Reconstruction and Development (Jackson 1998a: 14–15; Trebilcock and Howse 1999: 20).

The Atlantic Charter, Bretton Woods and the San Francisco 1945 conference establishing the United Nations (UN) all witnessed a repetition of the message that in order to secure peaceful relations amongst states, it was necessary to look at the nature of commercial policies between those states (Goldstein 1993: 215). 'Liberalization' was sedimented within the US identity, and provided the driving logic behind attempts to 'win the peace' post-1945.[17] It also provided the USA with an ideological launch pad from which to crack open new markets for its expanding industry (Ruggie 1983: 214).

The RTAA gave the US Administration a flexibility – freed from the constraints of immediate accountability to Congress – that allowed it to take full advantage of its rising hegemonic status and direct the shape of the post-war plans (Beane 2000: 57; Nivola 1986; Jackson 1998a: 15). The 1934 RTAA was originally passed on the proviso that it would be subject to re-evaluation after three years, as said earlier. Successful extensions (in 1937, 1940, 1943, 1945 and onwards) were helped by a growing US economy in which capital shifted over to large-scale industry keen to export, but the support of public opinion was won by framing the RTAA within a cooperative (and internationalist) project towards a peaceful and progressive world (Zeiler 1999: 6–19).[18] The 1940s began with much uncertainty as to the future of the MFN principle, a leading American political science journal publishing the pessimistic forecast that:

> As regards the future of most favored nation treatment … it may not survive the onslaught of economic and political changes, in which case it will be almost completely discarded in favor of the principle of bilateral bargaining. In all probability, the present war in Europe … [will] render inoperative many commercial treaties embodying the clause, and it will intensify policies of trade regulation which are antithetical to equality of treatment.
>
> (Snyder 1940: 96–97)

Though the RTAA achieved renewal, the MFN principle had not firmly sedimented itself, facing a dramatic reversal within Europe, which had traditionally led promotion of its use in trade between nations. That leadership role would now be subsumed by the USA.

1945 marked both the resolution of major military conflicts in Europe and the Pacific and the fourth renewal of the RTAA and, with that momentum, the USA invited representatives from several other states to begin discussions towards the creation of a multilateral agreement for the mutual reduction of tariffs, intended as a consolidation of the bilateral agreements negotiated under the RTAA (Jackson 1998a: 16). Hegemonic within the United Nations, formed that same year, the USA was able to use a subsidiary body of the UN – the Economic and Social Council (ECOSOC) – to call for an 'International Trade Organization' to facilitate multilateral trade negotiations (Jackson 1998a: 16).

The ideological vein of these discussions was distinctly tilted towards 'trade liberalization'. The British, influenced by Keynes, favoured a greater role for the domestic state in economic planning. Though its imperial ambitions were near-exhausted, Britain's demands additionally included the retention of colonial preferences, to maintain its territories (Zeiler 1999: 20–40; Hart 1995a: 132). On the other hand, the USA's foreign trade policy was increasingly in the hands of pro-export lobbyists keen to ensure the removal of trade barriers to expansion into Europe. US efforts also focused elsewhere on the possibility of entering the new markets promised by the decline of European colonialism (Ruggie 1983: 201–41). The USA promoted an ideological push towards minimalization of the state and a flourishing of universalism, exemplified in the logic of 'equality' germinating via the RTAA and figures such as Cordell Hull (Ruggie 1983: 202; Zeiler 1999: 41–58).

To structure the new economic order, the USA endorsed the creation of both an agreement to sediment the tariff reductions under the RTAA, and an institution to house that agreement – the International Trade Organization (ITO), an organization to be based in the UN that would act as a sibling to the IMF and World Bank.

The plans for the ITO were ambitious, incorporating the idealism of the UN with an intention to include not just trade policy, but labour policy and other issue areas that gave it far-reaching geopolitical goals (Hart 1995a: 162). Consequently, discussions over the ITO gained a high profile, giving the politics over its creation visibility (Beane 2000: 56; Zeiler 1999: 41–58). This exposed the process to an intense contestation that forced the eventual product to adopt many compromises (Goldstein 1993: 216–17; Cohn 2002: 22). Although many of the economically weakest states were represented only by proxy as colonial territories, the ITO received persistent demands that preferential treatment be given to those national economies on the periphery of global trade in order to aid their development.[19] The eventual product was signed at the United Nations Conference on Trade and Employment in 1948, at Havana, perceived by the USA as a compromise to its original intentions (Hart 1995a: 125–67; Cohn 2002: 50; Zeiler 1999: 75–88). To arrange its construction, the UN created an 'Interim Commission for the International Trade Organization' (ICITO) (Jackson 1998a: 19).

Whilst the ITO was in discussion, the multilateral agreement proposed to sediment the legacy of the RTAA – the General Agreement on Tariffs and Trade (GATT), was signed in 1947 (Hart 1995a: 125). With much contestation focused on the higher-profile ITO, the GATT was sedimented in a relatively narrow discursive environment in which the USA was able to ensure that the end product was responsive to its own position on global trade management.[20] Eleven of the original 23 contracting parties were 'developing states' (Michalopoulos 2001: 43). These 11 economically weaker states included: Brazil, Burma, Ceylon, Chile, China, Cuba, India, Lebanon, Pakistan, Rhodesia and Syria. The attractiveness of GATT for these states was the promise of increased access to the rich US market, just as the USA saw GATT as a means by which to launch its own trade invasion into Europe and emerging markets around the world (Keohane 1984: 180). These economically weaker states remained relatively inactive in a system that has been described as containing a 'club-like' elitism geared towards excluding any sense of a development agenda for its economically poorest members (Cohn 2002: 23). In 1947–48, any attempts by these states to change the direction of global trade management would have been over-stretched by efforts to affect the sedimentation of the ITO. The voices of these countries were constrained because of a lack of unity or coalition movement around 'development issues' as well as the subsumption of the needs of many smaller countries within colonialism (Cohn 2002: 49, 50, 53). There were no special provisions or exceptions in respect of the rights or obligations of these members; as such, difference (potentially articulated as 'material inequality') between the contracting parties was institutionally invisible (Michalopoulos 2001: 23). In effect, the identity 'developing country' lacked being in the GATT, with the agreement making no mention of 'development' (Narlikar 2004: 135).

The contestation around GATT was further narrowed by its head start over the ITO. GATT could place its origins in the RTAA, shaped by that earlier sedimentation so that some of the most potentially damaging contestations had been cleared from its path (Hart 1995a: 163). More pragmatic than the ITO, the GATT's initial singular concern with tariff controls meant that it was a comparatively modest agreement not completely distant from more traditional trade agreements (Jackson 2000: 21–24). Despite this, electoral changes in the USA brought in both a Republican Congress and president, creating uncertainty as to the extent of US legislative support for 'trade liberalization' and 'multilateralism'. Truman favoured GATT, but it was uncertain as to how the agreement might weigh with Congress. This potential source of contestation was, however, constrained by what authority over foreign trade policy the RTAA gave the Executive (Jackson 1998a: 16).

This modest approach to the regulation of global trade suited the often divergent positions taken by the different parties signed to GATT (Goldstein 1993: 202). There was no mention of 'free trade' – only a loose agreement that tariffs should be reduced (Hoekman and Kostecki 2001: 37; Cohn 2002: 378). Within the realm of tariffs, GATT was intended to increase predictability amongst the contracting parties by restricting their ability unilaterally to raise tariff barriers, as well as ensuring that via the agreement's legal standing, any future administration in those states would be bound by the GATT (Keohane 1984: 118). However, GATT was sensitive to domestic political representatives in the sense that its limited articulation of 'liberalism' meant that the agreement was unable to override domestic laws (Jackson 2000: 24). It was very much a product of its time, part of the then hegemonic discursive formation. GATT lacked any form of a 'development' agenda (Cohn 2002: 23, 53). As already stated, European colonialism weakened the position of those states that might otherwise have campaigned for a development agenda. Positioned as 'colonies', they effectively lacked the political subjectivity required for agency. Even those states that had achieved independence were still constrained in their actions by neo-colonial linkages. Many of the concessions made to economic disparity in the sedimentation of the ITO had been brought not by the weaker states themselves, but by Britain or France, which sought to maintain at least the economic component of their diminishing empires through providing trade preferences to their former territories (Zeiler 1999: 39). The USA had an imperial legacy via preferential trade arrangements with its former territory of the Philippines, but not to the same extent as the European powers, and so overwhelming US hegemony in the formation of the GATT gave the agreement relative immunity from such pressure.

The GATT combined 'reciprocity' with the concept of 'non-discrimination', in effect adopting the same practice from the RTAA (Winters 1990: 1289). Non-discrimination is effectively the same as non-conditionality, and, as agreed in the GATT, incorporated the MFN clause with the principle of 'national treatment'.[21] The MFN principle took on particular significance within the framework of the GATT because of the size of the agreement. Requiring that tariff concessions granted to one contracting party be given equally to all other states party to the GATT created a polity in which a particular approach to managing international trade was universalized to minimize the visibility of national particularity.

The specific arrangements for decision making in the GATT were never formally decided, left vague due to the fact that it was never formally articulated as an 'institution' in itself. It was understood that the ITO would provide this function. However, the 1947 Charter establishing the GATT as a multilateral agreement did contain provision for voting which, in contrast to the institutional arrangements for weighted voting utilized in the IMF and World Bank, operated on a 'one-member, one-vote' basis (Jackson 1998a: 41). The GATT formally provided each of its Contracting Parties with equal voting power. Zeiler views this as symptomatic of the GATT's success – a claim towards equal treatment despite overt dominance by the identity of particular nation-states (Zeiler 1999: 165–79). The particular concept of equality built within the GATT would prove to be an important legitimating logic empowering the development of the GATT/WTO regime.

Weapon of the free world

A changing historical situation in which nation-state identities were polarized around the creation of a Cold War axis dislocated the logic in which GATT had been formed as a multilateral regime, in which trade was peaceful cooperation. Trade was now to be a 'weapon', not facilitating an open community of nations, but constituting a closed club of nations equivalentially defined as the 'Free World', against an equivalential chain in which 'Communist World' acted as the empty signifier.

The ITO died a quiet death after a short and unfulfilled life of compromise, the end coming in 1950 and the US Executive's withdrawal of ratification of the proposed organization from Senate consideration (Hart 1995a: 125).[22] Refusal by the USA to support the organization dealt the blow that brought the ideal of the International Trade Organization seemingly to an end, but not the multilateral trade regime now tentatively established in the form of the General Agreement on Tariffs and Trade. As detailed above, the politics of the ITO were much more visible than that involved in the sedimentation of the GATT, leaving the end product dissatisfactory in the eyes of those within the USA who had originally led the push for a multilateral trade organization. Time was a factor, the ITO less able to capture the momentum for radical change that followed the economic depression of the 1930s and militant nationalism that was seen to have led to the Second World War. The GATT, though not a formal organization, did appear to fill the vacuum opened up in the wake of the crisis, with less force now present to empower the much more demanding idealism of the ITO (Hart 1995a: 165).

Whilst the GATT could speak to the same American liberal-capitalist ideology that had facilitated the RTAA, the ITO's inclusion of state inter-vention and special treatment of the colonial territories of the old European powers was easily articulated by its critics as a betrayal of the 'American way' (Hart 1995a: 164; Zeiler 1999: 146). With the onset of the Cold War and the construction of an ideological binary opposition between the Soviet Union and the USA, American feeling was particularly sensitive to anything that could be articulated as challenging the now sedimented 'free market' of US society.[23]

In the discursive formation of the Cold War, the US Administration's sense of its managerial role was heightened, as opposed to a more neutral form of engagement that had been present in the attempts to create the ITO (Zeiler 1999: 194). GATT fitted into this context as a tool for shaping the trade policy – and, thus, the identity – of foreign states. Boltho emphasizes the importance of the ideological dimension during the 1950s in the USA's foreign policy towards Europe; trade liberalization to be the preventative to further wars (Boltho 1996: 250). However, the US push for the opening of markets in Europe was also to cement relations between the continent and the capitalist global economy, in which the USA was hegemonic. The Marshall Plan, sup-ported by the grossly dominant political situation of the USA, allowed a structural adjustment of Europe, with the intention that, where shaped by the USA, Europe would serve as a 'bulwark against communism' (Zeiler 1999: 251). Against opposition from the Commonwealth, the USA brought Germany and Japan into the GATT as a means of 're-integration' and, in the case of Japan, 'Westernization' in order to contain communism in Asia (Zeiler 1999: 141, 172). In this context, the GATT operated as a tool for consolidation and reinforcement of US power, by promoting economic integration throughout the 'Western alliance', rather than as a universal (global) project. The value attached to GATT as a weapon to discriminate between allies and enemies had already been made clear as early as 1948 when the US Congress expressed disgust upon President Truman's failure to protest the accession of Czechoslovakia, then a close Soviet ally, as a contracting party to GATT (Zeiler 1999: 86). The principle of equal treatment thus found its parameters in the Cold War, its applicability constrained as a means to utilize the USA's economic strength (and lucrative domestic market) as a tool to reward allies and ostracize those deemed 'enemies'.[24]

Despite – or, perhaps, because of – its re-assignment as a weapon of war, GATT was operated with caution (Jackson 2000: 374). Although the agreement contained a mechanism intended to settle any disputes that might arise over the often vague wording of its content, disputes were typically settled outside the GATT, avoiding the visibility of disagreement within the institution.[25] The effect was to shift international trade away from the contestation of public scrutiny (Hart 1995a: 167). Despite the provision of voting on a 'one-member, one-vote basis', the actual practice of decision making that developed in the 1950s relied solely on a process of achieving consensus (Jackson 2000: 374). Disagreements are to be expected in negotiations over any agreement that includes more than 20 states and so, arguably, the fact that consensus was chosen over the formal process of voting suggests a deliberate intention from those hegemonic in the GATT's discursive formation to achieve an outward impression that not only did each contracting party receive equal treatment, but also that each was of equal opinion.

In 1955, the US Congress effectively tested the degree to which the GATT would appease US demands by passing trade legislation that placed the country in open and direct violation of the agreement (Beane 2000: 134). According to Beane, the other contracting parties had only two options: 1 to demand that the USA 'bring its laws into compliance with the system'; or, 2 'make the legislative actions legal within the system' (ibid.: 135). They chose the latter, acknowledging the initial violation, but papering it over with the authorization that the USA be given a waiver. For Beane, the waiver meant that 'the system at least was able to surround the US action with the illusion of some degree of legality and, therefore, by not ignoring the problem, at least on the surface, maintain to as greater degree as possible the integrity of the regime' (ibid.: 136). The survival of the GATT was based on a pragmatic approach to multilateral trade negotiation, emphasizing the attempt to adapt the discursive formation to a changing context. With this event, a fundamental shift took place away from procedure towards a much more flexible philosophical adherence to the basic principles of GATT (ibid.: 63). This does not just reflect the importance of the USA to the GATT, but also suggests the perceived importance of the agreement to those outside the USA.

Principally, Europe was returning to at least a semblance of its former economic status, and was already beginning to aggregate its negotiation position, and so increase its leverage within GATT (Beane 2000: 66). European nation-states may have also believed that they stood to gain from a GATT in which US determination was now questionable. The same was true for Japan, which signed up to the GATT in 1955. Beane argues that the actions of the US Congress greatly undermined the credibility and negotiating power of the US Executive, stating 'US trade policy was no longer seen as unified, and further questions were raised about US commitments to its negotiated schedules' (Beane 2000: 83, ft 54). Arguably, this moment represents a dislocation, however swiftly the discursive formation re-adjusted, because it showed the contingency of the USA's identity as 'manager', creating new political subjectivity in the form of post-war Europe and Japan. It also represents the sedimentation of the GATT as 'important' to the rearticulated identities of Western European 'nation-states' and Japan.

In 1954–55, the GATT was placed under review with the intention of sedimenting the procedures developed thus far, as well as devising a more concrete institutional framework within which the agreement could operate. Proposals were made for the creation of the 'Organization for Trade Cooperation' (OTC), to provide this framework (Zeiler 1999: 195). Though much less ambitious than the ITO, the OTC suffered the same fate as its predecessor, falling at the hurdle of the US Congress (Beane 2000: 67). However, that it was attempted represents a new push towards 'multilateralism'. The Review did produce significant reform to the GATT in, first, the US waiver already mentioned, but also it strengthened the GATT secretariat into a much more permanent body, putting into question whether the GATT was still merely an agreement, or whether it had become an 'institution' (Beane 2000: 67). This represented a further sedimentation of trade governance as exceeding the nation-state.

By 1955, apart from the emergence of a stronger Europe, the collapse of colonialism gave birth to a host of new independent states, some of which had by then become sufficiently stable to enter the process of multilateral trade negotiation under the GATT (Beane 2000: 66–67). This change fed into the Review and, by 1956, the agreement developed acknowledgement of the special 'development' problems faced by the economically poorest states.[26] For the first time in the GATT, developing countries existed as a group (Michalopoulos 2001: 25). Significantly, this acknowledgement did not amount to providing a definition or necessarily a single identity, but instead focused on a set of key issues of particular concern to economically poor countries (Michalopoulos 2001: 23). These countries existed as countries experiencing a set of problems seen here as indicating a lack of development – their identity provided not by a single definition but by a series of shared concerns involving such areas as primary commodities and infant industry. The logic of equality was to be rearticulated so that 'equality' now meant 'special and differential treatment'. The Review led to the insertion of Article XVIII in the GATT, which allowed those countries experiencing severe balance-of-payments problems (where much more was imported than could be exported, causing a monetary insufficiency) to operate certain quantitative restrictions on imports (Michalopoulos 2001: 25). Additional measures brought in under Article XVIII included acceptance of trade restrictions when used to support infant industry intended to raise living standards (Michalopoulos 2001: 25). Along with Article XVIII, the Review led to the adoption of the Resolution on Particular Difficulties Connected with Trade in Primary Commodities, which 'called for an annual review of trends and developments in commodity trade' (Michalopoulos 2001:

25). The resolution was seen as of particular relevance to the economically poorest countries because their economies were viewed as being dependent largely upon such 'primary commodities'.

The discussion on 'primary commodities' continued into the Harberler report, which in 1958 stated that 'there is some substance in the feeling of disquiet among primary producing countries that the present rules and conventions about commercial policies are relatively unfavourable to them' (quoted in Michalopoulos 2001: 25). This amounted to acknowledgement that global trade was weighted against those with the smallest share in it. This, however, led to few reductions in the criticized tariff barriers of the economically richer states (Srinivasan 1998: 23).

The 'weaker states' in the global economy remained lacking influence and demands that their special circumstances be acknowledged in the trade policy of the richer states proved ineffective beyond the actions discussed above. Multilateral trade management remained the prerogative of the richer states, only negotiating special treatment for the 'weaker states' on a bilateral basis and often under the pretence of a colonial legacy. However, from the late 1950s, the demise of European colonialism provided the emergence of new nation-state identities that led to a swelling of GATT's ranks so that a majority of the GATT's contracting parties consisted of the 'weaker states' (Beane 2000: 89). The attraction GATT held for these countries was, it seems, in part due to the pragmatically cautious manner in which it was applied, making few radical demands upon its signatories (Beane 2000: 89, 142). An additional factor will have been the lure of selling to the US market, but the importance of fresh independence for many of the new contracting parties should not be underestimated, each eager to prove itself a credible political entity to be acknowledged on the international stage. No longer would their negotiating voice be subsumed by proxy within the position of the European powers. The GATT was seen as new and its promise of 'multilateralism' and 'equal treatment' in management of the global economy would have been a tempting ideal for these states, even if an equal approach to trade policy disadvantaged them as experiencing particular unequal economic problems. The GATT had become important to the identity of nation-states, and newly emerging nation-states wanted recognition.

The 1950s confronted the GATT with an economic order and set of issues contrary to its thesis for trade liberalization. Equality was rearticulated within the parameters of the Western alliance that surrounded the hegemonic leadership of the USA. The new visibility of development issues faced this order with a challenge and potential disruption, brought by the arrival of the newly independent countries, but the pragmatic flexibility of the GATT was successfully able to accommodate many of these states within its multilateral framework. Article XVIII and the Harberler report claimed to have acknowledged the 'unequal' position of these countries in the global economy and thus pacified any disruption to the GATT's logic of equal treatment.

Development

Though the equivalential logic in which trade was a Cold War weapon continued, development became increasingly prominent in the 1960s, particularly as a North and South divide emerged in the concept of the nation-state which challenged both the logic of multilateralism and the alternative divide of Free World and Communist. In this context, trade became increasingly articulated as a 'tool for development'.

The Fifth Round (the 'Dillon Round') of GATT negotiations, in 1960–61, was held amidst a perceived worsening of the economic situation for many weaker states, which led to their increased desire to find export success via greater engagement in the multilateral trade negotiation process (Beane 2000: 71–72). The contracting parties reformed the principle-supplier line norm, which had up until then dictated that negotiations on any one product be led by the principle supplier in that market. As few of the 'weaker states' could claim to be a principal supplier in many goods areas, this practice had favoured the richer states taking a hegemonic role in negotiations over nearly all goods.[27] Abandoning the principle-supplier line norm appeared to open trade talks in the GATT to a greater number of state actors.

Dillon also institutionalized a general system of preferences (GSP) for the first time, responding to calls for special treatment of weaker country exports (Michalopoulos 2001: 25). The logic of equal treatment had been rearticulated as unequal, and thus to be ameliorated it required special treatment for particular countries. However, as in the 1950s, the GATT's formal response to the economic position of the weaker states in global commerce was ambiguous and unpredictable, so that it had very little effect upon trade relations. Dillon appeared contradictory, the GSP sitting alongside the creation of the Long-Term Agreement on Common Textiles, which endorsed the imposition of tariff barriers to protect the manufacture of textiles (Dunkley 2000: 35; Winters 1990: 1291). This agreement was seen to favour the economically richer countries, as a protectionist measure against the threat of cheaper imports of textiles from countries with lower labour costs. This violated the norm of 'non-discrimination' but, despite its apparent inconsistency, it would remain a fundamental principle within the GATT/WTO regime.

Dillon provoked more frustration than it resolved so that by 1964 and the Kennedy Round, which would continue until 1967, 'development' had become a political disjuncture in which the weaker states were able to aggregate a potent force in the management of global trade. This was the most ambitious round since the GATT's birth in 1947, with a mandate to consider amendments to cover non-tariff barriers to trade, including quotas and other areas of foreign trade policy not previously tackled (Winters 1990: 1294). In 1964, a senior US diplomat presented his country's position in the US journal *International Organization* as follows:

[A] substantial reduction of trade barriers in the Kennedy Round serves political as well as economic objectives. The collective security of the industrial countries of the North Atlantic Community and Japan and the defense of freedom in the less developed countries will be importantly influenced by the extent to which the *free world* can provide satisfactory alternatives to trade with the *communist bloc* ... The natural forces of interdependence have bound the United States, the industrial countries, and the underdeveloped countries of the noncommunist world into an intimate relationship. The weakness of that relationship is our weakness; its strength, our strength. The health of the other *free world* economies affects the health of our foreign markets and sources of supply and therefore our prosperity. It affects the capability of our allies to defend themselves as well as the political stability of the newly *independent* nations and therefore our *security*. It affects the material basis for the development of *freedom* abroad and therefore our own *freedom*.

(Gardner 1964: 686–87, emphasis added)

Trade was presented as a mechanism fundamental to the unity of the Western alliance, the US execution of the Cold War, and global 'freedom', echoing the rhetoric once used to justify the birth of the RTAA and the GATT. However, here GATT was not just a way to avoid war, but a weapon of war within a binary opposition between 'free world/freedom' and 'communist bloc'. In the same article quoted above, the US diplomat makes reference to GATT as a useful cloak by which state leaders can legislate trade policy normally infeasible in the full light of public contestation.[28] Allowing foreign trade policy to disappear into the marsh of so-called 'low politics' that relied on a complex cant of legal and economic terms will have helped to centralize the power of that policy throughout each of the contracting parties' legislatures, and freed a central plank of the USA's Cold War from contestation.

During the Kennedy Round, GATT faced competition for the management of global trade in the 1964 emergence of the first United Nations Conference on Trade and Development (UNCTAD) (Cohn 2002: 23, 72). The conception of UNCTAD had been contested along Cold War divisions, with support from the Soviet Bloc, but initial reluctance from the USA (Cohn 2002: 23; Lancaster 1992: 69). The US Administration was to have opposed the UN even considering the proposal for such a conference, but after advice from the US ambassador to the UN, President Kennedy agreed not to stand in the way of the United Nations secretary-general formally asking his members' views on the matter. The result was the first institutional response to development issues (Cohn 2002: 23; Lancaster 1992: 61–73).

UNCTAD criticized the GATT as unfair in its treatment of non-equals as equals, denying substantive special consideration of the particular needs of the weaker states within its management model of the global economy (Cohn 2002: 3; Fisher 1967: 852, 854). Driven by the Latin American dependency theorist Prebisch and the vigour of the newly emergent, but increasingly dissatisfied, 'weaker states', UNCTAD was able to aggregate divergent issues within the general platform of development. In this space, the 'weaker states' were able collectively to mobilize for the first time as a single body, which came to be known as the 'G77', which would prove a serious challenge to the identity of the GATT system.[29]

However, whilst UNCTAD might possibly have offered an alternative model of global trade management, the vast bulk of global commerce took place under the jurisdiction of the GATT, because much of that trade was operated by the richer states that dominated the agreement. Understood thus, it was difficult to articulate UNCTAD as an 'alternative' trade manager.[30] Though dissatisfied with their lack of sufficient representation in the agreement, the weaker states were also fearful of the danger of deliberately excluding themselves from GATT trade negotiations (Beane 2000: 142). This is perhaps why more and more of the weaker states continued to apply for accession to GATT, so that it now appeared a fully fledged multilateral organization with a body of contracting parties in which those weaker states were a large majority (Beane 2000: 138, 142, 170).

The 1964 arrival of UNCTAD was countered by the GATT within its own answer to development issues, through setting up the Committee on Trade and Development (CoTD) (Cohn 2002: 72; Michalopoulos 2001: 26). The CoTD provided a negotiating framework intended to express development issues within the GATT, and was later joined by a new Part IV of the GATT, on 'Trade and Development', which entered into force in 1966 with a pledge from the USA, Europe, Japan and other economically dominant states to lower import barriers to products of export interest to the weakest states (Cohn 2002: 72).[31]

However, as before, the material effects of these institutional changes were minimal at best. The Kennedy Round went into the history books as failing development (Cohn 2002: 74–76). The introduction of a 'development' norm sat uncomfortably next to the primary norm of 'non-discrimination', each seeming to contradict the other. A further tension arose, this time targeted at the weaker states, in which their demand for special and differential treatment was seen by some in the richer states as signalling a claim for the right to 'free-ride' the GATT without reciprocity (Finlayson and Zacher 1983: 285). This tension would not be resolved in the 1960s.

Multilateralism

In the 1970s, an unsuccessful attempt to stabilize the GATT's logic of multilateralism failed in a context in which alternate 'economic' perspectives emerged to contest the universalism of the GATT.

The 1974–79 Tokyo Round was initiated with the joint intention of sedimenting the multilateral trade regime normalized thus far, and to expand that regime with the proposal that the complexity of the GATT agreement be multiplied fourfold (Jackson 2000: 46–52). The Tokyo Round would be labelled the 'Multilateral Trade Negotiation' (MTN) and was to extend the GATT's remit to include government procurement, technical standards and subsidies.

Possessing such a far-reaching agenda, the Tokyo MTN Round was always going to be the subject of disputes, but this contestation was greatly intensified by a series of changes related to the global recession. A dominant reading of history viewed that 100 years earlier a recession amongst the leading trading powers had similarly threatened global trade, with the result that trade liberalization was replaced by entrenched 'economic nationalism' (Boltho 1996: 257). With a century having passed, it appeared that that history was about to be repeated.

In the context of a perceived 'recession', the discursive formation within the USA altered, so that it began to abandon multilateral arrangements of trade management, utilizing a series of unilateral measures argued to protect its domestic economy, viewed as hurt by both recession and the revival of European and Japanese 'competition' (Boltho 1996: 257). The US waiver of 1955 had created a precedence in which the GATT would attempt to accommodate this unilateralism, but it was uncertain how it would continue to do so if the recession continued. Also, in the context of the success of oil-exporting nations in articulating common concern within OPEC (Organization of the Petroleum Exporting Countries) and setting their own commodity prices for the first time, a dislocation followed in which nation-state identities were rearticulated and a new sense of agency was achieved – with several 'weaker states' appearing self-empowered. Many of the states now collectively mobilized under the OPEC banner had formally been submissive to US and European demands, tied by colonial linkages and foreign control over their oil production. Other producers of 'primary commodities', most of which stood submissively on the outer edges of the global economy, saw the oil-producing states now taking control of their own export prices and, with rising petroleum prices, actively affecting the economies of the richest countries.[32]

Using UNCTAD as a discussion forum, the Group of Seventy-Seven (G77), representing a large swath of states that perceived themselves as experiencing special 'developmental' problems, mobilized to launch the 'New International Economic Order' (NIEO) (Cohn 2002: 110). This 'order' demanded improved export markets for developing countries via special and differential treatment, and the creation of institutions favouring 'development' interests in international trade. Part of its programme included the proposal for an 'Integrated Program for Commodities' (IPC), which would regulate the commodity prices of the weaker countries to ensure that they received higher prices and an improved balance-of-payments situation (Cohn 2002: 111).

In the worsening economic situation, the French government called for an emergency Conference on International Economic Cooperation, to discuss the production of energy, with OPEC and representatives from both the 'rich' and 'poor' non-oil-exporting countries invited (Cohn 2002: 110). After an initial disagreement in which the 'weaker states' demanded that the meeting include the broader issues of primary commodities and development, endorsement by the OPEC summit meeting of 1975 ensured that these demands were met.

To overcome the NIEO, multilateralism in many of the negotiations taking place within the Tokyo MTN Round disappeared in favour of achieving agreement on a 'plurilateral' basis. Many of the Tokyo Round agreements existed between only a select group of contracting parties (Das 1999: 5). These plurilateral codes challenged the principle of non-discrimination, and diverged from the multilateralism of the GATT regime to the extent in which plurilateralism/discrimination was accepted within the institution (Winters 1990: 1295). The richer states threatened to abandon large-scale multilateralism in trade altogether, looking to the Organisation for Economic Co-operation and Development (OECD) – dominated as it was by those states – as an alternative facility for trade management. An additional suggestion considered was that of a GATT-Plus regime, which would remain part of the wider agreement, but operate with a narrowed group of states party to a rearticulated (and expanded) concept of global trade governance.[33] The closest things came to the creation of such a GATT subsidiary body was in the formation of the Consultative Group of Eighteen (CG-18), set-up as a temporary entity in 1975 (but made permanent in 1979), which was intended to serve as an executive for the GATT (Blackhurst 1998: 33). The CG-18 was an institutional response to the problems of reaching agreement in a GATT that possessed not only a larger number of contracting parties than ever before, but also a greater number that felt able visibly to assert their positions. The CG-18 is discussed further on.

Boltho argues that the reason GATT and multilateral trade liberalization survived, whereas recession in 1870 sparked 60 years of rising economic nationalism, is down to two factors: 1 the strength of its driving ideology; and, 2 a shift in the ownership of global capital (Boltho 1996: 257–58). The sedimentation of the GATT throughout Western Europe, Japan and the other leading trading states facilitated the spread of both multilateralism in the management of trade policy and trade liberalization. The end product was an ideological momentum that allowed the GATT regime to survive despite rising economic nationalism amongst key parties like the USA. However, also, the growth of 'export-led economics' maintained a shift in the ownership of capital away from entrenchment within the domesticity of the nation-state and towards transnationalism. In other words, Boltho argues the importance of multinational corporations as lobbyists within the national governments of the contracting parties and as key proponents of trade liberalization ideology (ibid.: 258). Trade liberalization had collapsed in 1870 because inward-looking industry in most countries favoured protectionism. This was no longer the case in the 1970s.

The 1970s offered a different historical context to that in the 1870s, with a quite different hegemonic discursive formation in which 'multinational corporations' constituted significant actors. In this discursive formation, trade liberalization was understood as equivalential with that identity and thus had firmer grounds than 100 years earlier.

Tokyo ended with a host of plurilateral agreements and many issues unresolved, threatening the concept of 'equal treatment', but the system had expanded so that it was clear that the GATT had emerged from an agreement into a fully fledged institution (Jackson 2000: 46). The long and drawn-out contestations of the MTN round had been weathered by a mixture of institutional flexibility, but also increased use of the dispute settlement mechanism, so that many interpretations now depended upon a process of jurisprudence rather than the legislature (Jackson 2000: 52).

Despite – or perhaps because of – the problems experienced in the Tokyo Round, the GATT entered into an eighth round (the Uruguay Round) which would provide the context for a rearticulation of global trade governance that was markedly different to the GATT pre-1980s, with a vastly expanded understanding of trade and a much more formalized institutional body to administer its management: the World Trade Organization (WTO).

The Tokyo Round was widely articulated as a 'crisis' for the GATT regime and multilateral trade management, increasingly seen as ambiguous and devoid of discipline (Jackson 2000: 38). Tokyo was described as 'GATT à la carte', its plurilateral salvation of the MTN suggestive of an arrangement of agreements vulnerable to variable selection and contrary to the founding principles of 'reciprocation' and 'non-discrimination' (Jackson 2000: 375). This problematization of the then current articulation of global trade governance took place in the context of a much larger problematization that encompassed not only the GATT regime but also the entire 'global economic system', including the barely sedimented collective identity of the developing countries and UNCTAD.

The global economic system was framed as increasingly 'turbulent' (Wilkinson 2002a: 129), subject to a growing 'economic nationalism', with increasing 'protectionist pressures' (Croome 1995: 7). According to Croome – a former GATT staff member who was actively involved in the trade negotiations at this point[34] – speeches had been made in the US Congress in which there had been talk of 'shutting off the world's largest market' from foreign competition, threatening the basis of international trade in the twentieth century (ibid.: 22). The USA threatened to abandon multilateralism in favour of unilateralism, embodied in the so-called 'Super 301' legislative provision, which 'authorised the President to restrict imports from countries whose trade policies *he* found unfair' (Croome 1995: 290, emphasis added). Also, nation-states such as the USA and commercial unions such as the European Community asserted their hegemonic position in trade via successfully negotiating a series of extensions to the 'Multifibre Agreement', which restricted access for cheap textile imports into those territories (Das 2003: 25–26; Croome 1995: 17, 30). This emphasized the threat of bilateralism to the other nation-states, exhibiting the difficulty that 'weaker states' would face in promoting their trade interests if multilateralism were further eroded.

In 1982, Mexico's threat to default on its loan repayments was articulated as the eruption of a global debt 'crisis', which helped to facilitate the disarticulation of the G77 and break equivalential links between nation-states that had been made possible under the collective identity of developing countries. This dislocation occurred as many of those nation-states abandoned their attempts towards independence from the 'rich' nation-states, and accepted recovery packages through the IMF and the World Bank, which advocated the liberalization of the domestic economy to 'foreign' finance and competition. The self-sufficient identity of the G77 was no more, eroded further by a growth in relations between nation-states that denied the developing country identity (Winters 1990: 1297). With a grossly weakened support base, UNCTAD was subjected to a barrage of intense criticism, led by the US Administration of Republican President Reagan, which accused it of exacerbating international tension, and of standing in the way of trade liberalization and economic development (Cohn 2002: 155). The attack was a success and UNCTAD underwent a change in its executive structure that left the UN sub-body more amenable to Western demands (Cohn 2002: 155, 188). The identity of international politics had changed from that in the 1970s. The logic of development became weaker in the 1980s (Das 2003: 32).

Resistance to liberalization was weakened as the alternative of special and differential treatment was problematized, based upon the articulation of apparent export-led economic success for several East Asian nation-states (Croome 1995: 10).[35] For Croome, this period witnessed a renewed enthusiasm for GATT from developing countries following a move from 'high protection, government direction of the economy and great suspicion of foreign investment', and the 'example of dynamic growth set by East Asian developing countries' (ibid.: 289).

In this crisis, the GATT regime was criticized as 'unwieldy' (Croome 1995: 145–46), with specific problematization focusing on the dispute settlement mechanism that had evolved to resolve contractual disagreements amongst the GATT's Contracting Parties regarding implementation of the agreement. Dispute settlement in the GATT was seen as ineffectual, with delays and blocking by various Parties resulting in resolutions grinding to a halt, as well as a failure to implement rulings when finally achieved (Lee 2004: 120). The process was also seen as lacking transparency, and being dominated by developed countries (Lee 2004: 120).

It was in this context that a new GATT round was to emerge that would lead to a significant rearticulation of global trade governance, which would conclude in the birth of the WTO. However, at the start of the 1980s, such a rearticulation was not evident. Several nation-states with developing country identities called for multilateral trade negotiations to be moved to the UN, retaining the impetus that facilitated the NIEO.

Articulated as a means to overcome the disagreement made visible during the Tokyo Round, those dominant over the shape of the GATT experimented with the Consultative Group of Eighteen (CG-18), which, although created first as a temporary body, operated until its suspension in 1989, by which time it had grown to 22 members.[36] The CG-18 has been described as a 'formal informal group' (Das 2003: 17), because it had a formal constitution and meeting agendas were prepared by the GATT director-general, though the meetings themselves were held informally with no official minutes and thus less pressure against agreement. The nation-states present were seen as equally representative of both developed and developing countries – selected on an annual basis by the GATT director-general – though the European Economic Community was defined as only one party, meaning that in praxis there was a greater representation of the developed countries (Das 2003: 17).

When it was first created, the CG-18 provided a means to produce decisions amongst a select group of nation-states prior to the decision being opened up to the much wider contestation of the full GATT Contracting Parties. Ostensibly, it existed to deal with the controversial work programme produced in the Tokyo Round (Croome 1995: 6–7). However, it was also active in restabilizing the GATT, by forming agreement amongst its select members towards calling for a meeting of government ministers of the GATT Contracting Parties to be held in 1982 (Croome 1995: 12). This was unusual because GATT had no provision for regular ministerial-level meetings except for at the start of major trade negotiations, thus setting the tone for intensive work (Croome 1995: 12).

Articulated within a crisis, the meeting itself was viewed as a 'crisis' – resulting in disagreement (Croome 1995: 13). For Croome, the meeting brought the GATT close to a serious 'breakdown' (ibid.: 14). Agreement was achieved, however, in that a crisis was now formerly acknowledged within the GATT. This sedimentation of the crisis developed within the problematization created a context in which there was a sudden perceived need for 'new initiatives', leading to a space for providing a 'more secure and less divisive basis' for future negotiations (Croome 1995: 14–15). In this context, the GATT Secretariat was strengthened by acting as the means for resolving such problematized disagreement, giving it the position to 'collect and publish detailed information about the trade policy actions of individual GATT members' (Croome 1995: 15). The wider series of problematizations were made more visible, with demands for not only an overhaul of the dispute settlement rules but also new progress on reducing tariffs on agriculture, and expanding global trade governance to include US demands on 'services', 'trade in counterfeit goods', 'investment' and 'high-technology' (Croome 1995: 16). The meeting produced a 'work programme' to discuss these new issues and future negotiations (Das 2003: 9).

In the articulation of the 'need' for a new round, limited access groups such as the CG-18 were central in forming agreement amongst a grossly narrowed set of nation-states. The potential for disagreement was fragmented, heightening the pressure against dissensus by making it more visible who was responsible for a lack of progress. In Croome's account, the identities Brazil and India are singled out as the principle instigators of dissensus (Croome 1995: 20). In Western Europe, contestation was limited via an aggregated negotiating position represented to the GATT by the European Commission.

Important, too, were such forums as the Group of Seven (G7), where the heads of state or government of the seven economically richest nation-states sedimented the possibility of new GATT negotiations (Croome 1995: 21). Additionally, in February 1984, the US Trade Representative organized a meeting between what would become known as the 'Quad' – the USA, Japan, Canada and the European Community (represented by the Commission) – where the possible content of these negotiations was further sedimented (Croome 1995: 21).

In the background to these different meetings, representatives of the USA were supposedly pushing for a new round of GATT negotiations in the context of informal discussions with business and other nation-states, in which the GATT director-general was present (Croome 1995: 17). Though there were no formal calls for a new round by these nation-states, a demand for new negotiations was increasingly articulated in speeches made by the GATT director-general (Croome 1995: 17). The GATT Director-General Arthur Dunkel commissioned a group of 'independent experts' to produce a report aimed at the domestic publics of nation-states to create pressure towards a new round (Croome 1995: 18). To avoid any expression of dissensus from those Contracting Parties that were less willing to engage in further negotiations, the group's identity as formally independent from the GATT was articulated by seeking its finance from outside the GATT Contracting Parties (Croome 1995: 18). The independent experts – the Leutweiler Group – was financed by such organizations as the Ford Foundation, and involved individuals identified as from both developing and developed countries (Croome 1995: 18).

The Leutweiler Group's report was presented by Dunkel at the GATT Council meeting in April 1985, where its call for a new round of negotiations, 'provided they are directed toward the primary goal of strengthening the multilateral trading system and further opening world markets' (quoted in Croome 1995: 19), met with a mixed response from the Contracting Parties, with disagreement framed along a developed/developing country divide (ibid.: 23). The OECD had been used to sediment support for a new round from the industrialized countries, actively working on proposals for new GATT negotiations, and this was supported by further endorsement from the G7 (Croome 1995: 23). Increasing the pressure within the GATT, at the July 1985 GATT Council the USA called for a vote on whether to launch a new round (Croome 1995: 25–26). This was unusual in that decisions in the GATT were normally taken by consensus, and so the call for a vote represented a significant statement of US determination. Without actually holding a vote, the demand for a vote led to the establishment of a preparatory committee for new negotiations, 'to determine the objectives, subject-matter, modalities for and participation in the multilateral trade negotiations' (Agreement for Preparatory Committee, quoted in Croome 1995: 26).

The Preparatory Committee, open to Contracting Parties, was to produce a declaration for a GATT ministerial conference to be held in September 1986.

Uruguay was chosen as the host of the conference, in order to express that the round had 'developing-country endorsement' (Croome 1995: 28). This was significant because representatives of Uruguay had at the May 1984 GATT Council taken a visible leadership position for developing countries by demanding that earlier commitments made by ministers to help developing countries be implemented or 'any initiative such as a new round of negotiations in GATT would be lacking in credibility and devoid of relevance, particularly for developing countries' (statement by representative of Uruguay, quoted in Croome 1995: 22).

At the Uruguay ministerial conference – held in the tourist town of Punta del Este where plenary meetings were hosted in a casino – pressure to produce a consensus towards new negotiations was created by the extension of the Multifibre Agreement on textiles for another five years, as well as a US threat to negotiate elsewhere unless there was progress in GATT (Croome 1995: 30). The Punta del Este declaration that appeared on 20 September 1986 came out of a series of small meetings during the ministerial, and laid the foundations launching what was now formally known as the 'Uruguay Round', and set a timetable of four years for its completion (Croome 1995: 32).

Two years later, in December 1988, at Montreal, a mid-term review was held. Originally called by the USA as a ministerial meeting that would allow an 'early harvest' of what had been agreed so far in the negotiations that had been ongoing in Geneva since Punta del Este, disagreement from those that wanted the round to be seen as a whole package meant that the meeting was no more than a formal assessment of the negotiations (Croome 1995: 167). This disagreement continued, with failure to reach consensus on the issue of agricultural trade, so that the Montreal mid-term review was halted (Croome 1995: 173). However, in the period that followed, informal small group meetings were used to facilitate a basic agreement on agriculture so that a mid-term package formally stating what had taken place thus far in the negotiations was adopted by the GATT Contracting Parties in April 1989 (Croome 1995: 179). Disagreements on agriculture persisted despite this April agreement, and appear to have been responsible for the collapse of the Brussels GATT Ministerial Conference in December 1990, and the subsequent prolonging of the round beyond its original four-year mandate (Croome 1995: 275–79).

Despite much of what would become the Uruguay Round agreement being completed in the latter half of 1991, disagreement over agriculture persisted until it was resolved via bilateral negotiations between the USA and European Community at the end of 1993 (Hart 1995c: 232; Croome 1995: 291–369). Pressure towards agreement was maintained via a problematization where, for example, as late as 1990 a commentator questioned whether or not the era of liberal and multilateral trade had died (Winters 1990: 1288). The final text of the round was drawn up on 15 December 1993, and signed in April 1994 in Marrakech, Morocco (Croome 1995: 377).

Radically rearticulating global trade governance

The initial demands made by the USA for the inclusion of 'services', 'trade in counterfeit goods', 'investment' and 'high-technology' to be covered within the GATT's sphere of global trade governance underwent a significant process of sedimentation in the Uruguay Round due to separate projects to increase information on each of these areas. Prior to Uruguay, tradable commodities had been defined as 'manufactured products, raw materials and agricultural products' (Krugman and Obstfield, in Sapir 1999: 51). At the 1982 GATT Ministerial Conference, a group of Contracting Parties formed as the G77 – continuing from the 1970s – to oppose any rearticulation of trade that might favour the industrialized countries seen to be dominant in these sectors (Croome 1995: 16). They argued that inclusion of these new issues in the GATT 'would not only be detrimental to the interests of developing countries in international markets, but would hamper efforts aimed at reforming GATT in order to adapt it more closely to the needs and interests of developing countries' (statement by the G77 ministers, quoted in Croome 1995: 16).

Despite this initial resistance, the inclusion of trade in counterfeit goods as a subject relevant to the GATT was sedimented in the process leading up to the Uruguay Round, and expanded into the term 'intellectual property', and framed as motivated by a desire to prevent 'theft' (Croome 1995: 121). The intellectual property debate had originally been framed as favouring developing countries, though representatives of the USA, in particular, again made use of offering greater access to its textiles markets – as both a bargaining chip but also a means to argue that whilst intellectual property offered a 'competitive advantage' to developed countries with companies that owned a larger percentage of patent rights, textiles offered a similar advantage to the developing countries with their cheaper labour and, thus, mutual gain could be won by producing a deal based on a bargain between the two issues (Croome 1995: 120). This example illustrates that the identities 'developed' and 'developing' country are not necessarily divisive, but have been articulated as mutually beneficial. Agreement was also reached that work could begin on exchanging information among interested countries regarding services, without any formal commitment to launch negotiations on the matter (Croome 1995: 16). It was in this process that interests were formed in this area previously not touched by the GATT. The sedimentation of trade in services represented a significant shift in the articulation of global trade governance.

Trade in services

According to Sapir, the concept of 'trade in services' has only become established within the terminology of economists and trade lawyers after several decades of activity from 'US-based service multilaterals', primarily targeted at the US government (Sapir 1999: 52). This led to the eventual inclusion of trade in services in the Uruguay Round. However, this was far from an inevitable process. As Drake and Nicolaïdis argue:

[The articulation of services as 'trade'] was a revolution in social ontology: it redefined how governments thought about the nature of services, their movement across borders, their roles in society, and the objectives and principles according to which they should be governed.

(Drake and Nicolaïdis 1992: 38)

The formation of trade in services as a concept increasingly recognized within the governance of global trade required a long and gradual rearticulatory process. A series of equivalential links needed to be built up between what had previously been seen as separate sectors, such as telecommunications, construction, management consulting and finance, so that they might be seen to all constitute trade (Drake and Nicolaïdis 1992: 38, 44). Appearing first within a report produced by a group of economists within the OECD in 1972, the concept of trade in services came to act as the empty signifier at the centre of what has become a vast equivalential sequence. Prior to this rearticulation, those sectors – such as telecommunications – that would come to be brought together as services were understood to require management through state regulation rather than as trade, and subject to the rules of the market (Drake and Nicolaïdis 1992: 44). Consequently, prior to their rearticulation, as objects of governance these various sectors were understood as subject to sector-specific regulatory regimes.

In 1972, the OECD group that gave one of the first formal expressions to the category trade in services did so in the context of a problematization of the current discursive formation. A view in which industrial structures were seen to be shifting had become increasingly sedimented, where OECD member states were seen to be losing their traditional dominance in the production and export of goods (Drake and Nicolaïdis 1992: 45). The category trade in services appeared also in the context of the then upcoming GATT Tokyo Round and a US shift away from multilateralism in the face of a perceived recession. 'Services' were effectively articulated as a new frontier in liberalization. The report stated: 'Given that services are a sector which seems likely to expand rapidly in countries' economies, the main need is to avoid any tendencies to protectionism and to aim at achieving a more thorough liberalization' (OECD report, quoted in Drake and Nicolaïdis 1992: 45). Services were seen to be offering new economic vitality to the OECD members in a situation where traditional industries suffered apparent decline and growing foreign competition.[37]

Soon after this initial expression, a community of different identities began to converge around the new category. This was actively promoted by, for example, the Office of the US Trade Representative. The community included, according to Drake and Nicolaïdis, 'trade officials', 'politicians', 'industry analysts', 'academics' and 'corporate lobbyists' (Drake and Nicolaïdis 1992: 46). Representatives of US transnational corporations (TNCs), eager to ease their entry into foreign markets, showed a high degree of political activism in their attempts to widen the community. Articulating their joint activities as trade facilitated a coalition between companies from 'diverse industries by underscoring their common problems and justifying their individual demands' (Drake and Nicolaïdis 1992: 46). Additionally, Drake and Nicolaïdis emphasize that the category 'trade in services' worked to give these companies:

> each a *potent discursive weapon* with which to advance these demands by redefining industry-specific policies as 'protectionism', a charge that was less easily ignored by foreign governments than were ad hoc appeals for regulatory flexibility.
>
> (Drake and Nicolaïdis 1992: 46, emphasis added)

This corporate activism operated on two fronts, working towards those other TNCs selling services, but also towards those purchasing such services. A changing economic structure in which many TNCs had externalized formerly internal functions meant that a growing number became either sellers or buyers of services.[38] This activism was not limited to the US environment alone, but took the form of specific seminars and conferences organized with US corporate representatives visiting their foreign contemporaries. This involved promoting liberalization, as well as underlining that market access given to US services was a price that had to be paid to guarantee the access to the large US market that had been built up since the late 1940s.

Considering the gradual pace of this articulatory process it would be wrong to suggest that corporations represented a single identity. It took almost 10 years from the initial expression of trade in services in the OECD economists' report for the International Chamber of Commerce, to endorse GATT negotiations on services in 1981. Despite the OECD's early involvement, US policy makers were slow to accept the category of services. The category lacked sufficient sedimentation, with few studies produced. Consequently, the 1970s and onwards witnessed a string of conferences and publications by which services became a legitimate object of trade governance at the global level. The crisis of the 1982 GATT Ministerial meeting provided an impetus to services because whilst the G77 opposed the new category as a distraction from 'protectionism' in agriculture and manufacturing, agreement was reached that GATT contracting parties could voluntarily submit data on their service industries. Services were now linked to the GATT. This opened up a new space for identity formation in which national interests were to be rearticulated.

The desire for information on services empowered those who had already been active in the sedimentation of this category. The category shifted from being perceived as in the material interests of specific actors towards achieving a level of 'scientific objectivity', which in turn empowered further sedimentation of the category within global trade governance. It became increasingly difficult for those opposed to the new category as new technological developments in such sectors as telecommunications were used to convey the sense of a general shift within global economics towards new industries. The production of data that followed the 1982 Ministerial helped to re-align national interests so that the European Community moved from a general reluctance towards active engagement, coming to view itself as 'the biggest world exporter of services' (Drake and Nicolaïdis 1992: 57).

In the mid-1980s, the political environment of services shifted from US dominance towards a cleavage between developed and developing countries, which, respectively, supported or opposed any inclusion of the new category within the global governance of trade. The body of publications acknowledging trade in services took on the 'attributes of a social science literature' (Drake and Nicolaïdis 1992: 59–60), so that the public debate moved away from the question of whether or not services served as a legitimate category of trade to the detailed conceptualization of the category. This was made possible via further conferences and research sponsored by new organizations dedicated to promoting the new category, such as the US Coalition of Services Industries (CSI), as well as the Liberalisation of Trade in Services Committee (LOTIS) in the UK, the European Services Forum (ESF) and, globally, the Services World Forum. These various organizations and the networks through which they operated represented a dynamic process of articulation, Drake and Nicolaïdis writing that the 'academics', 'corporate representatives', 'trade officials' and so on:

> self-consciously shared causal and principled beliefs, validity tests, and a policy project ... There was a real sense of excitement in these meetings and in the expert network generally, as participants were intrigued by the conceptual and bargaining challenges and pleased to be seen as involved in a 'cutting edge' issue.
>
> (Drake and Nicolaïdis 1992: 60)

In this context, it became increasingly difficult to oppose the new category. Drake and Nicolaïdis (1992: 64) argue that for many identities there was 'little to be gained professionally from aligning with a [now] dissident view at the margins'. Though many developing countries remained opposed, such a position appeared particularistic whilst supporters of the new category were now able to claim a degree of objectivity with reference to the shifting understanding of global trade governance. As such, the identities of supporters and opponents of trade in services had switched with respect to their identities as 'particularistic' or 'universal'.

It was debated whether current rules dealing with traditional trade (trade in goods) should simply be reworded to acknowledge goods and services – and, thus, dealt with in the same negotiations – or if trade in services should be negotiated separately (Sapir 1999: 52). This has relevance because not all nation-states perceive a similar interest in trade in services, because any market liberalization in this sector naturally favours those with a service industry. Consequently, trade in services tends most to favour those countries in Europe, North America and Australasia that seek new markets for their domestic services industries. Many other nation-states, by comparison, have only an emerging service industry. If tied into a single agreement with trade in goods, however, trade in services would acutely be part of a 'grand bargain' approach unpopular with developing countries because of the explicit assumption that access for their primary commodities (such as grain) could only be achieved in return for market access given to foreign services firms substantially able to out-compete their own still-emerging service industry.[39]

For Croome, the delay on negotiating services was ultimately beneficial to the agreement because it allowed time for support to be built up, the work programme started in 1982 persuading 'some key countries, in addition to the United States, that services negotiations could be rewarding' (Croome 1995: 16). Further exchange of information on services was endorsed in the April 1985 GATT Council despite disagreement on the larger question of whether or not to launch a new round (ibid.: 27). However, it was only at Punta del Este that agreement was reached to include services in the new negotiations, with the text launching the Uruguay Round placing services into its own separate track of negotiations away from goods (Croome 1995: 32, 119; Sapir 1999: 52). Agreement was reached on services via using access to the textiles markets of the industrialized countries as a bargaining chip (Croome 1995: 119).

The issue of services was framed in terminology developed in the GATT related to goods, using terms such as 'national treatment', 'non-discrimination', 'progressive liberalization', amongst others (Croome 1995: 243). This was achieved at the Montreal mid-term review, as well as the first articulation of the agreement that was to cover services: the General Agreement on Trade in Services (GATS) (Croome 1995: 244–51). Despite this apparent consensus, Croome sees that the GATS benefited from the problems with other areas such as agriculture, which absorbed much of the disagreement, so that, for example, the collapse of the Brussels Ministerial Conference in 1990 was a 'blessing in disguise' because it prevented the services negotiations moving onto more contentious issues (ibid.: 282).

Opposition to the inclusion of new issues was such that services was not formerly discussed within the GATT until after the early 1980s, only becoming acceptable for negotiation in the Punta del Este declaration in 1986 (Croome 1995: 119–23). Attempts to prevent the launch of a new round were tied into the dissensus against the expansion of the GATT. According to Narlikar (2004: 135), it was the new issues that 'shook' many countries formerly inactive in the GATT forum into an active engagement with the regime that stretched beyond demanding special and differential treatment. At the first formal debate in the GATT regarding the possibility of a new round, at the GATT Council meeting in June 1985, India stated its opposition on behalf of 24 other developing countries,[40] demanding that moves first be made on reducing restrictions to textiles and that the GATT should focus only on goods (Croome 1995: 24). However, six months later, 14 of those developing countries had given up their dissent, with only the remaining 10[41] now demanding that the Preparatory Committee not discuss the new issues, which they, according to Croome (1995: 28), 'insisted were outside GATT's competence'. However, this opposition was weakened by both the successful extension of the Multifibre Agreement on textiles until 1991, meaning that textiles remained less relevant during most of the Uruguay Round, and the US threat to walk away from the negotiations unless they included the new issues (Croome 1995: 31). Therefore, the idea of a new round had been sufficiently sedimented to mean that the USA was no longer required to advocate for its launch, instead being able to threaten its success unless that round reflected its demands.

Articulating the need for an organization

Beyond the rearticulation of trade, the Uruguay Round was significant because of the emergence of a formal institutional body to manage that trade – the World Trade Organization (WTO). The articulation of the need for a specific organization – as opposed to the contractual status of the GATT that was administered by a quasi-institutional secretariat set up originally to facilitate the creation of the never-born International Trade Organization – can be separated into three elements: an improved dispute settlement mechanism; a trade policy monitoring body; and a formal organization with a Secretariat.

The mechanism for resolving disputes between GATT Contracting Parties regarding the implementation of its rules had been problematized as slow and frequently blocked (Croome 1995: 144). There seems to have been little disagreement on the need for reform of the mechanism that had evolved in the history of the GATT, with agreement being reached on this need as early as August 1987 (Croome 1995: 148). However, the exact nature of this reform remained more contentious, with disagreement emerging between representatives of the USA who demanded that decisions taken by the dispute resolution mechanism be received as legally binding on the relevant parties, rather than merely advisory conclusions, as was then the case (Croome 1995: 149). Against this 'legalistic' approach were the European Community and Japan (Croome 1995: 149–50). Such dissensus was, however, relatively minor compared to the much larger series of battles being fought over in the Uruguay Round, meaning that dispute settlement was not to provide a focus point for disagreement. The most potentially controversial idea made was that direct access (and thus rights) be given to non-state actors including individuals and companies to bring disputes to any reformed resolution mechanism, though this proposal suggested by Switzerland found little resonance amongst a hegemonic understanding of the GATT as an 'intergovernmental' regime (Croome 1995: 265).

At the Montreal mid-term review, agreement was reached on both strengthening the dispute settlement mechanism as a legal entity, and a new practice of regularly reviewing the domestic trade policy of the nation-states party to the GATT (Croome 1995: 261). This contrasts with overall disagreement caused by agriculture, thereby emphasizing the institutional reforms to the GATT system as a point of solidarity amongst the negotiating delegations (Croome 1995: 146). The concept of systematized monitoring of trade policy was first articulated during the Tokyo Round and was endorsed by the Leutweiler Group that led up to the launch of the Uruguay Round (Croome 1995: 145). The greatest controversy came from those representing nation-states then undergoing structural adjustment programmes imposed by the IMF, which were most sensitive to the possibility that the role of the GATT Secretariat in monitoring domestic trade policy might involve a similarly intrusive process (Croome 1995: 158). The role of the GATT Secretariat in monitoring domestic trade policy was articulated in two ways: as ensuring 'peer pressure' from fellow GATT Contracting Parties towards certain trade policies; and as a means to enforce GATT rules (Croome 1995: 157). Promoting the latter articulation, the USA found 'wide sympathy' for a 'central registry in GATT that would clearly show how governments were living up to their obligations' (Croome 1995: 159). Monitoring was sedimented within the Punta del Este declaration, which called for 'better monitoring of trade policies' (quoted in Croome 1995: 145).

Reform of the dispute settlement mechanism and a new role for the GATT Secretariat in monitoring domestic trade policy provided the impetus for problematization of the informal identity of the GATT institution, left as a contract with a Secretariat described as a 'phantom agency' that had lost its original role with the collapse of attempts to launch the ITO (Croome 1995: 145). Ministerial meetings were rare, leaving much left to the civil servants representing the various Contracting Parties to negotiate in what was seen as an 'unwieldy' institution (Croome 1995: 145). The first public call for an organization came in 1987, made by Canada in a proposal for reform of the GATT, where the brief suggestion was put that efforts be made to 'examine proposals to establish an international trade organization' (quoted in Croome 1995: 156). Rather than a formal organization, most other proposals suggested strengthening the GATT Secretariat, for example, enforcing the powers of the director-general (Croome 1995: 156).

The name 'World Trade Organization' was first suggested not within the GATT itself but by a US law academic, John Jackson, who was a noted expert on the GATT legal code (Croome 1995: 272). However, the representatives of the USA at the GATT were not supportive of such a proposal, fearing the creation of a powerful new international agency that would not gain support of the US Congress (Croome 1995: 272, 325). The idea for a new GATT organization was more popular within European politics, where the Italian Trade Minister Renato Ruggiero – who would become the first WTO director-general – supported proposals being developed within the European Commission for an organizational treaty (Croome 1995: 272). Reflecting that the idea for an organization remained relatively low down on the list of negotiating priorities in the Uruguay Round, the European Commission's proposal – for a 'Multilateral Trade Organization' (MTO) – was only made in June 1990 (Croome 1995: 273). The proposal was legitimated on the grounds that the growing number of trade agreements developed in the round required a strong institutional body at the centre, as well as one that would reflect an expanded role due to the monitoring function of the GATT and a demand that the GATT needed to work more closely with the IMF and World Bank and thus required a similar institutional basis (Croome 1995: 273).

For its part, the USA proposed the creation of a limited-membership executive to direct the expanded GATT, though this was unable to garner sufficient support amongst the Contracting Parties (Croome 1995: 274). The CG-18 had played a diminishing role in the Uruguay Round after its initial work in launching the project, suggesting the potential problems of an executive body as either, according to Croome, 'too large to be effective or too small to be representative' (Croome 1995: 155). Additionally, it appeared that the idea for an 'MTO' would be left until after the round (Croome 1995: 274). However, the expansion of trade appeared a problem where the dispute settlement process was to cover the old and new issues and yet there was no single institutional framework to manage the overall set of agreements, being that the GATT itself was no more than an agreement (Croome 1995: 322). In this context, a draft 'Agreement establishing the Multilateral Trade Organization' was submitted to the negotiating process on behalf of Canada, the European Community and Mexico (Croome 1995: 325). Though the USA, as well as Japan, expressed opposition, they took part in the negotiations articulating the proposed organization (Croome 1995: 325). In the end, an MTO agreement was included as an annex at the very back of the Final Act of the Uruguay Round, in the absence of further dissensus expressed by either the USA or Japan (Croome 1995: 327). Again, with attention focused on the specifics of the trade agreements, institutional matters remained relatively free of disagreement (Croome 1995: 335). The decision to change the proposed name to the 'World Trade Organization' came as a last-minute demand from the USA, where it was noted in a meeting between the heads of delegations and with minimal discussion (Croome 1995: 377–78; Jackson 1998a: 6). As an annex to a much larger text, and as a comparatively late proposal, the WTO emerged quietly. Perhaps indicative of how some viewed the new body, the European Community described the outcome of the Uruguay Round as 'economic democracy' (quoted in Croome 1995: 379).

Emergence of new identities

The Uruguay Round was dependent upon the emergence of several new identities that were visible within its articulation. First, in the wake of the problematization that followed the Tokyo Round, the GATT Secretariat had gained a status unparalleled in its history. This was reflected in the larger-than-life personality of Arthur Dunkel, and later Peter Sutherland, who served in the position of director-general during the round. Dunkel was appointed as GATT director-general in 1980, having been actively involved in the GATT on behalf of Switzerland, and was instrumental as an identity visiting capitals advocating for the launch of a new round to the extent that he had to employ 'independent experts' in the Leutweiler Group to create a more 'impartial' demand for a new round (Croome 1995: 8). Where disagreement stalled the negotiations, Dunkel organized informal small group meetings within his office to drive parties into agreement (Croome 1995: 286, 293). To appease those who originally opposed the launch of a new round with new issues, formally the GATT was separated from the round by giving Dunkel two job titles: director-general to the GATT Secretariat and official-level chair of the Trade Negotiations Committee facilitating the round (Croome 1995: 33). Dunkel's position was extended throughout most of the round but eventually came to an end in 1993, and he was replaced by Peter Sutherland as director-general (Croome 1995: 344–46). The higher profile of the GATT director-general made evident in Dunkel's role in the round was carried over to his successor, with Sutherland actively courting domestic publics by writing a series of newspaper articles arguing the cost of 'protectionism' to 'consumers' – 'How governments buy votes on trade with the consumer's money' (Croome 1995: 350; Hart 1995c: 240–47).

Second, in the context of the developing country identity that had proven so strong in the 1970s, the emergence of the Cairns Group[42] – representing several countries largely dependent on agricultural exports – in 1986 cut across this divide by articulating an alternative form of solidarity in the Uruguay Round (Cohn 2002: 189–90).

Third, the emergence of 'new issues' in the Uruguay Round represented the emergence of industrial/corporate lobbies as actors within the GATT process, maintaining what Croome (1995: 122) has called 'unremitting pressure for substantial agreements on services and intellectual property'. Though industrial lobbyists had been important throughout GATT history, it was in the Uruguay Round that they became most apparent as actors through the pressure placed on the USA and European Community for the rearticulation of global trade governance (Qureshi 1996: 11–13; Das 2003: 8). Hoogvelt (2001: 148) argues that, through the legacy of GATT, a transnational business 'culture' had emerged within the institution. This culture, and successive lobbying by its advocates, ensured a collective belief in the legitimacy of a particular articulation of global trade governance amongst those de/contesting the future of the GATT regime at Uruguay (Beane 2000: 111).[43]

The Uruguay Round was facilitated via an intense problematization of the status quo, framing the GATT as unreflective of a changing world. Trade governance was articulated to cover a much greater sphere of social activity, so that the identity of the GATT regime was radically transformed. The emergence of the WTO will be considered in greater detail in Chapter 3, which traces the articulation of the GATT/WTO regime from 1995 (the formal birth of the WTO) onwards. The purpose of this section focusing on the Uruguay Round has been to emphasize the decontestatory process at play in both making possible that round, as well as the rearticulation of global trade governance to include further activities.

Conclusion

The purpose of this genealogy has been to trace out the historically contingent articulations through which global trade governance has been made possible, underlying what appears as the present-day WTO. The RTAA signalled a discursive shift in which trade has been alternately articulated as 'national security', 'peaceful cooperation', 'Cold War weapon', 'development tool' and 'anti-terrorist'. These articulations have been contextualized in a wider discursive context, in which ideational and material factors can be seen to co-exist effectively, as in the example of the Cold War, where trade became a free world weapon.

The emergence of development demands – centred in the developing country identity and contextualized by the emergence of new nation-states (post-independence) – forced further dislocation and rearticulation of global trade governance, and provided the discursive context in which the Uruguay Round and the WTO itself would eventually appear. Rearticulation has occurred in moments of crisis, whereby the former discursive formation is shown to be contingent. This is most evident in the Uruguay Round, where the feared collapse of multilateralism facilitated a significant expansion of the category 'trade' to include many new spheres of social activity, including those equivalentially grouped under the new category of 'trade in services'. The current crisis facing the Doha Round may, on this basis, lead to a further rearticulation of global trade governance, though clearly it is impossible to say how that articulation will appear.

The articulatory process is immensely complex and diffuse. Much of the articulatory process has taken place in formal and informal forums external to the GATT. In the case of services, much has relied upon a vast network of identities far exceeding the nation-states. In the same process, new actors have emerged, including the agency of the GATT/WTO Secretariat, as well as transnational corporations.[44]

Having now considered the historically contingent articulatory process underlying the WTO, the next chapter will continue the analysis by concentrating on the WTO in its present-day operation. It will argue that the WTO exceeds its formal legal institutional arrangement and show how it has been rearticulated since its emergence in 1995.

Notes

1 Quentin Skinner (1998) *Liberty Before Liberalism* (Cambridge: Cambridge University Press), 117.
2 WTO Secretariat, *WTO News: Speeches – DG Pascal Lamy, 13 December 2005 Opening Ceremony, Ministerial Conference, Sixth Session, Hong Kong*, www.wto. org/english/news_e/sppl_e/sppl15_e.htm (accessed December 2012).
3 As defined in the previous chapter.
4 For Foucault, the social world is imbued with interpretation, which may be historicized via genealogy. He writes: 'The development of humanity is a series of interpretations. The role of genealogy is to record its history: the history of morals,

ideals, and metaphysical concepts, the history of the concept of liberty or of the ascetic life; as they stand for the emergence of different interpretations, they must be made to appear as events on the stage of historical process' (Foucault 1991: 86).

5　For a more detailed summary of *iterability*, please see Critchley 1999: 33–34.

6　Krasner defines an international regime as consisting of: 'implicit or explicit principles, norms, rules, and decision-making procedures around which actors' expectations converge in a given area of international relations' (Krasner 1983: 2). Though MFN lacks a formal procedure for decision making, it does sediment a body of norms affecting those state actors party to agreements signed in which it is included, constituting the tentative beginnings of a regime.

7　Beane writes: 'These started with agreements such as the 1890 treaty Concerning the Creation of an International Union for the Publication of Customs Tariffs. There were also various international congresses, on problems of customs cooperation, held in 1900, 1908, 1913, 1920, 1922, 1923, 1927, 1930, and 1933. In the 1920s, there was also an International Finance Conference in Brussels, a 1923 Geneva conference, and another 1923 Conference on Customs Formalities. The latter, sponsored by the League of Nations, sought to reduce "excessive and arbitrary formalities associated with national tariff policies", but it did not specifically attack tariffs' (Beane 2000: 52–53).

8　This account is based upon Goldstein 1993: 227, ft 16.

9　Ibid.

10　Trade governance understood as dictated by whatever was argued to be in the 'interests' of the 'nation-state'.

11　For a detailed account, see: Sen 2003: 116; Trebilcock and Howse 1999: 20; and Cohn 2002: 34.

12　On Roosevelt, see Zeiler 1999: 9.

13　Account from Dunkley 2000: 23; and Wolman 1992: 197. See also Goldstein 1989.

14　For a fuller account on Cordell Hull, see Allen 1953.

15　Haggard 1988: 100.

16　This is exemplified in contradictions in the implementation of the RTAA, where controls placed on the import of Japanese textiles ran contrary to non-conditionality. See also Haggard 1988: 92.

17　See Zeiler 1999: 42; Hoekman and Kostecki 2001: 37–4; and Beane 2000: 51.

18　See also: Haggard 1988: 118–19.

19　Michalopoulos states: 'The draft charter of the International Trade Organization (ITO) … provided for exceptions to be made to the general trade rules when dealing with issues of development. For example one provision allowed Contracting Parties to use protective measures during the establishment, development or reconstruction of particular industries or branches of agriculture, provided they obtained the permission of the other Contracting Parties'. C. Michalopoulos (2001) *Developing Countries in the WTO* (Basingstoke: Palgrave), 23.

20　On elitism, see Hart 1995a: 160–61. On GATT's responsiveness to US demands, see Goldstein 1993: 223.

21　National treatment ensures that, having passed border measures, foreign goods are 'treated no less favourably than like or directly competitive goods produced domestically in terms of internal (indirect) taxation' (Hoekman and Kostecki 2001: 30).

22　See also Zeiler 1999: 75–88, 147–79.

23　For more, see Zeiler 1999: 147–64.

24　In his account of the development of trade liberalization in the context of the Cold War, Zeiler describes the GATT as: 'A weapon in the arsenal of democracy … Its humble beginnings and modest nature belie the fact that GATT proved crucial to the Free World's victory in this great conflict' (Zeiler 1999: 199).

25　This was particularly true in legal matters of any complexity. See Cohn 2002: 38.

26 This is discussed by the WTO itself in: WTO Secretariat (1999) *High Level Symposium on Trade and Development – Geneva, 17–18 March 1999* (WTO Publications: Geneva), 12, www.wto.org/english/tratop_e/devel_e/tr_dvbadoc_e.doc (accessed December 2012).

27 See Winters 1990: 1291.

28 He writes: 'Eric Wyndham White, GATT's Executive Secretary, likes to tell of a visit with the foreign trade minister of a leading GATT member. In the presence of numerous trade officials, the minister criticized GATT at length for preventing him from taking various actions ardently advocated by important domestic groups. The minister seemed somewhat shaken when Wyndham White assured him that none of the actions he proposed actually violated the GATT rules. After the meeting had concluded, he took Wyndham White aside and whispered, "Why on earth did you have to say that? I don't really want to do those things anyway!" GATT's administrative procedures are no proof against protection; but they do provide a handle to government leaders who "really don't want to do" things which would impede pursuit of the general welfare' (Gardner 1964: 694–95).

29 On the G77, see Cohn 2002: 74–75.

30 As illustration of the contingency of the discursive formation whereby UNCTAD was not successfully articulated as a real 'alternative' trade manager, there is no pre-discursive reason why the management of tariff controls on the international exchange of 'goods' should reflect not already existing trade but *potential* trade, and thus give an equal role to those that are understood to gain from that potential as those who already 'gain' from that trade.

31 On the Committee on Trade and Development, see Michalopoulos 2001: 26; and Srinivasan 1998: 24.

32 The richer states had the oil storage capacity to soften the full blow of these price increases, leaving many of the weakest states bearing the greatest negative effect of OPEC's action. However, all the world could see the importance that commodity-based multilateral mobilization had in affecting international politics, having previously seemed only susceptible to military and economic might.

33 This is discussed in Steinberg 2002: 358.

34 John Croome was a senior official in the GATT, starting as its press spokesman. In the Uruguay Round, he was to have administrative involvement in several negotiating groups, as well as helping to produce the draft documents that would become the WTO. He was also secretary to the Leutweiler group, which was central to making the Uruguay Round possible in the first place (Croome 1995).

35 Present here is a contingent articulation. It should be noted that it is debated whether the so-called 'Asian Tiger' phenomenon – where formerly economically impoverished nation-states in Asia shifted to become industrially strong, exporting capital-intensive goods to the USA and Europe – can be understood as export-led or due to more complicated factors. For a good comparative discussion on this topic, please see: Veltmeyer *et al.* 1997.

36 See Hoekman and Kostecki 2001: 60; and Blackhurst 1998: 33–34. 'The number of annual meetings ranged from two to four. One of the most important features of the group's work was that it was able to bring together high officials from a number of capitals. This greatly increased the value of its discussions and the force of its recommendations' (Blackhurst 1998: 33–35).

37 Unless stated otherwise, the account on the emergence and sedimentation of trade in services is based upon Drake and Nicolaïdis 1992.

38 In respect to this point, though there is not space in this particular account to do so, it might be interesting to examine the articulatory process underlining the shift in business practice whereby formerly internal functions were externalized.

39 Although a similar process of bargaining was possible by offering progress on issues affecting GATT rules on the primary commodities (e.g. agriculture) of

developing countries in return for progress in the GATS, separating them this way would have involved less pressure than if 'goods' and 'services' had been more officially tied into the same negotiating process via being within the same agreement.

40 These 24 were Argentina, Bangladesh, Brazil, Burma, Cameroon, Colombia, Côte d'Ivoire, Cuba, Cyprus, Egypt, Ghana, India, Jamaica, Nicaragua, Nigeria, Pakistan, Peru, Romania, Sri Lanka, Tanzania, Trinidad and Tobago, Uruguay, Yugoslavia and Zaire (Croome 1995: 24, ft 2).

41 The remaining 10 were Argentina, Brazil, Cuba, Egypt, India, Nicaragua, Nigeria, Peru, Tanzania and Yugoslavia (Croome 1995: 28, ft 3).

42 Its members included Argentina, Australia, Brazil, Canada, Chile, Colombia, Fiji, Hungary, Indonesia, Malaysia, Philippines, New Zealand, Thailand and Uruguay (Cohn 2002: 189).

43 The role of issue groups (e.g. environmental, development non-state organizations) contesting the Uruguay Round is discussed in Chapter 4.

44 The chapter has not discussed the emergence of issue groups contesting the WTO because such is its utility to understanding the discursive formation of the WTO that it will be focused on in Chapters 4 and 5.

3 The WTO as an uncertain political project

Introduction

To understand the WTO as embedded within a specific historical and social context, this third chapter shows how since its creation the WTO has undergone a continual process of rearticulation. It exceeds any finite political structure and appears as what is described here – an uncertain political project constituted by a changing amalgam of social practices that each alters what the WTO means for those actors it impacts. Despite possessing a formal institutional structure, the WTO cannot be reduced to that structure, as this chapter shows. What is more, the purpose or function of the WTO is constantly subject to rearticulation as it buffets between the thunderous political storms that have enveloped its path. As the book argues overall, the WTO is not passively subject to external forces but is, rather, intimately tied into these social practices as constituting – and reconstituting – the conditions of possibility that made it a political project with being. This third chapter, then, draws heavily open the methodology developed in the Introduction to this book whilst advancing further by looking at both the formal and informal character of the WTO as an institution – showing that the WTO as a political entity exceeds a conventional legal-institutionalist model. Attention is placed on empirically observable practices attributed to the social practice of the WTO. These practices underline uncertainty in defining precisely what is meant by the 'WTO', exhibiting an open articulatory process.

Uncertainty exists despite 26,000 pages of negotiated texts – formalized at the end of the GATT Uruguay Round on 1 January 1995 – stipulating the regime of global trade governance to be facilitated by the WTO, as well as an appendix laying out the formal practices of the WTO as an organization (Croome 1995: 3). As discussed in Chapter 1, when defining the social practice of the WTO, the literature gives much attention to the formal rules and procedures outlined in these negotiated texts. Additionally, attention is given to the informal norms shaping the WTO. The presence of informal norms is sometimes used to argue that the WTO is no more than the product of 'power politics' (Kwa 2003), privileging the material over the ideational.[1] In such criticism, formal rules and procedures appear as superficial, subject to informal norms much more sensitive to the whims of those actors 'possessing' the most (material) capabilities in a given decision domain. This position – reliant as it is on a material-ideational divide – is problematized within a post-structuralist discourse theoretical approach to the WTO. No social practice can be defined by a finite set of formal rules/procedures and informal norms, but consists of a much more complex and diffuse articulatory process, as argued in Chapter 1. Consequently, the WTO is constitutively *uncertain* – exceeding any finite set of practices and subject to rearticulation.[2]

To construct this argument, the chapter will first introduce the formal rules/procedures and the informal norms through which the WTO is typically defined. Discussion of informal norms in the operation of the WTO helps to illustrate its character as a diffuse social practice. However, better to appreciate uncertainty, it is necessary to trace out the shifting discursive formation of the WTO post-1995, including where the WTO Secretariat has attempted alternately to present the WTO as 'development-friendly' or 'democratic'. This will be done in the second half of the chapter. The discourse of transparency is particularly interesting here. Whilst the articulatory process cannot be limited to public relations, such carefully formed rhetoric does give a useful impression of the wider discursive practices through which the WTO operates and the forces through which it is shaped. The analysis draws attention to, in particular, contestation over the WTO's constituent social practices – mapping out the WTO's conditions of possibility, in the sense developed by Laclau and Mouffe, as discussed in the first chapter.

The WTO as formal rules and informal norms

This first section appears similar to an international regimes theoretical approach[3] to the WTO by outlining a mixture of formal rules/procedures and informal norms. Defining the WTO thus may be problematized in two ways: 1 discursive practices exceed rules, procedures and norms to include a much more nuanced series of social activities;[4] and, 2 no social practice can be defined by a finite set of practices due to the overlap of overdetermination.[5] However, this does not necessarily negate the utility of analysing rules, procedures and norms if they can be acknowledged as parts of the discursive formation constituting the WTO rather than a static representation of its political operation. The first section, therefore, serves to begin tracing the articulatory shape of the WTO that emerged in 1995.

The WTO as a body of formal rules/procedures

Established in Article II of the Marrakech Agreement, the WTO is intended to provide a 'common institutional framework for the conduct of trade relations among its members in matters for which agreements and associated legal obligations apply' (quoted in Hoekman and Kostecki 2001: 51). This involves a consolidation of the body of law and practice that had evolved in the nearly 50 years of the GATT, but also a series of significant additions to the institutional regulation of global trade relations (Footer 1997: 653). These additions included: an increased legal institutionalization of the dispute set-tlement mechanism; the rules of the WTO were consequently to be much more legally binding than those under GATT (Jackson 1998a: 36); a deepening/widening of issue coverage, to include intellectual property and services;[6] and, most importantly, the single undertaking – also known as the 'single package' – approach, which commits all Members to accept agreed obligations.[7]

The WTO has four functions: 1 to facilitate negotiations amongst Members on current issues/agreements and proposals for future agreements; 2 to administer the system of dispute settlement, enforcing those agreements; 3 to monitor Members' trade policy via the Trade Policy Review Mechanism; and 4 to maintain cooperation with the IMF and World Bank (Matsushita *et al.* 2003: 9). The multilateral trade agreements produced within the WTO serve as a body of rules, with the four functions listed above acting to ensure their implementation and remedy any flaws in their design (Hoekman and Kostecki 2001: 51). The consequence is an organization that, on the formal level, may accurately be perceived as a legal institution – a juridical system with a minimum of political structure (Winham and Lanoszka 2000: 27). GATT was influential in international trade diplomacy as a formal code of behaviour (Curzon and Curzon 1973: 298), or rules, and the WTO was intended at least equally to satisfy, if not increase, this role.

The institutional structure of the WTO is hierarchical, with nearly all sub-bodies open to all Members. The functions of the different bodies reflect the different aspects of the various agreements contained within the organization's remit, which are all intended as the product of negotiation between Members. At the head of the organizational structure of the WTO is the Ministerial Conference, which has supreme authority over all the other bodies within the organization. The Ministerial Conference is open to all Members and is used to negotiate new issues, as well as decisions regarding waivers from agreement obligations. However, the Ministerial Conference meets only once every two years and so governance of everyday affairs falls under the authority of the General Council. The General Council exists as itself, supervising the running of a series of other bodies under it, but also convenes in two different guises: as the Dispute Settlement Body (DSB),[8] and as the Trade Policy Review Body (TPRB).[9] The General Council meets about 12 times a year, as 'appropriate' (Matsushita *et al.* 2003: 10), and attendance is open to all WTO Members. This remains true for when the General Council also meets as the DSB or TPRB. Reflecting the key functions of the WTO and the intentions of the Uruguay Round that launched the organization, there are three further councils that act as subsidiary bodies to the General Council: a Council for Trade in Goods; a Council for Trade-Related Aspects of Intellectual Property Rights; and a Council for Trade in Services (Matsushita *et al.* 2003: 10). Beneath these councils are the various committees, such as the Committee on Trade and Development or the Committee on Trade and Environment, which have been set up in response to focus on specific issues contained within the various agreements held within the WTO. The working parties are where the 'new' (and least sedimented) issues – such as investment and government procurement – are placed within the organizational structure. In terms of everyday decision making, the specialized councils and committees have responsibility, reporting only to the General Council as required.[10]

In accordance with agreement produced at the Fourth Ministerial Conference in Doha, 2001, a Trade Negotiations Committee (TNC) was created to oversee negotiations of the so-called 'Development Agenda', and prepare agreement on the key issues to be discussed at Ministerial Conferences, including those at the Fifth Ministerial, in Cancun, 2003.[11] It reports to the General Council.

The majority of these bodies are plenary, in that they are open to the participation of any Member, though this is not true of all the various organs.[12] Despite exceptions, participation in the majority of everyday decision making within the WTO is formally open to the entire Membership.

The WTO is administered by a Secretariat with offices in Geneva. The powers of the Secretariat are intended to be minimal, though sufficient to fulfil such tasks as providing the facilities necessary for the various councils, committees and working parties to meet, which includes the venue, recording of minutes and distribution of information.[13] This information includes that on agreements, but also concerns their implementation via the WTO's monitoring role. In line with the intention to keep the Secretariat as minimal as possible, its staff size is no fewer than 550 in number (WTO Secretariat 2003: 2). However, the size of personnel actually involved in the operation of the WTO is far greater when counting the two ways in which this principle body of staff is augmented by both the Geneva delegations of the WTO Members and the civil servants located in Members' capitals, who are assigned to various tasks related to the WTO. Therefore, the administration of the WTO can be accurately described as consisting of a network that involves the work of at least 5,000 people (Hoekman and Kostecki 2001: 55). The organization is described as 'Member-driven', which significantly means that it is the responsibility of the individual Member delegations, and their domestic civil service, to operate the substantive mechanisms of the WTO.[14]

The most senior role within the WTO is that of the director-general, who is the head of the Secretariat and is appointed by consensus in the General Council.[15] It is the General Council that decides the powers and terms of office of the director-general, but it is s/he who appoints the staff and directs the duties of the WTO Secretariat (Matsushita *et al.* 2003: 10). Those staff, including the director-general, swear the oath of impartiality required from all those employed in the international civil service (Matsushita *et al.* 2003: 10).

In all the councils and committees, including the General Council, a chairperson administers proceedings. In negotiations, the chair has an influential position due to their managerial role over the negotiating space, ascertaining the optimal arrangement for achieving agreement via separating issues out for select discussion, as well as the sequencing of the different actors. Consequently, guidelines exist to require representation of the overall membership within the selection of the chairs (Narlikar 2001: 3).[16] Selection for the various chair appointments is achieved via consensus within the General Council, and so open to all members in attendance.[17]

Rules of decision making

The rules for decision making in the WTO include a combination of procedures based upon majority voting, unanimity and consensus. Except for those decisions that require voting, as will be discussed, consensus is the dominant of these mechanisms.[18]

Consensus is distinct from unanimity as it includes only those Members present at the time of taking the decision, the WTO stating that '[t]he absence of a Member will be assumed to imply that it has no comments on or objections to the proposed decision on the matter'.[19] Unanimity (full agreement of the entire membership) is only required for certain amendments to WTO agreements.[20] A simple majority vote is allowed for in the General Council and Ministerial Conference in the event that consensus cannot be reached (Das 1999: 429). Voting is intended to operate on a 'one member-one vote' basis, with no formal arrangement for weighted voting (Hoekman and Kostecki 2001: 57). In the following decisions, it is necessary to hold a vote amongst the entire membership.[21] A three-quarters majority vote of the Members,[22] to be taken within the Ministerial Conference or General Council, is required for the adoption of an interpretation of an Agreement. However, waivers, which also require a three-quarters majority vote, may only go before the Ministerial Conference. Those amendments that do not require unanimity may be decided by a two-thirds majority vote of Members, though this is complicated in respect to an ambiguous clause which states that if an amendment is adopted, any member who votes against it, and can claim that adopting the amendment would fundamentally change their rights and obligations, may default from adoption of the amendment (Das 1999: 430).[23] A three-quarters majority vote is then required to declare that:

> [T]he amendment is of such a nature that if any Member does not accept it within a specified period (the period to be specified by the Ministerial Conference), the Member is free to withdraw from the WTO.
>
> (Das 1999: 431)

In order to remain within the organization, the dissenting Member must receive consent to do so from the Ministerial Conference (Article X:6). Technically, this allows for the expulsion of any Member who refuses to accept an amendment agreed upon by three-quarters of the membership.[24] Decisions on the accession of new members are taken by the Ministerial Conference on a two-thirds majority (Article XII:2).

These rules need to be seen as not only shaping the political operation of an institution, but reflective of a much wider discursive context in which the WTO exists. In this respect, those rules and procedures emphasizing a logic of 'inclusivity' or 'equal responsibility' for decision making are particularly interesting, suggesting that such logics are somehow important to facilitating the political operation of the WTO. These logics become even more interesting when considered in the light of what follows. That is, next the chapter discusses the role of informal norms in WTO, and the role in facilitating a much less egalitarian model of policy formation in the WTO. This suggests that the WTO exists in a discursive context in which these logics are important, even if informal norms contradict their substantive operation.

The role of informal norms in WTO decision making

Since there is no formal weighted voting in the WTO – not being dependent upon either a 'member's contribution to international trade, or its contribution to the budget of the WTO', Qureshi (1996: 6) concludes that '[p]rima facie ... the decision making process is democratic'. The specific question of 'democracy' is highly contentious with respect to the WTO and will be specifically discussed in the context of examining the articulation of the WTO at key moments post-1995. However, Qureshi's comment is useful here because it highlights a distinction between the formal institutional arrangement of the WTO and its much larger identity dependent upon informal mechanisms for ensuring agreement. Sedimented within the Marrakech Agreement establishing the WTO was the norm of consensus – developed within the GATT but never formally acknowledged as the default means for reaching decisions amongst participating nation-states – which, Qureshi (1996: 6) argues, acts as a 'latent' form of weighted voting. A footnote to Article IX of the Marrakech Agreement defines consensus in WTO decision making as follows:

> The body concerned shall be deemed to have decided by consensus on a matter submitted for its consideration, if no Member, present at the meeting when the decision is taken, formally objects to the proposed decision.
>
> (Quoted in Jackson 1998a: 115, ft 29)

This would appear to provide any Member, as long as it ensures its presence at the relevant meeting, with veto power and, consequently, a decisive bargaining chip via the threat to dissent. To understand how consensus operates in the decision-making mechanisms of the WTO, it is necessary to understand it as a form of diplomatic negotiation. This places all decisions in a multi-stage process that places emphasis on the pre-negotiation stage of agenda setting, which is crucial to affecting which matters reach the negotiating arena.[25]

Consensus emerged as a proactive and deliberate negotiating strategy.[26] This differs from a negative form of consensus, where decisions are based on the passive non-objection of those participating in the meeting. It requires a positive strategy of 'mediation' (Footer 1997: 659). Mediation demands pre-formal negotiation arenas in which not only the agenda may be set, but information may be gained as to what proposals are most likely to succeed, and what is necessary to ensure they reach consensus (Footer 1997: 667). An issue that cannot achieve consensus outside the forum is unlikely to be submitted for expression inside the forum. The privilege that proactive consensus gives to mediation external to the institution is important because it prevents disputes that may potentially damage the institution if they become visible (Footer 1997: 667). Therefore, consensus in the WTO is utilized to displace dissensus from the formal arena, limiting the extent to which it can be expressed beyond the informal, and low-visibility, domain of international diplomacy (Jackson 1998a: 58). The principle of consensus as proactive, which is utilized for decision making in the WTO, allows the organization to exist at the centre of global trade governance, overcoming the differences otherwise expressed between nation-states.[27]

However, Qureshi (1996: 6–7) argues that even if consensus were to be replaced by voting, decisions in the WTO are taken not by secret ballot but by a show of hands of those Members in dissent. This places significant diplomatic pressure on those Members in disagreement with the overall proposed agreement, with Qureshi concluding that voting in the WTO would also have the same effect as a weighted voting system (ibid.: 7). In one respect, this means simply that one should not be 'confused' by the formal decision-making mechanism and instead view the WTO as being as subject to the opaque nature of international diplomacy as any other international regime, though it also opens up an important question as to why it is even necessary to create a formally 'democratic' system in the first place. This will become clearer when discussing the articulation of the WTO post-1995.

An uncertain identity

The role of informal mechanisms is far from unusual in the context of international diplomacy. What makes the role of informal mechanisms in the WTO interesting, however, is that they clearly demonstrate that the WTO is much more complicated than suggested by any organogram or discussion of the formal legal codes. This is despite the majority of WTO studies focusing only on its formal legal-institutionalist identity. What, then, is the identity of the WTO? For Wilkinson, the WTO that emerged in 1995 was to be:

> the centre piece of a much consolidated and significantly widened regulatory framework designed not only to administer a series of legal agreements, covering trade in goods, trade in services, trade-related intellectual property rights, and oversee the wherewithal to settle trade disputes, but also to provide a permanent forum in which further liberalisation could be pursued through periodic negotiation.

> (Wilkinson 2002a: 129)

The 'regulatory framework' that includes a greatly expanded set of legal agreements exhibits both a rearticulation of global trade governance and the contingency of that construction, making clear that 'trade' is not pre-discursive.[28] This has significant ramifications for the rest of the definition, with the identity of the WTO clearly being far from static or pre-discursive.

The preamble to the Marrakech Agreement establishing the WTO is less legally binding than the full Uruguay text, but it does frame the general intended purpose of the body. It states:

> [R]elations in the field of trade and economic endeavour should be conducted with a view to raising standards of living, ensuring full employment and a large and steadily growing volume of real income and effective demand, and expanding the production of and trade in goods and services, while allowing for the optimal use of the world's resources in accordance with the objective of sustainable development, seeking both to protect and preserve the environment and to enhance the means for doing so in a manner consistent with their respective needs and concerns at different levels of economic development ... [T]hat there is need for positive efforts designed to ensure that developing countries, and especially the least developed among them, secure a share in the growth in international trade commensurate with the needs of their economic development ... [and, the need for] entering into reciprocal and mutually advantageous arrangements directed to the substantial reduction of tariffs and other barriers to trade and to the elimination of discriminatory treatment in international trade relations.
>
> (Quoted in Qureshi 1996: 196)

This presents a complex equivalential chain (WTO = 'raising standards of living' + 'full employment' + 'growing real income and effective demand' + 'expanding production of trade in goods and services' + 'optimal use of the world's resources' + 'sustainable development' + 'protect and preserve the environment' + 'mutually advantageous arrangements', etc.), reflecting the contestation that took place during the 1980s as well as a discursive context in which 'environmentalism' emerged as a potent political identity with the phrase 'sustainable development' included in the preamble (Wilkinson 2002a: 135). The preamble is ambiguous, with 'optimal use of the world's resources', for example, open to interpretation as either supporting an environmentalist critique against wasteful polluting industry or embodying the theory of comparative advantage (Qureshi 1996: 4; Croome 1995: 361). Outside the preamble, the WTO has been articulated as on the edge of a frontier against 'protectionist siren calls', acting as a 'mast' to which 'governments can tie their hands' to escape such calls (Esty 2002: 11; Wilkinson 2002a: 138). Linked with the 'protectionist siren calls' as the 'other' is 'discrimination', with the 'most-favoured nation' and 'national treatment' principles articulated to embody 'non-discrimination' (Qureshi 1996: 22).

Beyond such a formal statement, the identity of the WTO encompasses such sub-bodies as the Trade Policy Review Mechanism – giving the WTO Secretariat the legitimation to review domestic trade policy of its Members (Hoekman and Kostecki 2001: 63–64; Narlikar 2004: 136), as well as an administrative capacity reliant on not just the WTO Secretariat but also the domestic trade departments in the nation-state capitals, as discussed. The outcome of the reform of the dispute settlement mechanism that had evolved in the GATT was the Dispute Settlement Body (DSB). The DSB represents a significant shift towards a more law-based form of global trade governance, where the various trade agreements contained within the WTO effectively become law because the body ruling on disputes between WTO Member states uses those agreements as the basis of its rulings which are articulated as 'legally binding'.[29] Additionally, DSB rulings feed into how those agreements are to be interpreted later, so that WTO agreements have been described as 'law as process' (Footer 1997: 667).

Central to the identity of the WTO is what might be described as a logic of agreement, embodied not only in the name of the various texts representing the rules of global trade governance held under the GATT/WTO regime, but also unique to the WTO in the formalization of the consensus principle as well as the practice of including the vast bulk of the texts within a single undertaking. The principle of consensus, as Footer writes, 'will mask any differences which may exist between [Members]', and, as such, allow 'participants in the process to identify with the result as a whole', regardless of their initial position (Footer 1997: 667). Regardless of the effect of this logic, it is significant that the WTO – understood as a series of rules and institutional bodies – should be articulated as a collective undertaking, supporting the idea of a collective identity, reflected in the phrase 'mutually advantageous arrangements' stated in the preamble to the Marrakech Agreement.

Ford argues that the Uruguay Round represented the emergence of a 'new collective identity ... as the boundaries between developing and developed countries were re-formed and both groups became part of a Self of multi-lateral traders' (Ford 2003: 133). Whilst the account of the various Ministerial Conferences that have followed the WTO's birth in 1995 suggest that this might be somewhat of an exaggeration, quite clearly the WTO identity includes a sense of a collectivity within its political operation.

The single undertaking approach means that the expansion of trade that was facilitated via its rearticulation in the Uruguay Round affects all nation-states party to the WTO. This rearticulation of global trade governance is itself a significant feature of the WTO identity that emerged in 1995. Whereas the GATT was more concerned with reducing restrictions to trade between nation-states, the WTO had a much broader concept of trade governance at the global level that 'extended into intellectual property, environment, competition rules, and health care policy' (Esty 2002: 14). The rearticulation of trade – reflected in the growth of texts with the phrases 'trade and ...' or 'trade-related ...' within them – has led some to argue that the WTO faces an 'identity crisis' with its expanding definition of trade (Qureshi 1996: 13). This warning appears to be evidenced in many of the conflicts over the shape of the WTO since 1995, which will be discussed next.

Singapore

The first WTO Ministerial Conference – the biennial meetings that serve as a stocktaking exercise and negotiation of new regulations and issues unresolved within the daily workings of the organization – was held in December 1996. The event involved the completion of expanded rules (the Agreements on Basic Telecommunications and Financial Services), as well as the launch of the WTO's logo (Wilkinson 2002a: 130). Multilateralism was articulated as unity, with the then WTO Director-General Renato Ruggiero, stating in his conference address that:

> The unity of industrialized, developing, least-developed and transition economies is the most valuable asset of this organization. It is because of this unity that membership in this organization is proving so attractive to the 28 candidates for accession, who include some of the world's largest economies as well as some of the smallest.[30]

This was repeated within how Ruggiero viewed the formalized 'consensus' practice for decision making, which he viewed as providing all Members with 'shared responsibility'.[31] The concept of 'liberalization' was included within his address, articulated to be equivalential with 'progress' and 'empowerment' of the 'world's peoples'.[32] The WTO was articulated as at the centre of a 'global community'. Interestingly, the presence of non-state actors was given special reference, as the means by which engagement with this community would be achieved:

> A world trading system which has the support of a knowledgeable and engaged global community will be in a far stronger position to manage the forces of globalization for everyone's benefit. This is why the presence here of so many representatives of non-governmental organizations, the business sector, and the media is so important.[33]

This engagement appears to have been articulated in line with multilateralism, at least in a cosmopolitan sense that viewed the role of the WTO as at the centre of the management of trade, removing it from nation-states. This is particularly clear in the following quotation:

> It is about recognizing that our national interests are increasingly global interests and that our economic security increasingly hinges on the strength of others.[34]

Thus, particularisms are erased and the WTO is conceived as a universal, apolitical manager of trade.

The identity of developing countries as political actors re-emerged at Singapore only in the immediate aftermath of the conference, with criticism articulated by some Members that the outcome of the Ministerial disproportionately favoured developed countries by stalling liberalization of agriculture and textiles (Narlikar 2004: 136–37), as well as introducing new issues to be considered for future negotiation that were seen as supportive of industry in those developed countries (Qureshi 1996: 13–14). These issues included 'investment', as well as 'competition policy', 'government procurement', 'trade facilitation' and 'social clauses' (labour standards) (Qureshi 1996: 13–14). The latter issue proved most contentious and was abandoned, distracting pressure from the remaining four on which a study process was launched at Singapore (Qureshi 1996: 13–14). Singapore concluded with a statement in the official declaration that 'social clauses' remained the policy domain of the International Labour Organization (ILO) (Wilkinson 2002a: 134), abstracting labour demands outside global trade governance.

Emerging dislocations

Following Singapore, a series of events threatened to show the contingency of multilateralism and trade as articulated within the discursive formation of the WTO and thus force its dislocation. A dispute was brought to the DSB by the USA against the European Union for restrictions placed on its beef exports. The EU had restricted the imports on the grounds that the US farmers were using growth hormones in their cattle. This dispute, whilst not in itself necessarily a problem because of the DSB – which was designed specifically to deal with such disputes, and thus was potentially strengthened by acting out its role – provoked a tension between the articulation of global trade governance as separate from the domestic state that managed human health. The tension was increased because of recent food scares, particularly in the United Kingdom, which had framed food as a potential health hazard. Protection from potentially dangerous food was understood to be the preserve of the nation-state, rather than a trade-focused body, yet this appeared to contradict the notion of global trade governance upon which the WTO was based. A widely traded 'good' such as beef was being articulated as more than a trade issue.

Another dispute, this time brought against the USA – by India, Pakistan, Malaysia and Thailand – on the basis that a ban against shrimp imports caught with nets, argued by environmental groups to be dangerous to turtles, was adjudicated by the WTO DSB, which ruled that the ban was 'illegal' under the terms of WTO agreements (McGrew 1999: 201). The original ban had been brought after nationally focused campaigning by US environmental groups, which found themselves positioned against an international organization few had previously considered within their demands.[35] Trade appeared an increasingly tenuous category. This has been described by Esty, in an article published within the WTO's own journal, as the collapse of 'technocratic rationality', and as the cause of a 'legitimacy crisis' for the WTO (Esty 2002: 13).

The multilateralism of the WTO was threatened in disagreement concerning the appointment of a successor to Renato Ruggiero as director-general of the WTO Secretariat. A divide emerged between developed and developing countries which formed behind, respectively, Mike Moore (briefly prime minister of New Zealand) and Supachai Panitchpakdi (a former deputy prime minister of Thailand) (Hoekman and Kostecki 2001: 56). Majority support for Panitchpakdi amongst the developing countries was articulated via a demand for a vote, abandoning the consensus principle (Georgiev 2003: 29). However, the USA successfully opposed the call for a vote (Georgiev 2003: 29). In the end, consensus was only reached after a formal suggestion by Australia that rather than give the director-general the statutory appointment of five years, the two candidates would both be appointed, each serving only three years consecutively. In consequence, Mike Moore came to the post in 1999, with Supachai Panitchpakdi succeeding him in 2002. This dispute left the WTO with its most senior administrative role vacant long enough that the organization appeared weak and incapable of agreement, as well as undermining multilateralism.[36]

The battle for Seattle

Hosted in Seattle, the Third WTO Ministerial Conference collapsed because of a failure to reach consensus amongst its Member states, which fell into separate identities with the re-emergence of a divisive articulation of the developed and developing country categories. The WTO also faced a serious challenge to its articulation of global trade governance. Seattle has become synonymous with either the power of civil protest to disrupt international organizations, or the difficulties of achieving agreement amongst a large membership of nation-states.[37]

Of relevance to this discussion is how 'environment' and 'labour' were articulated so that the WTO was forced to argue its democratic credentials. This took place via a series of dislocations. First, the series of issues normally contested at the level of the nation-state but affected by the WTO created the conditions in which new identities emerged, so that environmentalists became increasingly relevant to global trade governance. This was reflected in the series of equivalential demands articulated by the different groups. One such set of equivalential demands was 'Beef, Bananas, and Burma' (Danaher and Mark 2003: 269–72). Slogans were displayed reading 'Teamsters and Turtles – together at last' (Danaher and Mark 2003: 223). 'Teamsters' referred to the trade unions, and 'turtles' to the environmentalists. Seattle provoked the equivalence between a series of wide demands (Danaher and Mark 2003: 224). The hegemonic formation of global trade governance in which the environmental and labour demands appeared abstract faced dislocation. Environmental actors emerged as actors within the sphere of global trade governance at the borders of how trade is to be understood. Trade unions became mobilized as they found their own ability to demand improved labour conditions weakened due to the increasing mobility of capital. Issues previously seen as outside the remit of trade entered the contestation of trade governance at the global level. This is not to say that the WTO explicitly acknowledged these issues within its mandate, but that the categorization of trade as distinct from categories such as labour or the environment appeared increasingly tenuous.

Although many more specific demands were made by those emerging identities articulated as the critics of the WTO, overall there was a central underlying critique that the WTO was undemocratic. For example, the US advocacy group Public Citizen published 'Whose Trade Organization? – Corporate Globalization and the Erosion of Democracy', framing the WTO as a threat to democracy (Danaher and Mark 2003: 269). This critique best illustrates the dislocatory moment here in the discursive formation of the WTO, where trade as an exclusive field requiring supranational management appears contingent, and trade comes to cover many more spheres of social life.

A key contributing factor to its collapse was pressure placed on the US president, who gave a seemingly insubstantial concession to the trade unions that the WTO might consider inclusion of labour standards within its trade agreements (O'Brien *et al.* 2000: 140). In the context of an upcoming selection of the Democrat candidate for the US presidential elections, pressure was applied by trade unions on US President Clinton who sought their support for Al Gore (Danaher and Mark 2003: 285–87). The demand for labour rights in global trade governance was being equivalentially linked to the demand for a Democrat presidency. This gave US labour groups more leverage by which to promote its demands for 'labour' language to be included within the WTO agreements. During the first few days of Seattle, as the protests began that linked labour to the demand for labour rights to be acknowledged as a relevant consideration in global trade governance, Clinton responded to a press question by suggesting the possibility that labour conditions were relevant to trade agreements and might be used as conditions for determining access to US markets (Danaher and Mark 2003: 285). This unexpected statement sparked protests internally within the WTO from many Members, which viewed labour conditions as outside the jurisdiction of the WTO. According to Danaher and Mark, the tension was greatest for those low-income Members that perceived cheap labour as their 'comparative advantage' (ibid.: 285). This demand for something already decontested as beyond WTO jurisdiction at Singapore was articulated as a sign of US insensitivity to the interests of other Members, and fitted into a context where arguments were also made that the Seattle Ministerial was overly dominated by informal small-group meetings to which developing countries had only limited access (Hoekman and Kostecki 2001: 51, 108; Schott and Watal 2000: 1; Esty 2002: 14). This undermined the logic of agreement by making visible inequalities amongst Members, and was significant in facilitating the re-emergence of a strong developing country unity that prevented any substantive consensus at Seattle.

A group of Latin American and Caribbean Members complained that the US hosts had used too much pressure in trying to force a consensus at 'any cost' (Das 2003: 170). The use of informal small-group (or 'Green Room'[38]) meetings was criticized as indicating a lack of transparency with the overall WTO process, favouring certain Members (e.g. USA and European Union) over others (Das 2003: 170–75).

The turbulence marked not only the collapse of a single Ministerial Conference but also an attempt to launch a new round of trade negotiations, titled the Millennium Round (Wilkinson 2002a: 131), which had the potential to include the additional issues introduced for working groups at Singapore: investment, competition policy, government procurement and trade facilitation. Since they remained at the working group stage, all four issues remained to be sedimented, though collectively they constituted a shift towards increasing involvement of the WTO in the domestic policy of nation-states, under the auspices of global trade governance. Seattle effectively stalled the sedimentation of these issues.

The day before Seattle became a front-page news story, WTO Director-General Mike Moore responded to growing criticism from civil society groups targeting its articulation of global trade governance, by arguing that the WTO was no more than the product of decisions taken by its Member-states, arguing: 'the WTO is not a supranational government ... Our decisions must be made by our Member States, agreements ratified by Parliaments and every two years Ministers meet to supervise our work.'[39] The management of trade was being articulated so that it could be connected back to the nation-state even if it exceeded that identity. In the speech, the WTO is also connected to 'freedom', Moore stating:

> Of course *economic freedom* is not the only freedom. But it is an indispensable part of all the other freedoms we hold important – *freedom of speech*, *freedom of conscience*, the *freedom of choice and opportunity.*[40]

In combination with freedom, the WTO is articulated as 'rationality' or 'order':

> Our dream must be a world managed by *persuasion*, the *rule of law*, the *settlement of differences peacefully by the law and in co-operation.*[41]

The 1999 protests in Seattle outside the Ministerial Conference exposed fractures within the organization, but they also showed the contingent categorization of 'trade' as distinct from 'labour' or the 'environment'. The emerging identities would force a rearticulation of 'trade management', so that non-state actors would be increasingly acknowledged within the management of trade. The politicization and emergence of civil society at Seattle is discussed in greater depth in the next chapter, though it should be noted here that whilst there were multiple possible causes for the collapse of the Third Ministerial Conference, Seattle does suggest a rearticulation of who/what constitutes an actor in the WTO by the Secretariat's particular engagement with non-governmental organizations.

Democracy and development post-Seattle

At the time of writing, there had been five WTO Ministerial Conferences following Seattle – Doha (2001), Cancun (2003), Hong Kong (2005), and two most recently in the organization's host city of Geneva (2009 and 2011) – and nearly two decades of General Council meetings and countless informal and formal negotiations further articulating the WTO. Despite this, Seattle remains a key historical moment, haunting the shifting identity of global trade governance embodied in the WTO. In the aftermath of Seattle, the world has witnessed a further Ministerial collapse – at Cancun – and a sedimentation of the issues introduced at Singapore within what has been articulated as the 'Development Round', launched at the Doha Ministerial that immediately proceeded in the wake of Seattle. The WTO has, to different degrees, been articulated as democratic and supportive of development since its inception, but it is in the wake of Seattle that this has been most acute. The Doha Round has brought with it, however, a new sense of crisis to global trade governance, where the ongoing failure to reach a definitive conclusion to negotiations has left the future of the WTO seemingly more uncertain than ever.

Transparency in the aftermath of Seattle

Post-Seattle, a number of actions took place that can be seen within the context of an attempt to rearticulate the discursive formation of the WTO, which followed the dislocation threatened at that Ministerial.[42] Together, these actions show a response to an accusation that the WTO lacks transparency. First, agreement was reached that the derestriction of WTO documents would be sped-up. Second, the organization's website was expanded to include online and unrestricted access to a large percentage of these documents. Most documents are translated into French, Spanish and English, and can be easily downloaded via an electronic database. There is also technical assistance via e-mail and telephone for those seeking more complicated information. Third, a series of pamphlets[43] and more extensive guides[44] to the WTO were produced for a public not versed in the technical language of trade negotiations. Fourth, the WTO produces a regular e-mail bulletin with press releases and announcements regarding news on trade disputes or agreements, to which anyone may subscribe via the website. Fifth, with each Ministerial Conference since Seattle there has been a growing amount of material produced for public consumption. This includes informal-style diary entries from the director-general, as well as engagement in online discussion forums, where members of the public are, on certain occasions, given access to talk with officials from the WTO Secretariat. There is also an annual 'public symposium' to which journalists, NGO representatives and academics are eligible to apply. Related to the issue of democracy, these practices have been presented by the WTO as an attempt to become transparent.

The WTO does not make the claim to *be* transparent, but relies instead on the claim that it is *working* to be transparent. This is evidenced within its main pamphlet intended for public consumption, called 'Understanding the WTO', where it states:

> On 14 May 2002, the General Council decided to make more documents available to the public as soon as they are circulated. It also decided that the minority of documents that are restricted should be made public more quickly – after about two months, instead of the previous six. This was the second major decision on transparency. On 18 July 1996, the General Council had agreed to make more information about WTO activities available publicly and decided that public information, including derestricted WTO documents, would be accessible online.
>
> (WTO Secretariat 2003: 110)

More specific engagement with the question of democracy is evident in the following speech by then WTO Director-General Mike Moore, in 2002, and illustrates the organization's rearticulation as democratic:

> The WTO does not tell governments what to do. Governments tell the WTO. All decisions from the creation of the GATT to last year's launch of the Doha Development Agenda have been taken collectively by the member governments themselves. No decision is taken unless all member governments agree, effectively every Member from the largest to the smallest has the power of veto. Even the enforcement of rules is undertaken by the members themselves. Sometimes enforcement includes the threat of sanctions but those sanctions are imposed by Members not by the organization. These are all features of a highly democratic organization and system … It is not a 'world democracy' in the sense of being a government of the world's people but it is the most democratic international body in existence today.[45]

The equality of the MFN principle is carried over to this democratic discourse, so that the end product, the power of the GATT/WTO regime, is a consensual amalgamation of all parties' interests. In a publicity document produced by the WTO Secretariat and intended for mass consumption, entitled '10 Common Misunderstandings About the WTO', the organization argues that:

> It would be wrong to suggest that every country has the same bargaining power. Nevertheless, the consensus rule means every country has a voice, and every country has to be convinced before it joins a consensus. Quite

often reluctant countries are persuaded by being offered something in return. Consensus also means every country accepts the decisions. There are no dissenters.[46]

The acknowledgement of unequal bargaining power is undermined by the claim that the organization provides its members with an equal right to a 'voice'. Central to the WTO's discourse on democratization, important as it is for legitimation in contemporary politics, is the statement that by consensus, 'There are no dissenters'. The end product of negotiations is, therefore, equality of opinion.

WTO executive

Beyond the articulation of transparency, attempts have been made to introduce an executive body with limited membership in order to ensure agreement. Influential think-tanks such as the Institute for International Economics have argued that the difficulties with achieving agreement within the WTO are the product of an increasingly assertive group of developing countries – made so because of the higher participation required of them under the terms of the single undertaking approach to trade obligations under the organization, binding all Members to obligations contained within an agreement (Schott and Watal 2000: 3). The small-group meetings, though important to negotiation, fail to express adequately this new participation from the developing countries (Schott and Watal 2000: 3). The authors of the Institute's report suggest the creation of a formal executive body, representative of the composition of the membership, but containing a much reduced number of participants (Schott and Watal 2000: 5).[47]

This idea, however, generally has been opposed within the WTO, possibly because of the loss in legitimacy it would involve, undermining multilateralism and the logic of agreement through which it is made possible (Steinberg 2002: 364). One fear is that it would lead to an institutionalization of 'power asymmetries' between Members, giving representation to only a specified elite (Narlikar 2001: 17).

Non-governmental organizations

Responding to the emergence of civil society at Seattle, a prominent question has been whether – and how to – engage non-governmental organizations (NGOs) more actively within the WTO. Other than the public symposia, the WTO attempted this project of engagement via: 1 meetings with NGO representatives; 2 inviting those representatives to seminars on technical issues related to WTO agreements; 3 workshops on specific issues to which NGOs were invited; and, 4 including an NGO section on the WTO website (Wilkinson 2002a: 133).[48]

An NGO presence has been maintained at all Ministerial Conferences, exercised via a series of briefings and meetings with WTO Secretariat staff and Member state delegates during the course of the negotiations, though NGOs do not have any form of official observer status at the negotiations themselves.[49] In his article asserting the existence of a 'legitimacy crisis' in the WTO, published in the WTO's journal *World Trade* Review, Esty argues that shifts in the world where 'state power has been weakened' means that new actors have emerged, so that '[d]erivative legitimacy built on the popular sovereignty of [sometimes] unelected Trade Ministries in distant national governments is simply no longer adequate' (Esty 2002: 15). Rather than focusing on the WTO as a body consisting of nation-states, he suggests it gives a greater role to 'communities of interest defined by an issue focus', which he sees as better representing contemporary identity formation, and to be embodied in the NGO (Esty 2002: 15–17). Given that the WTO is nothing but the sedimentation of social practices, this proposal, even if not adopted, does indicate the fluidity of the WTO identity.[50]

Rule of law

Another response to Seattle has been to emphasize the WTO as based on the 'rule of law', as illustrated in the Mike Moore quotation listed above, and linking back to what has been seen as one of the reasons for the longevity of the GATT: 'a sense that international economics and trade policy making were highly technical realms best left in the hands of an elite cadre of qualified experts', as expressed in Esty's (2002: 10) article. The DSB has been articulated as the dominance of consensus-based law over force or politics, and therefore making the WTO more responsive to developing countries than would otherwise be the case (Lee 2004: 125). In its constitution, the DSB is also to give representation to developing countries in panels deciding rulings where one of the parties includes a developing country (Lee 2004: 125).

Doha, development and the articulation of a new round

The 2001 Fourth WTO Ministerial Conference, in the capital of Qatar, launched what was to be branded as the 'Doha Development Agenda' by the WTO Secretariat for a new round of negotiations (Kwa and Jawara 2004: 199). This signalled a notable rearticulation of the round since its failed launch at Seattle, when it was named the Millennium Round. The WTO Secretariat had launched a new programme of cooperation with UNCTAD, articulating the WTO as concerned with development. In his address to the Ministerial Conference, Director-General Mike Moore stated:

> Trade rules offer only the gift of opportunity. That has to be backed up by an effective civil service infrastructure, to negotiate, implement and benefit from the rules. We have excellent cooperation with UNCTAD in our JITAP [Joint Integrated Technical Assistance Programme] programme. The new Integrated Framework will be a model of inter-agency

cooperation and coherence, enabling us to multiply our modest resources by working with other agencies to assist developing countries on the ground.[51]

In this opening speech, developing countries were singled out as a problem to be solved, their lack of influence at the WTO articulated as a matter of 'technical capacity', as due to a weak civil service infrastructure that was unable to engage fully with the multilateral trade regime. The solution was framed as a need to extend the 'full benefits of ... [the WTO] system to countries now marginalized by poverty'.[52] Furthermore, the WTO is articulated as trade rules, repeating the strategy utilized to legitimate WTO global trade governance in the immediate aftermath of Seattle, as argued above.

With reference to Seattle, the WTO was presented as a dialogue, Moore's address admitting that: '[S]ome of our critics are correct. We learned lessons in Seattle which ... we must not forget over the next few days.'[53] Additionally, the statement argued:

> A mature and confident organization should welcome scrutiny – that is healthy, it's how you improve our service. And in the end, some years out, parliaments and congresses must ratify the final agreements [of the Doha Round].[54]

Emphasis is thus placed upon the identity of the WTO as no more than the product of its Member states which, in this paragraph, are equated with domestic 'parliaments and congresses'. The role of the WTO in global trade governance is downplayed.

Despite this articulation, the launch of what was framed as a new round indicated a significant expansion of the WTO, if understood via its governance mandate. Within the Uruguay Round text, new negotiations began on 1 January 2000 – immediately after Seattle – to consider the more contentious issues (such as government procurement) left open in the GATS 1994 package. GATS would therefore feature within the Doha Ministerial. The issues introduced at Singapore, which had caused dissension from many developing countries returned in the Doha negotiations. Doha began controversially. Two mini-ministerial meetings were held unofficially in the build-up to the conference, which were open to only invited Members (Kwa and Jawara 2004: 58–62). Following the first meeting – held in Mexico – the Chairperson of the General Council, Stuart Harbinson, released a first draft of the text that would form the basis of the Doha Ministerial Declaration, representing the outcome of the then upcoming conference (Kwa and Jawara 2004: 63). This document, produced in a select and closed forum, was controversial because it was seen to bias the Singapore issues seen to favour developed countries (Kwa and Jawara 2004: 63). Additionally, the document did not express disagreement between the Members on these issues (Kwa and Jawara 2004: 64). In preparations for Seattle, disputed issues included bracketed comments acknowledging the differing positions on which agreement was left open.

A second mini-ministerial meeting was held, again with only invited Members, from which a new draft appeared, and which was then discussed within the WTO General Council open to the wider membership (Kwa and Jawara 2004: 69). Despite further objections being expressed, the second draft was submitted to the trade ministries of WTO Members without any specific brackets, though it did include a letter acknowledging that there were general disagreements to be resolved (Kwa and Jawara 2004: 69; Das 2003: 178). Stuart Harbinson defended the text on the grounds that it was necessary to achieve agreement (Kwa and Jawara 2004: 75–76). When the Doha Ministerial Conference began, the draft was unexpectedly presented as the working text of the event at the grand opening ceremony (Kwa and Jawara 2004: 89).

The framing of Doha as friendly to development has been supported by the apparent success of several Members in advocating for acknowledgement in the intellectual property text (TRIPS) that provision be made for the production of generic drugs within developing countries to provide affordable drugs to deal with, for example, the AIDS epidemic in Africa (Narlikar 2004: 137). Doha also saw a reaffirmation of the special and differential treatment principle in the context of a high-profile acknowledgement of development problems experienced by certain Members (Narlikar 2004: 137). Linking TRIPS to public health was particularly significant because it was seen as a victory against the pharmaceutical industry lobbyists who opposed any such provision for the manufacture of generic drugs (Kwa and Jawara 2004: 122). This was in the context of an anthrax scare in the USA, where the government had broken its own patent rules to ensure production of an anthrax vaccine, as well as growing public awareness of the AIDS epidemic in Africa (Kwa and Jawara 2004: 100).

An agreement at Doha remained elusive until the very end, when the WTO Secretariat took the decision to extend the conference for an additional day. This limited the field of contestation because many delegates and trade ministers of Members were already due to leave on scheduled flights (Kwa and Jawara 2004: 103–4). Negotiations ran overnight, until no further dissensus was expressed (Kwa and Jawara 2004: 104). The end product remained ambiguous, with a statement made by the chairperson of the conference, that negotiations on 'investment', 'competition policy', 'government procurement' and 'trade facilitation' could not proceed without a further decision to be taken by the Members at the next Ministerial (Kwa and Jawara 2004: 111). This was ambiguous because the final Doha Ministerial Declaration included a statement that such negotiations would take place after the next Ministerial (Kwa and Jawara 2004: 237–38). This ambiguity would be reflected during a mini-ministerial meeting in Sydney, in 2002, in a dispute between India and the EU representatives over whether or not the mandate existed for negotiations to begin on these issues (Kwa and Jawara 2004: 238–39).

Despite effectively achieving agreement to launch a new round, since Seattle many Members became united under the developing country identity, where a general demand for implementation was becoming central to its articulation

(Wilkinson 2002a: 137; Das 2003: 67–107). As articulated, 'implementation' concerns the extent to which the Uruguay agreements had been fully put into effect by the developed countries opening up their domestic markets, though part of the demand does include a call for 'assessment' of the impact of liberalization upon Members (Wilkinson 2002a: 131; Das 2003: 74). The strength of the demands was in its ability to dislocate the single undertaking and multilateralism of the WTO. Against this equivalential identity, a frontier was drawn against the developed countries which demanded expansion (e.g. the 'new/Singapore issues', 'new round') (Wilkinson 2002a: 137–38). In the wake of Seattle, a review mechanism was launched within the WTO to accommodate the demands for implementation, which included a report to be presented at Doha (Wilkinson 2002a: 138). The demand for implementation issues to be addressed was potentially detrimental to the possibility of launching a new round at Doha because it questioned the ability of the first round at Uruguay to have 'liberalised trade' on a fair basis (Kwa and Jawara 2004: 54–55). Access to agriculture and textiles markets featured prominently in disagreements during the Uruguay Round and remain present within the demand for implementation, where complaints have been made that the developed countries have made only technical changes whilst stalling on liberalization (Das 2003: 74–88). In this context, a cleavage emerged between those Members that advocated for greater liberalization on agriculture, and those Members that demanded expansion of the services agreement (Wilkinson 2002a: 138).

However, the developing country identity appears to have been effectively disempowered at Doha via the articulation of the new negotiations as supportive of development. Trade was formed into an equivalential relationship with development, as illustrated in the following extract from an address made by the US trade representative during the Ministerial:

> Trade is about more than economic efficiency, it reflects and encourages a systems of values: openness, peaceful exchange, opportunity, inclusiveness and integration, mutual gains through interchange, freedom of choice, appreciation of differences, governance through agreed rules, and a hope for betterment for all peoples and lands.[55]

Thus, global trade governance as embodied in the WTO is equated with economic efficiency, openness, peaceful exchange, opportunity, inclusiveness, integration, mutual gains, freedom of choice, appreciation of differences, governance via agreed rules, and betterment for all.

Cancun and the re-emergence of developing countries

The Fifth WTO Ministerial Conference, held in the Mexican tourist resort city of Cancun, has been noted for the emergence of the G20 and the re-emergence of the G90 – both collectives of Members based upon the developing-country identity (Kwa and Jawara 2004: xv). The development agenda launched at

Doha continued into Cancun. The new WTO Director-General Supachai Panitchpakdi contextualized the event in the framework of development projects such as the United Nations Millennium Development Goals, stating: 'We can make a significant contribution towards achieving these vital goals by removing the shackles on world trade ... Aid is certainly necessary but it is trade that will generate decisive results for sustainable development.'[56] These sentiments were repeated by other officials, including the United Kingdom's representative, who made the statement that: 'Success in the DDA [Doha Development Agenda] could help 300 million people in developing countries to lift themselves out of poverty.'[57] Despite these attempts to avoid the emergence of any divisive identities amongst the membership by creating an antagonistic frontier between developed and developing, the Fifth Ministerial Conference collapsed. The collapse was marked by disagreement over investment issues, and was heralded by some as indicating a new political mobilization by the weaker countries.[58] Its future appeared uncertain, with the *Financial Times* commenting that:

> At best, the organization seems likely to face an indefinite period in limbo. At worst, the WTO may be threatened with marginalisation, as its divided and disenchanted members look instead to bilateral and regional deals to promote trade.[59]

The contingency of multilateralism was made visible with the consequence that the Members were articulated into divisive identities. The dislocation of multilateralism is reflected in the following comment made by the US trade representative, stating:

> It's fair and appropriate to report that, since Cancun, America may take the bilateral route. But it's important to note that this has been an important part of our policies for two years. The US plays countries off against each other. It's competitive liberalisation. Countries know that if the US is slowed up with the WTO there is still much to be done. We're not going to be sidetracked by countries like India and Morocco.[60]

The Ministerial collapsed after the Mexican conference chairperson halted the event, announcing irreconcilable differences on the last day (Kwa and Jawara 2004: xvi), though it followed growing dissensus towards the draft Ministerial Declaration, with delegates of Members such as India, for example, publicly declaring:

> We are disappointed that the draft text ignores several concerns expressed by us and many developing countries. I note that the pretence of development dimensions of the Doha Agenda has finally been discarded confirming the apprehension expressed by me at the plenary session that this is mere rhetoric.[61]

Disagreement centred around the so-called Singapore issues, though a newly empowered developing country identity appears to have been important, with a new slogan appearing amongst several delegates declaring 'No deal is better than a bad deal', challenging the logic of agreement (Kwa and Jawara 2004: xxiii). Prior to Cancun, the USA and EU had bilaterally agreed changes to their subsidization of domestic agriculture, which was critiqued as protectionist by a group of 20 Members (the G20) (Kwa and Jawara 2004: xxvi). No similar response had been made by the Cairns Group, which was internally split by those of its members who advocated tariff reductions on agricultural imports and those who wanted to protect their own domestic markets (Kwa and Jawara 2004: xxvii). In this context, the G20, which included many lower-income countries – as compared to the Cairns Group which contained a wide range of incomes amongst its membership – was able to articulate development as a unifying demand.[62] The statement argued that the USA and EU were not adhering to implementing liberalization of their agricultural sectors, and thus it was able to reduce pressure from developing countries to accept any expansion of the WTO with the new issues (Kwa and Jawara 2004: xxvii). Additionally, whereas 'TRIPS and public health' were articulated as evidence of the development-friendly nature of Doha, the agreement appeared uncertain when the US trade representative suggested that African ministers renegotiate directly with the pharmaceutical transnational corporations if they wanted to ensure what was agreed at Doha (Kwa and Jawara 2004: xxxii).

Hong Kong

However, as the 2000s progressed, there was an ever more active attempt to promote the logic of development with trade liberalization, so that events like the UK-led Africa Commission and the 2005 G8 Summit reiterated the logic. At the Sixth Ministerial Conference, held at the end of 2005 and hosted by Hong Kong, Director-General Pascal Lamy articulated the WTO as a collective project, representing the amassed wishes of its membership. He stated:

> [Let us] try to combine our hopes and our powers, your hopes and your powers, to advance the negotiations so that they can be completed in 2006 ... This Ministerial Conference is your Conference – it is therefore in your hands and in the hands of your negotiators to work as best you can ... You have also inherited a well-oiled machine that oversees and ensures the implementation of a balanced system of rights and obligations. You have every reason to be proud of the past achievements of your collective enterprise.[63]

The address also specifically described the WTO as 'democratic', articulating this as the reason why it was sometimes difficult to reach agreement amongst the entire membership.

The WTO decision-making process, as you all know is, let us say, difficult. The difficulty stems from the fact that all stakeholders – all of you – have decided that you have exactly the same right, no matter how big or small, no matter how powerful or weak, no matter how rich or poor you are: you all have the right to speak, the right to agree, the right to disagree. In sum, in spite of all criticism, the WTO decision-making process is democratic. If it were different, taking decisions on the negotiations would probably be easier. But it would not be as legitimate. Reaching agreement in the WTO is difficult because it is done bottom-up – and it is good this is so. It takes more time, it is more burdensome and cumbersome, but I am convinced it remains the best way to take decisions that impact directly the lives of billions of people.[64]

Thus, at Hong Kong, the WTO was legitimated as both a collective and democratic. Thus, this rhetoric suggests the articulatory process at play: the WTO has faced a series of dislocations to its discursive formation of global trade governance, which have led to a rearticulation in which a logic of democracy and development appear increasingly central. Whilst a cynical observer might view such a shift as superficial, discourse theory suggests that such an assumption is overly one-sided, ignoring the interaction of identities affecting the constitution of the WTO.

Staying at home

Since Hong Kong the WTO's rearticulation has been dominated by the changing fortunes of the Doha Round. In the nearly 10 years since Hong Kong, the Secretariat has only risked exposing negotiations to the light of day in two Ministerial Conferences – both of which were hosted at the WTO's headquarters in Geneva in 2009 and then 2011.

At both the Seventh and Eight Ministerial Conferences, in 2009 and 2011 respectively, the WTO director-general post remained occupied by Pascal Lamy. It is intuitive to compare his public addresses at each event with that presented above from 2005. In an open letter to journalists attending the 2009 Ministerial, Lamy began by stating that the event was not to deal with Doha but to provide a more general reflection on the future of the organization's work.[65] In the letter Lamy reiterates the themes of a collective identity ('Our organization') and development ('millions have been lifted from poverty'), but connects them to a view of the multilateral trading system as a vehicle for peace ('building bridges rather than barriers between countries'), which reflects the original discourse present in the formation of the GATT, demonstrated in the previous chapter. The above is illustrated in the following excerpt from Lamy's letter:

Our organization is the guardian of a trading system that dates back to the end of World War II. The agreements we administer have contributed greatly to the economic prosperity and geopolitical stability of the last 60 years. Following the War, the architects of the multilateral system sought to put in place rules which would encourage governments to open their economies, building bridges rather barriers between countries. The result has been that trade has risen more than 30 fold and hundreds of millions have been lifted from poverty.[66]

These themes were repeated in Lamy's speeches to the Member states but with a particular emphasis on the WTO as a collective project and the principle of multilateralism.[67] Much the same message was repeated at the Eighth Ministerial Conference, when in 2011 Lamy addressed the opening plenary. The one significant difference was the impact of broader events, with Lamy making direct reference to both the ongoing financial crisis and the growth in social movements demanding reform in the global political economy.[68] Lamy concluded his speech as follows:

My call today is for all of us to stand up for the values of multilateralism. For major players to exercise leadership and to muster political courage to act together for greater trade opening and reform. To place the interests and needs of developing countries and, in particular, those of the poorest, at its heart. And to start thinking seriously about the dire consequences of not doing so in the midst of a worsening crisis. To act now in favour of a stronger multilateral trading system tomorrow.[69]

The WTO is directly linked with multilateralism and presented as the solution to the global financial crisis, as well as the bulwark against growing citizen unrest. This accords with a general move within the discourse around the WTO – that it is a technocratic body through which to escape the dangers of politics rather than a realm in which to conduct politics. Since December 2011, there has been a succession of mixed reports from commentators, Member states and the WTO Secretariat as to the health of the ongoing Doha negotiations. The next Ministerial Conference is scheduled for December 2013, to be hosted by Bali, Indonesia. The year 2013 will also see the election of a new director-general to replace Pascal Lamy. To try and renew momentum behind the Doha Round, the current director-general initiated in April 2012 a special advisory group consisting of 12 prominent figures from the works of politics, economics and business, called the Panel on Defining the Future of the WTO. Critics have feared that the group will be used to produce a framework for concluding the Doha Round that limits the options of developing countries, as some claimed occurred when Arthur Dunkel used the Leutweiler Group to push the Uruguay Round out of its own crisis (see the previous chapter).[70] Whatever occurs at Bali or is announced by the new special advisory panel, it is safe to say that the WTO will remain an uncertain political entity at the heart of a contestatory process that exceeds its own finite institutional borders.

Conclusion

Formal rules/procedures and informal norms are part of the same discursive practice constituting the WTO. However, no social practice may be defined by a finite series of rules/procedures and norms. Instead, these mechanisms should be taken as only indicative of the articulatory process through which that social practice is made possible. In articulatory process, formal rules/procedures and informal norms are part of the same political operation. Together, they exist as both a product of a wider, historically contingent discursive context and a means to legitimate the political operation of the WTO within that context. If the informal mechanisms exist to express a certain relationship between the actors not made possible through the formal arrangement, this is because of the shape of those relations in the wider discursive context.

To understand the implications of this uncertainty, it has been necessary to consider the rearticulation of the WTO post-1995. The second half of the chapter has provided a narrative tracing attempts by the WTO Secretariat to articulate the WTO at different moments since its birth in 1995. Public relations are part of discourse but discourse cannot be limited to public relations since it exceeds the linguistic. However, the account of such rhetoric does have utility in as much as it illustrates the constitution of the WTO within a social-historical context external to the institution. The re-naming of the Millennium Round as the Development Round suggests that it has become increasingly necessary to the discursive formation of the WTO that it incorporates a development demand. Speeches by senior Secretariat staff following the collapse of the Seattle Ministerial suggest a discursive context in which it became necessary for the WTO to acknowledge a democratic aspect to its identity. These moments are significant because of the change they suggest within the discursive formation constitutive of the WTO.

Having considered the articulation of the WTO, the next chapter will focus on the question of who/what constitutes an 'actor' within the WTO. The chapter will specifically look at the emergence of an NGO identity within the WTO, tracing the formalization of this identity as well as the discursive context constitutive of its emergence. This next part of the investigation is particularly important because it will help to trace out the discursive context shaping the rearticulation of the WTO noted in this chapter.

Notes

1 As defined in Chapter 1.
2 This was discussed in Chapter 1 through the concept of 'overdetermination'.
3 As discussed in Chapter 1.
4 As discussed in Chapter 1.
5 See Chapter 1 for discussion on overdetermination.
6 Respectively, these are included under the following agreements within the WTO: Intellectual Property Rights (TRIPS); General Agreement on Trade in Services (GATS). These all represent a rapid expansion in the issue interest of the GATT/WTO system.

7 However, Jackson (1998a: 6) has argued that the WTO was less ambitious than the never-ratified ITO, describing the former as a 'mini-charter' with little substantive content in itself.

8 The Dispute Settlement Body is responsible for administration of the Dispute Settlement Understanding, through which the WTO adjudicates trade disputes that may arise amongst its membership. Rulings are intended to be based on the agreements contained within the WTO, and therefore the DSB serves as an enforcement body for those agreements. However, the DSB has no enforcement capacity itself, being Member-dependent. Enforcement is made via rulings granting the successful complainant Member permission to launch retaliatory trade measures against the offending Member. Cases may only be investigated if brought by a Member.

9 The position of enforcement and monitoring of agreements at the top of the WTO illustrates the importance of regulation within the WTO, but also the articulation of these two functions as open to all members via the General Council.

10 This will be to report decisions and if agreement cannot be reached, then the General Council will be asked to intervene in order to produce a decision.

11 Doha Declaration, paragraph 46 states the TNC's mandate: 'The overall conduct of the negotiations shall be supervised by a Trade Negotiations Committee under the authority of the General Council ... It shall establish appropriate negotiating mechanisms as required and supervise the progress of the negotiations'. Available online at: www.wto.org/english/news_e/news02_e/tnc_01feb02_e.htm (accessed December 2012).

12 Those with limited membership include the Textiles Monitoring Body (TMB), the plurilateral committees, the dispute settlement panels and the Appellate Body (Winham and Lanoszka 2000: 39). The dispute settlement panels and the Appellate Body consist of Members appointed through the General Council to fulfil the various functions of the judicial process of the Dispute Settlement Understanding (DSU). Participation to the TMB is by appointment, given by the Council for Trade in Goods. The committees relating to plurilateral agreements involve only those members who have plurilaterally signed up to these agreements.

13 In the build-up and administration of a Ministerial Conference, the Secretariat re-channels its resources to accommodate the extra demands placed upon it, thereby causing the organization to set aside matters unrelated to the specific conference. The operation of a Ministerial remains the ultimate responsibility of the Members, but administrative matters will, depending on their level of importance and the availability of resources, be shared between the Secretariat and the host Member.

14 'Only officials from member governments can deal with the important routine tasks of the organization: accession of new members; initiation of disputes or complaints; interpretation of WTO rules; judgements on waivers of obligations; or working parties on free trade areas' (Winham and Lanoszka 2000: 28).

15 If consensus cannot be reached, the option exists for a vote, though this has never occurred and remains only a very last option within the official procedures for appointing a director-general. For more information, please see WTO Secretariat document WT/L/509 – 'Procedures for the Appointment of Directors-General, Adopted by the General Council on 10 December 2002'.

16 Also, see WTO Secretariat document WT/L/31, 'Guidelines for Appointment of Officers to WTO bodies, approved by the General Council on 31 January 1995', as well as WT/L/510 'Guidelines for Appointment of Officers to WTO bodies, adopted by the General Council on 11 December 2002'. For an illustrative list of chairperson appointments, see WTO Secretariat document Press/273 'WTO chairpersons for 2002', or 'Chairmanships of the WTO bodies under the TNC' in

WT/GC/M/82 'General Council – Minutes of Meeting held in the Centre William Rappard on 25, 26, 27 August 2003', 104.

17 Decisions regarding the appointment of persons to such bodies as the Appellate Body also operate via consensus, though in the case of the Appellate Body in particular, this occurs first via a selection committee. It is the responsibility of the selection committee (comprising the chairpersons of the councils, as well as of the DSB) to interview candidates and reach a consensus upon who to appoint. This process, however, invites delegates of any interested Member to attend and express their wishes.

18 Article IX.1 of the WTO Agreement states: 'The WTO shall continue the practice of decision-making by consensus followed under GATT 1947. Except as otherwise provided: where a decision cannot be arrived at by consensus, the matter at issue shall be decided by voting' (quoted in Jackson 1998a: 136).

19 WTO Secretariat document WT/L/93 'Decision-Making Procedures Under Articles IX and XII of the WTO Agreement – Statement by the Chairman, As agreed by the General Council on 15 November 1995'.

20 'Amendments to (i) the provisions on waivers ... ; (ii) provisions relating to tariff binding in GATT 1994; and (iii) MFN provisions related to goods, services and intellectual property rights will come into effect only when accepted by all Members. A similar process also applies to amendments to the provision on amendments' (Das 1999: 430).

21 However, in the case of decisions relating to financial regulations and budget estimates for the Secretariat, not all the membership need vote as long as a two-thirds majority decision is achieved which comprises more than one-half of the total membership. See Blackhurst 1998: 57.

22 As opposed to merely three-quarters of those present at the meeting.

23 The ambiguity is in defining exactly what constitutes a fundamental change to a Member's rights and obligations. Without specific definition, it would seem to be potentially applicable to any amendment.

24 To date, this has never occurred within the WTO. Das has also argued that it is unlikely ever to occur, at least as far as the largest trading states are concerned (Das 1999: 432). To expel such a state would severely undermine the legitimacy of the organization and significantly reduce the share of world trade over which it currently presides. Therefore, the larger trading states are under much less pressure than their smaller rivals to accept an amendment perceived to be against their interest.

25 Hoekman and Kostecki (2001: 113) divide trade negotiations into four stages: 1 catalyst; 2 pre-negotiation; 3 negotiation; and, 4 post-negotiation. The *catalyst* stage takes place on the domestic level, between the interest groups within a state and the appropriate governing bodies within that state. Within their model, it is here that policies and interests are preliminarily defined. *Pre-negotiation* refers to the series of informal negotiations that take place between states over the agenda for the much more formal *negotiation* stage, where policy packages change as required. It is in *post-negotiation* that attention is given to the problem of implementation at the domestic level. This model serves to illustrate the multi-level character of WTO negotiations. Business and other special interest groups, including NGOs, influence the process principally via their lobbying activities at the domestic level, influencing and offering initiatives to the capitals of Members (ibid.: 120). Furthermore, the WTO provides a framework in which negotiators return to confront each other in a repeated game, and the model described above illustrates that this is also a multi-stage game. As a result, players gain reputations and gather information about other sides, as well as being able to use a multiplicity of strategies between stages in order to offer incentives and threaten sanctions as required (ibid.: 137).

26 Consensus developed as the default norm of decision making in the GATT, despite it, too, containing provision for majority voting. Unlike the WTO, though, the GATT did make use of this provision, if only rarely. However, when a vote did formally occur, agreement would always be arranged beforehand (Jackson 1998a: 46, 50; see also Steinberg 2002: 334). Consequently, majority voting has never played a significant factor in the governance of the multilateral trading system. The sedimentation of the consensus norm in the GATT, which was never legally defined until the birth of the WTO in 1995, was principally a response to the expansion of those states contracting to the agreement (Jackson 1998a: 46). Developing states rapidly grew to form a significant majority with the technical ability easily to outvote the USA and other large trading states (ibid.: 42). Still, this does not explain why consensus arose. Voting may allow a majority of developing states to dominate decision making, but consensus would give not only this majority decisive power, but every single one of those states a veto over decisions. Where consensus makes sense is as a proactive strategy for negotiations, which goes well beyond the passive form of simply acknowledging non-objection. For description of consensus in the WTO as a proactive negotiating strategy, see Footer 1997: 665.

27 For example, Georgiev argues: 'Consensus as the principal method of decision-making in the WTO is the most significant expression of its *intergovernmental* character' (Georgiev 2003: 28, emphasis added).

28 The legal framework of the WTO as 1 January 1995 included: Final Act of the Uruguay Round of Multilateral Trade Negotiations; Marrakech Agreement Establishing the World Trade Organization; Multilateral Agreements on Trade in Goods (including: General Agreement on Tariffs and Trade 1994; Agreement on Agriculture; Agreement on the Application of Sanitary and Phytosanitary Measures; Agreement on Textiles and Clothing; Agreement on Technical Barriers to Trade; Agreement on Trade-Related Investment Measures; Agreement on Implementation of Article VI of the GATT 1994; Agreement on Implementation of Article VII of the GATT 1994; Agreement on Preshipment Inspection; Agreement on Rules of Origin; Agreement on Import Licensing Procedures; Agreement on Subsidies and Countervailing Measures; Agreement on Safeguards); General Agreement on Trade in Services; Agreement on Trade-related Aspects of Intellectual Property Rights; Understanding on Rules and Procedures Governing the Settlement of Disputes; Trade Policy Review Mechanism; Plurilateral Trade Agreements (including: Agreement on Trade in Civil Aircraft; Agreement on Government Procurement; International Dairy Agreement; International Bovine Meat Agreement); and, Ministerial Decisions and Declarations (Wilkinson 2002a: 130).

29 For more on the Dispute Settlement Body, please see Lee 2004.

30 Address by Renato Ruggiero, Director-General, World Trade Organization at the Singapore Ministerial Conference, December 1996, www.wto.org/english/thewto_e/minist_e/min96_e/sing_dg_e.htm (accessed December 2012).

31 Ibid.

32 Ruggiero stated: 'This new economy will be different from the old because knowledge is both a resource and a product – the new capital of economic growth, but capital which can be made accessible to all. In the economy of the twenty-first century, knowledge, like water, will be an essential resource. Our challenge is to extend and widen the global aqueducts – to help to irrigate parched soil. For example, by liberalizing telecommunications we can help put a telephone in every village – something that can make the difference between life and death. By liberalizing information technologies we can educate our people on a scale unimaginable ten or twenty years ago, empowering them to compete in the global economy. This is the human dimension of globalization. This is why liberalization is the wellspring of progress for all the world's peoples' (ibid.).

33 Ibid.

34 Ibid.
35 The political subjectivity and emergence of civil society groups contesting the WTO is discussed further in Chapter 5.
36 Though eventually resolved, the dispute became a case study for much criticism alleging that agreement was only reached after the USA had forcefully persuaded several Members originally supportive of the Thai candidate to switch sides (Kwa 2003: 13). It has been further claimed by the then Thai secretary of state that the proposal for a shared candidacy was produced during a phone call between her and the US secretary of state, and presented as an Australian idea in order to provide a third party author (Kwa and Jawara 2004: 186–91).
37 The role and emergence of civil society campaigning during the Seattle Ministerial will be discussed in more detail later in the book, in Chapter 4.
38 Named so because many of the small-group meetings held during the Uruguay Round took place in the office of the GATT Secretariat's director-general, in which one wall was olive green. 'Green Room' has become a shorthand for the small-group process by which a limited number of Members are informally invited to discuss negotiations behind closed doors with the WTO Secretariat in attendance. Consequently, it both expresses the nature of international trade negotiations as well as providing a source of much controversy amongst those who might argue that the WTO is the product of only a select group of nation-states.
39 WTO Secretariat Press Release (29 November 1999), *The WTO is not a World Government and No One has any Intention of Making it One, Moore tells NGOs,* www.wto.org/english/thewto_e/minist_e/min99_e/english/press_e/pres155_e.htm (accessed December 2012).
40 Ibid., emphasis added.
41 Ibid., emphasis added.
42 This account is based upon Wilkinson 2002a: 131–32.
43 WTO Secretariat (April 2003) *10 Common Misunderstandings About the WTO* (Geneva: WTO Publications). Also: WTO Secretariat (April 2003) *10 Benefits of the WTO Trading System* (Geneva: WTO Publications). Both downloadable from the WTO Secretariat website: www.wto.org (accessed December 2012).
44 WTO Secretariat (September 2003) *Understanding the WTO,* third edn (Geneva: WTO Publications). Downloadable from the WTO Secretariat website: www.wto. org (accessed December 2012).
45 Extract from speech taken from 'Democracy, Development and the WTO' (presented 26 April 2002), www.wto.org/english/news_e/spmm82_e.htm (accessed December 2012).
46 Taken from WTO Secretariat (April 2003) *10 Common Misunderstandings About the WTO* (Geneva: WTO Publications), 10.
47 Along the same lines, Matsushita *et al.* have suggested that: 'The Members of the Executive Body should be chosen according to objective criteria based on such factors as (1) GDP; (2) share of world trade; and (3) population. Other criteria could assure representation by developing countries and a geographic balance. The Executive Body should have both permanent Members and a rotating group of Members that would serve fixed terms. Thus, every WTO Member would have a seat on the Executive Body at regular intervals. A weighted voting system could be devised to replace consensus decision-making' (Matsushita *et al.* 2003: 15).
48 However, Wilkinson argues that these arrangements have had little impact on expanding access to the WTO because: 1 most forums take place in Geneva, thus favouring a select set of NGOs already based in Geneva, which includes many corporate lobbies; 2 the WTO selects participants, so that contestation is minimized; and, 3 the majority of WTO meetings are held behind closed doors amongst a limited group of Members, thus limiting the transparency benefits potentially gained (Wilkinson 2002a: 134).

49 The only exception to this point is where a Member state delegation includes an individual from, for example, an industry lobby group or a trade union (both not defined by the WTO as an NGO if part of a Member state delegation, since the composition of delegations is meant to be the choice of that Member state). See Barfield 2001: 143.

50 There has been much criticism against the idea of giving greater status to NGOs – as either observers or decision makers – because of the argument that most NGOs working on the WTO are geographically based in either North America or Europe, so that further NGO involvement would only further tilt negotiations towards one set of Member states. Also, Barfield has argued against allowing NGOs (whether issue groups, trade unions or corporate bodies) greater participation with voting rights, stating that few NGOs are themselves exemplars of accountability (Barfield 2001: 108, 142, 143). Whilst this point is open to contestation, it illustrates how the problem of NGOs has been articulated.

51 Address by the WTO Director-General Mike Moore at the Inaugural Session, Ministerial Conference, Fourth Session, Doha, 9–13 November 2001. WT/MIN (01)/12. Available at: www.wto.org (accessed December 2012).

52 Ibid.

53 Ibid.

54 Ibid.

55 Statement by HE Mr Robert B. Zoellick, United States Trade Representative. Ministerial Conference, Fourth Session, Doha, 9–13 November 2001. WT/MIN (01)/ST/3. Available at: www.wto.org (accessed December 2012).

56 Address by Dr Supachai Panitchpakdi, Director-General, Ministerial Conference, Fifth Session, Cancun, 10–14 September 2003. WT/MIN(03)/10. Available at: www.wto.org (accessed July 2005).

57 Statement by Mr Mike O'Brien, Minister for Trade, Investment and Foreign Affairs, United Kingdom. Ministerial Conference, Fifth Session, Cancun, 10–14 September 2003. WT/MIN(03)/ST/11. Available at: www.wto.org (accessed July 2005).

58 Oxfam adviser and newspaper columnist Kevin Watkins declared that: 'WTO negotiations will never be the same. Developing country governments representing most of the organizations' 146 members have found a voice. Led by India, Brazil and China, the group of 21 has emerged as a formidable negotiating force.' See K. Watkins (2003) 'Cancun was where the WTO Found Glasnost – and a Chance for Renewal', *The Guardian* (London), 22 September.

59 G. de Jonquieres (2003) 'Poorer Countries are Likely to be the Biggest Losers from the Unexpected Breakdown in the Doha Round', *Financial Times* (London), 16 September.

60 N. Mathiason and F. Islam (2003) 'West Wins Trade War in Secret', *The Observer* (London), 21 September.

61 Statement made by a WTO delegate of India, at the Heads of Delegation Meeting, Cancun, Mexico, 13th September 2003. Quoted in Kwa and Jawara 2004: xvii.

62 Statement available online at: www.g_20.mre.gov_br/conteudo/19082005_Breviario. pdf (accessed July 2006).

63 WTO Secretariat, *WTO News: Speeches – DG Pascal Lamy, 13th December 2005 Opening Ceremony, Ministerial Conference, Sixth Session, Hong Kong*, www.wto. org/english/news_e/sppl_e/sppl15_e.htm (accessed December 2012).

64 Ibid.

65 WTO Secretariat, *Director-General's Letter to Journalists, 30th November 2009, Ministerial Conference, Seventh Session, Geneva*, www.wto.int/english/thewto_e/ minist_e/min09_e/dg_letter_e.htm (accessed December 2012).

66 Ibid.

67 WTO Secretariat, *WTO News: Speeches – DG Pascal Lamy, 30th November 2009 Opening Ceremony, Ministerial Conference, Seventh Session, Geneva*, www.wto.int/

english/news_e/news09_e/mn09a_30nov09_e.htm#dg_stat   (accessed   December 2012).

68 WTO Secretariat, *WTO News: Speeches – DG Pascal Lamy, 15th December 2011 Opening Ceremony, Ministerial Conference, Eighth Session, Geneva*, www.wto.int/ english/news_e/sppl_e/sppl212_e.htm (accessed December 2012).

69 Ibid.

70 C. Raghavan (2012) 'From Bicycle to Snowball Approach to Policy', *TWN Info Service on WTO and Trade Issues 18th February*, www.twnside.org.sg/title2/wto. info/2012/twninfo120207.htm (accessed December 2012).

4 The emergence of new actors in the WTO

The NGO identity

Introduction

The WTO is not abstract to its wider context, as has been argued thus far. The validity of this argument, and the utility of a discourse theoretical framework to help understand what it means, is made evident in this chapter by exhibiting the contingency of who (or what) constitutes an 'actor' within the discursive formation of the WTO. The value of this analysis is that it helps better to understand both the discursive formation of the WTO, and the changing definition of an actor within its management of trade. In so doing, the WTO is seen as intimately tied into its historically contingent discursive context through a mutually constitutive relationship in which the WTO is both shaped by, but also shapes, that context.

Beginning with a critical examination of the claim that the WTO is no more than the product of its Member states, the argument is developed by considering the emergence of new actors within the WTO. This can be seen in the formalization of an NGO (non-governmental organization) identity that was initially sedimented within the agreement establishing the WTO but which has since been further elaborated to form a series of guidelines and procedures for both NGO attendance at Ministerial Conferences and how individuals operating under that identity may interact with the WTO. The literature suggests a process in which the WTO has been 'forced' both to respond to events outside of its institutional remit, and has itself expressed agency in this 'emergence' – the NGO identity both opening up and closing off various forms of political contestation around global trade governance.

The second half of the chapter approaches the question of the actor via considering a wider politicization of trade governance at the global level, which serves as the background to the emergence of the NGO identity. However, this process stretches far beyond the WTO, to include a series of political campaigns critiquing other regimes of global trade governance. Within this narrative, events such as Seattle (the protests sometimes viewed as the authors of the collapse of the Third Ministerial Conference) are but a small part of a much wider politicization of global trade governance. It is this politicization that exhibits the contingency of not only the constitution of actors within the WTO, but its overall discursive formation.

The question of the 'actor': a problematization of the primacy of the Member state identity

Though formally the question of who/what constitutes an actor with respect to the World Trade Organization is answered within the Marrakech Agreement – that decisions in the WTO are the product of the Member states – much of the literature acknowledges agency enacted with varying degrees of expression by such other identities as the Secretariat (Bronckers 2000: 297; Hoekman and Kostecki 2001: 54), 'Business Lobbies' (Scholte *et al.* 1999: 110), 'International Organizations' (Croome 1995: 21–23), and '[International] Non-Governmental Organizations' (Wilkinson 2005; Marceau and Pedersen 1999; Scholte 2004; Das 2003: 229). As is often argued, it might be said that though it is true that other actors attempt to influence the WTO, the formal institutional structure means that even the Secretariat must submit to the interests as expressed by the Member states, which act as the ultimate filter on decisions since it is they who must accept or reject any final agreements (Winham and Lanoszka 2000: 28).[1] On this basis, Members remain the ultimate actors within the WTO via being in the position to balance competing interests expressed from these other actors. Earlier in the book, in Chapter 1, this particular understanding of 'agency' in the WTO was represented as a two-stage flow model, where Member states effectively act as the gatekeepers to the WTO (Hoekman and Kostecki 2001: 120). In this model, focus was on the Member states as nation-state governments balancing competing national interest groups, so that the flow of influence affecting political behaviour constitutive of the WTO might be modelled as in Figure 4.1.

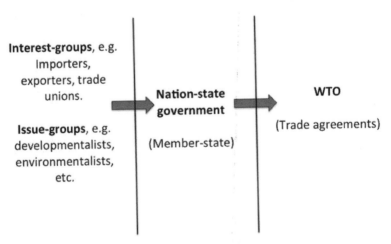

Figure 4.1 Member states as 'gatekeepers' to the WTO

The model is potentially complicated by the agency of other actors less easily categorized as interest groups. Contained within the legal document establishing the WTO – the Marrakech Agreement – is a formal requirement to maintain cooperation with the World Bank and the IMF (Matsushita *et al.* 2003: 9). Additionally, the literature acknowledges the agency of the WTO Secretariat, where its civil servants are able to influence decision making via, first, its technical skills, but also its institutional memory and familiarity with the often highly complex issues under discussion (Bronckers 2000: 297; Hoekman and Kostecki 2001: 54).[2]

Hoekman and Kostecki (2001: 121) note the agency of, in particular, financial corporations such as American Express and Citibank in the Uruguay Round that provided the sedimentation of those practices that would become the WTO. This does not necessarily threaten the primacy of the Member state. Indeed, as discussed in the literature review, Hoekman and Kostecki – proponents of the two-stage flow model – recognize the WTO as a network consisting of a multiplicity of actors – 'official representatives of members based in Geneva, civil servants based in capitals, and national business and non-governmental groups that seek to have their governments push for their interests at the multilateral level' (Hoekman and Kostecki 2001: 53). The influence of American Express and Citibank might then be understood as operating within the two-stage flow model, with the Member state remaining the 'primary actor' as far as the WTO itself is concerned. The same could be said of the WTO Secretariat, which might be described as a 'sub-actor' compared to the Member states.

Yet, as is argued in the earlier discussion, this model appears increasingly untenable if one acknowledges the transnationalization (or globalization) of businesses and non-governmental organizations, so that their respective influence exceeds the nation-state basis of the Member state as gatekeeper to the WTO, and moves to the supranational level so as to be able to affect multiple nation-states and thus play one off against the other – effectively, reversing the competitive process in the two-stage flow model. Rather than adopting a narrow model, a much more promising approach to understanding the forces behind the shape of the WTO is to view it as a network in which the concept of the 'political actor' is *malleable*, moving beyond a blind state-centrism and narrow focus on the legal-institutional arrangement, to acknowledging a wider (and more diffuse) plurality of actors. In this wider understanding of the actor in the WTO, the WTO might be modelled as at the centre of a convergence between such categories of actor as Member states, interest groups, issue groups, WTO Secretariat and international organizations (IOs), appearing as in Figure 4.2. Though the identities will operate differently within the WTO, the diagram represents the basic principle of intersection between the alternate subject positions. In Chapter 1 it was noted that even sub-identities within these categories, such as business within interest groups, cannot be taken as homogeneous but involve a contestation between identities at a lower level where, for example, exporters and importers have divergent

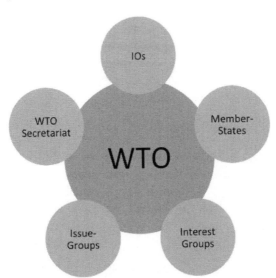

Figure 4.2 The WTO at the convergence of multiple subject positions

interest positions within their identities. A high degree of heterogeneity is evident amongst those identities categorized as Member states.

The literature has made attempts to understand gross differences in the ability of Member states to affect 'agreements' despite a certain formal equality expressed in the consensus principle and equal-voting power (Jackson 1998a: 45; Jackson 1998b: 73; Hoekman and Kostecki 2001: 58; Kwa 2003; and Dunkley 2000). As the representation of particular nation-state governments within the WTO, Member states vary in two general ways: 1) differences external to the WTO, relating to the nation-state itself; and, 2) differences internal to the WTO, relating to the composition of the individual delegation as well as its access to WTO decision-making bodies. In the literature, the influence of a Member state is understood as reliant as much on the wealth or percentage of overall trade controlled by its respective nation-state, as being affected by the stake that nation-state has in the particular matter under discussion (Curzon and Curzon 1973: 330). These external differences feed into creating internal differences between the Member state representatives, with richer countries being better equipped to provide the (generally English-speaking)[3] highly educated lawyers and economists required to engage with trade negotiations (Dunkley 2000: 217; Blackhurst *et al.* 1999; Narlikar 2001; Kwa 2003). The literature explains the inability of the consensus principle to ameliorate such differences as due to the predominance of informal negotiations within the WTO, where any formal equality has a diminished impact (Footer 1997: 667; Qureshi 1996: 6; Kwa 2003; Steinberg 2002). This further highlights the importance of adopting a perspective that moves beyond the formal legal-institutional arrangement of the WTO.

Heterogeneity of the Member state identity

Internal differences between the constitution of Member states can be further categorized into issues relevant to quantity, and quality. Certain Member states have many more delegates than others, meaning that not only are they better equipped to be present in more meetings (many WTO meetings overlap), but they are also able to negotiate for longer (Kwa and Jawara 2004: 104; Dunkley 2000: 217). The spread of a Member state across a large number of meetings not only gives that Member access to the formation of agreements on which they will be asked to give a final acceptance or rejection, but also the ability to form a wide negotiating position capable of offering side payments. Second, the quality of a Member may vary greatly, not only with respect to the legal or economic expertise of the individuals comprising the delegation, but also other identities through which these individuals are positioned as actors. The identity of a Member state as made present in WTO committees and working groups includes more than government officials, as many delegations also contain individuals who are otherwise positioned as civil society, such as trade union officials or business lobbyists (Barfield 2001: 143; Scholte 2004: 148). Indeed, this is well illustrated in the history of the Dispute Settlement Understanding (DSU). Marceau and Pedersen point to a process in which a series of rulings within the DSU have meant that individuals from non-governmental organizations (including environmentalists and business lobbyists) may be present as representatives of a Member party to a dispute, and therefore present at otherwise closed-door meetings, and submit amicus briefs, as amicus curiae ('friends of the court'), independently of any Member (Marceau and Pedersen 1999: 34–42). Although only Members have a formal right of action in the WTO (ibid.: 31), this does not mean that NGOs lack agency in praxis. This does not negate the primacy of the identity Member state within the discursive formation of the WTO, but it does help enlighten a more complex understanding of agency in the WTO.

As argued earlier in the book, interests cannot be taken as 'pre-given', as they do not exist outside of social practice. Instead, they are discursively structured, being produced within a sedimented discourse and bearing witness to their historical contingency. In this respect, interests are effectively the same as identity, being that they are mutually constitutive and only present within discourse. Thus, when one speaks of identity, one also speaks of interests. This has significance for the above discussion, because it helps to make sense of the uncertainty exhibited within the constitution of the Member state identity. It can be argued that Member state identities are different to one another because each is the product of a distinct sedimentation. However, in addition to this, it should be stated that the Member state is but one of many identities operating within the discursive formation of the WTO. Implicit within this argument, then, is the initial argument made in Chapter 2 – that the WTO cannot be understood via its formal legal-institutional arrangement alone. The Member state identity is but one of several identities capable of enacting agency within the WTO. It has primacy as the most sedimented and institutionalized identity through which agency may be given, though in this it could effectively become emptied of content, serving multiple other identities.

Having problematized the Member state identity within the WTO, the remainder of the chapter is divided into two sections. First, it will consider the formalization of the NGO identity within the WTO. At Marrakech, the charter establishing the WTO included formal acknowledgement of an NGO identity. Though this identity remained highly ambiguous at a formal level, the years that followed have witnessed the sedimentation (and contestation) of this identity within various WTO arrangements, including the Ministerial Conferences. Second, the chapter adopts a wider perspective incorporating Laclau and Mouffe's understanding of identity formation to ask how identities such as 'environmentalist group' have emerged as actors to contest the shape of global trade governance. This emergence is traced through a series of campaigns that exceed the WTO itself to include other regimes of global trade governance, including the Canadian-United States Free Trade Agreement, the North America Free Trade Agreement, the Multilateral Agreement on Investment, and the Third WTO Ministerial Conference.

Formalization of NGOs in the WTO

As stated above, this section of the chapter is intended to trace out the formalization of an NGO identity within the WTO. The identity has been sedimented into a particular articulation through a series of different expressions including the Marrakech Agreement establishing the WTO, but also the arrangements defining who/what constitutes an actor eligible to attend various WTO events, such as the Ministerial Conferences or Public Symposia. As will be discussed, those working under the auspices of the WTO Secretariat have been active in shaping this articulatory process. However, rather than suggesting free agency on behalf of the Secretariat, it is argued that the emergence of an NGO identity in global trade governance signals a contestation in which the discursive formation of the WTO has altered.

The emergence of an NGO identity in global trade governance

The 1948 Havana Charter meant to have established the International Trade Organization (ITO) contained a provision (Article 87) empowering the intended organization to develop relations with NGOs (Wilkinson 2002a: 158–59; Scholte *et al.* 1999: 110; Danaher and Mark 2003: 243). A note to the Charter expressed that 'it is clearly desirable that the ITO should be able to take full advantage of the knowledge and expertise of the non-governmental organizations in … various fields' (quoted in Marceau and Pedersen 1999: 9). Despite the formalization of a non-governmental organization identity, any definition remained elusive, the article left ambiguous and open to interpretation (Marceau and Pedersen 1999: 9). Though the 1947 General Agreement on Tariffs and

Trade (GATT) emerged out of the collapse of the never-ratified ITO and would be administered by the Secretariat (the Interim Commission for the International Trade Organization), which authored the above note, the identity 'non-governmental organization' was never formally present within either the GATT or its Geneva headquarters (Marceau and Pedersen 1999: 5).

The Marrakech Agreement that gave birth to the WTO institution in 1995 did include a provision (Article V:2) expressing the NGO identity, though it remained equally ambiguous without further definition. Article V – 'Relations with Other Organizations' – is concerned with both intergovernmental organizations and NGOs, and on the latter identity in paragraph 2 it simply states:

> The General Council may make appropriate arrangements for consultation and cooperation with non-governmental organizations concerned with matters related to those of the WTO.[4]

At the 1994 GATT Marrakech Ministerial meeting at which the WTO was signed into existence, those individuals present who were not formally affiliated with one of the GATT Contracting Parties or the Secretariat required press credentials to attend (Marceau and Pedersen 1999: 10). Article V:2 meant that with the birth of the WTO there would be a new identity through which to be positioned in respect to the multilateral trade regime.

The NGO identity gained greater clarity in the series of General Council meetings preparing for the first WTO Ministerial Conference, in Singapore, December 1996. Six '[g]uidelines for arrangements on relations with NGOs' were accepted by the WTO General Council on 18 July 1996 (Marceau and Pedersen 1999: 11; Wilkinson 2005: 164). The guidelines fail to define NGOs, though by repeating the language of Article V:2 in the first guideline ('consultation and cooperation with non-governmental organizations concerned with matters related to those of the WTO'), the principle was established that the WTO need only engage with those under the NGO identity if they could demonstrate their relevance to the work of the WTO (Marceau and Pedersen 1999: 12). Whilst introducing a new actor identity to the WTO, Wilkinson argues that this is limiting, because it negates more informal and under-financed expression of political demands, privileging groups already positioned as 'important' (e.g. business groups, large charities) (Wilkinson 2005: 163).

Within the July 1996 rules, the role of NGOs is to 'increase the awareness of the public in respect of WTO activities' (Guideline II) and 'as a valuable resource … [which] can contribute to the accuracy and richness of the public debate' (Guideline IV). Though it was stated that the '[WTO] Secretariat should play a more active role in its direct contacts with NGOs' (Guideline IV), guideline VI subordinates this relationship to the 'national level'. Emphasizing that the WTO is a 'legally binding intergovernmental treaty', Guideline VI includes the phrase: 'there is currently a broadly held view that it would not be possible for NGOs to be directly involved in the work of the

WTO or its meetings.' NGOs are articulated as 'national level ... public interest' bodies, as is evident in the concluding statement: 'Closer consultation and cooperation with NGOs can also be met constructively through appropriate processes at the *national level* where lies *primary* responsibility for taking into account the different elements of *public interest* which are brought to bear on trade policy-making' (Guideline VI, emphasis added).

In his analysis of the guidelines, Wilkinson argues that they articulate a relationship firmly in favour of the WTO, which is given agency over who/what constitutes an NGO eligible for engagement, as well as utilizing NGOs as a 'resource' rather than ascribing any rights to NGOs (Wilkinson 2005: 163–65). The form of this engagement is left ambiguous within the guidelines, except for a suggestion that they be through 'an *ad hoc basis of symposia* on specific WTO-related issues, informal arrangements to receive the *information NGOs may wish to make available for consultation by interested delegations* and the continuation of past practice of responding to requests for *general information* and *briefings* about the WTO' (Guideline IV, emphasis added). A principle of 'transparency' is established in Guideline III, which both goes beyond the NGO identity by referring to the 'public' and, at the same time, contextualizes the NGO identity as part of this transparency. Transparency is defined as 'making available documents which would be derestricted more promptly than in the past ... [via an] on-line computer network ... accessible to the public' (Guideline III). Wilkinson argues again that the guidelines place distinct limits on the contestation of global trade governance, where here 'transparency' refers only to the derestriction of certain documents rather than making more visible the working procedures that operate mainly via informal negotiations and thus produce minimal documentation (Wilkinson 2005: 163).[5]

Whilst Wilkinson (2005: 165) critically characterizes WTO relations with NGOs as 'managerial', with the former expressing considerable agency over the latter, thus constraining that relationship, it remains significant that the 1996 Guidelines gave new content to this relationship and, consequently, to the NGO identity. A more explicit definition of the NGO identity was attempted in the series of General Council meetings leading up to Singapore, with a decision that they be 'non-profit' organizations (Marceau and Pedersen 1999: 14) (Wilkinson 2005: 163). When applications were received from different groups wishing to attend the first Ministerial, the 'non-profit' principle achieved a certain degree of sedimentation as, according to Marceau and Pedersen – both WTO Secretariat staff – the Secretariat had to inform 'private companies and law firms ... that in order to qualify for accreditation they would have to register through their respective industry association or professional grouping' (Marceau and Pedersen 1999: 14). This adds both content and a further ambiguity to the NGO identity, since it negates private companies and law firms, yet rearticulates their demands within the identities 'industry association' and 'professional grouping', which may operate equivalentially under the NGO identity.

An NGO identity at WTO Ministerial Conferences

Ministerial Conferences have provided the most visible and active space in which to sediment a particular articulation of the NGO identity. A list of 159 NGOs applying for attendance at Singapore was produced by the Secretariat and informally distributed amongst the General Council, with apparently no Members objecting to any of the applicants (Marceau and Pedersen 1999: 13). However, it would appear that the Secretariat took an active role in selecting which NGOs were eligible to appear on this initial list. For example, the international trade union body Education International was omitted on the grounds that its activities 'were not directly related to the trade activities of the WTO' (WTO Secretariat quoted in O'Brien *et al.* 2000: 93). The General Council discussions preceding the Ministerial produced the result that NGOs were able to attend but not observe (Marceau and Pedersen 1999: 13). The ad hoc basis for WTO-NGO relations expressed in the 1996 Guidelines was used to legitimate a decision that the NGO presence at Singapore did not constitute a precedent and that NGO presence at future events would be left for a later decision (Marceau and Pedersen 1999: 13–14).

Singapore

At Singapore, each NGO was to be represented by no more than four persons, so that the total number of people in attendance was 235 (Marceau and Pedersen 1999: 14–15). Data from the WTO Secretariat show that 44 percent of the NGO identity consisted of what they define as 'business' (Marceau and Pedersen 1999: 46),[6] whilst O'Brien argues that 'business organizations' made up 65 percent (O'Brien *et al.* 2000: 94). 'Attendance' meant that those carrying the NGO badge had access to the plenary sessions of the Ministerial Conference, as well as two rooms in which they could arrange meetings with Member delegations, as well as formal entrance to the press room,[7] the floor of the conference venue, a supply of documents outside the rooms housing the informal negotiations, and the formal social events (Marceau and Pedersen 1999: 15). A separate building housed the NGO Centre, which provided computer access, a conference room for NGO use and an area for distributing documents (Marceau and Pedersen 1999: 15). Therefore, physical contact between NGOs and the WTO was channelled via: 1 NGO attendance at the plenary sessions; 2 a daily briefing given by a Secretariat staff member to the NGOs;[8] 3 informal NGO meetings with Member delegates; and, 4 a two-way supply of documents. An NGO identity was not present at the informal meetings at which any negotiations occurred – the plenary meetings consist of prepared speeches given by national trade ministers and are not themselves part of the decision-making process. Additionally, a TV channel broadcasted proceedings from the plenary session and was made available for NGOs to make two-minute statements (O'Brien *et al.* 2000: 93). The tone of expression was confined by an actively enforced Singaporean ban on any form of public protest, meaning that contestatory activity was limited to disseminating critical publications or lobbying (O'Brien *et al.* 2000: 93).

According to Marceau and Pedersen, 'the prevailing sentiment among NGOs was that the Singapore Conference marked a significant step towards acknowledging civil society' (Marceau and Pedersen 1999: 15). Whilst this can certainly be problematized by arguing that the NGO identity is not the same as the much wider 'civil society' identity, as Wilkinson (2005: 165) suggests above, the NGO identity sedimented at Singapore was maintained for the second Ministerial Conference, at Geneva in 1998.[9]

Geneva 1998

The 1998 Geneva Ministerial Conference was used to mark 50 years since the emergence of the GATT[10] – the '50th Year Celebration of the multilateral trading system' (Marceau and Pedersen 1999: 17). Geneva was attended by 362 persons present under the NGO identity, though this time the Secretariat had been free to select amongst the applicant NGOs without consultation from the Members (Marceau and Pedersen 1999: 17). With the Secretariat acting as a filter upon NGO attendance at Ministerials, the WTO side of the WTO-NGO relationship effectively – at least at the registration stage – is embodied by the Secretariat rather than the wider series of identities (e.g. Members) equivalentially linked within the discursive formation of the WTO. In contrast to the ban on public demonstrations enacted by the Singaporean government in 1996, a different discursive context meant that Switzerland was less able to prevent such expression, with the consequence that contestation was made visible outside the conference hall. Marceau and Pedersen (1999: 18) describe the demonstrations as 'against the WTO and globalisation ... [and] organized by a relatively large, but loose coalition of international NGOs and local squatters, [who] succeeded in capturing some headlines due to the violence and extensive property damage which ensued'. This raises important questions not only about the NGO identity but also the emergence of a wider series of identities contesting the shape of the WTO, which will be discussed in the second section of this chapter. However, in terms of the formalization of the NGO identity, Wilkinson argues that these demonstrations provided the context of a series of overtures made by individuals associated with the WTO which articulated acknowledgement of 'public concern' (Wilkinson 2005: 166–67). For example, Renato Ruggiero, the director-general of the WTO Secretariat, included in his opening address to the conference a list of 'challenges' facing the WTO: 'financial instability, development, marginalization, the environment, employment, health and cultural diversity' (Wilkinson 2005: 167). Wilkinson notes that in a statement supported later by both the USA and EU, Ruggiero suggested that a strengthened WTO-NGO relationship was one answer to these challenges (ibid.: 167). The speech came in the context of other suggestions for the launch of a new round at the next Ministerial Conference, with the possibility posed that new negotiations in the near future might offer a means to address these issues (ibid.: 167).

Seattle

Dubbed the Millennium Round, the new round of negotiations was to be launched with the Third Ministerial Conference at Seattle, in November 1999. Seattle has been introduced earlier in the book (Chapter 3) and will be returned to in the second half of this chapter because of its significance within the narrative of a global civil society emerging to contest the WTO. With respect to the formalization of an NGO identity in the WTO, it became much harder at Seattle for the Secretariat to hegemonize the articulation of this emergent identity. This will be later explained in the context of domestic US politics and the emergence of identities equivalentially linked to contest the shape of global trade governance – in which 'trade unions' and 'environmentalists' featured prominently. Of relevance here is how efforts by those associated with the WTO were made to re-hegemonize the articulatory process. For example, a few days before the Ministerial, the then Director-General of the WTO Secretariat Mike Moore gave a speech at a meeting organized by the International Confederation of Free Trade Unions (ICFTU). This was in response to growing demands for labour rights to be acknowledged within WTO management of trade. Moore argued that the issue was a 'false debate', on the premise that poor working conditions are the product of poverty rather than trade, with the side argument that they would improve if trade were allowed to help lift countries out of poverty (Wilkinson 2005: 168). At a wider meeting consisting of the NGO identity, Moore repeated this approach as well as attempting to distance the WTO from environmentalists, by stating:

> The WTO is not a world government, a global policeman, or an agent for corporate interests. It has no authority to tell countries what trade policies – or any other policies – they should adopt. It does not overrule national laws. It does *not* force countries to kill *turtles* or lower *wages* or employ *children* in factories. Put simply, the WTO is *not a supranational government* – and no one has any intention of making it one.[11]

According to Wilkinson, these attempts to re-hegemonize the NGO identity were partially responsible for the street protests that followed during the Ministerial itself, because they were viewed as 'insensitive' and 'patronizing' (Wilkinson 2005: 168), failing to acknowledge the arguments by which environmentalists and trade unions articulated their demands. Moore's words ran counter to the greatly expanded global trade governance remit made possible via the Uruguay Round, and suggested that there was no place for consideration of turtles (the environment) or wages/children (labour rights) within the Millennium Round that would expand this management.

Post-Seattle

The series of procedural amendments that followed Seattle can be seen as a second attempt to re-hegemonize the NGO identity, as well as a more assertive drive to turn around the claim put by many protesters on the streets of Seattle that the WTO was 'undemocratic'. First, these arrangements include: 1 'lunch-time dialogues' where selected NGOs have been invited to discuss their work with delegations and Secretariat staff attending at their own discretion; 2 'open dialogue' where NGOs are briefed on either specific WTO issues or the meetings; 3 'stand alone' workshops for NGOs on specific issues; and, 4 an NGO section on the WTO website (Wilkinson 2005: 169; Wilkinson 2002a: 133). These events provide an expression of the NGO identity which, at the same time, remains constrained by both WTO Secretariat selection of the invited parties and the Geneva location for the vast majority of the dialogues, so that those able to afford offices in Geneva are disproportionately advantaged to be represented within that expression (Wilkinson 2002a: 134).

Furthermore, the logic of transparency – embodied in the derestriction of documents discussed in Chapter 3 – was turned around so that as of a May 2001 decision by the WTO General Council, those wishing to attend WTO Ministerial Conferences under the NGO identity were required not only to argue their relevance to the WTO, but also provide information on the 'institutional structure of their organization, including details of national, regional, and international representation, the number of staff, size of membership, financial statements, as well as a statement of whether they have previously attended WTO Ministerial Meetings' (Wilkinson 2005: 169).[12] Therefore, whilst the WTO has been rearticulated to incorporate an NGO identity within its discursive formation, the Secretariat has been actively attempting to shape that articulation.

The location for the Fourth WTO Ministerial Conference in a state intolerant of public demonstration – Qatar – might be seen as part of the effort to sediment firmly a narrow articulation of the NGO identity. The lack of street battles in Doha might be attributed to the nature of the local political regime, but Wilkinson has pointed out that no large protest took place outside of Qatar despite there having been large demonstrations in Paris and elsewhere expressing solidarity with the Seattle protests in 1999 (Wilkinson 2005: 170). This, he suggests, was because Doha took place at the end of 2001, in the immediate aftermath of the 11 September 2001 terrorist attacks in the USA, where public protest seemed to lose its momentum in a new discursive context (ibid.: 170). Whatever one ascribes to be the cause, the consequence was greater leverage for the Secretariat to articulate the NGO identity. For example, whereas NGO representation was allowed to include four persons at previous Ministerials, Doha was to allow only one person per NGO (ibid.: 170). However, it should be noted that some groups were active in helping to inform and support the negotiating positions of several African and Asian Member states prior to Doha. For example, the agreement to allow developing countries to manufacture generic drugs for domestic use was based upon informational resources provided by Oxfam and Médecins sans Frontières to Asian and African Members (Das 2003: 229).

The collapse of the Fifth Ministerial Conference, in Cancun, was in many ways similar to Seattle, in that it occurred in the context of large-scale protests. Of these protests, the most famous was that of a South Korean farmer who killed himself in public on the streets of the Mexican resort city. Scholte (2004: 149) has argued that street protests at Seattle and Cancun can be understood as a response to the marginalization of the more critical demands forbidden access to the NGO identity as articulated by the WTO. Though heavily policed by the authorities, it is interesting, then, to consider that the Sixth Ministerial Conference, held in Hong Kong at the end of 2005, witnessed street protests, though these do not appear to have been repeated outside of Asia. Furthermore, despite broader politicization seen in the wake of the global financial crisis of 2007, neither the Seventh nor Eighth Ministerial Conferences, in 2009 and 2011, saw more than relatively small protests.

Evident throughout the discussion thus far is the role that the WTO Secretariat has played in framing the emergence of the NGO identity in the WTO. It is therefore important to consider specifically how the Secretariat has taken on this role.

An active Secretariat

WTO Secretariat staff have been active towards engaging NGOs within the WTO. First, the language used in formal events and reports frequently acknowledges NGOs. Since 2000, the WTO annual reports have included a section on relations with NGOs (Scholte 2004: 153–55).

Second, NGOs have been recognized at Ministerial Conferences via formal accreditation to enter the plenary sessions, for example, as well as an NGO centre. In this aspect, the Secretariat has been extremely active in determining who/what may attend as an NGO.

Third, the 'symposium' concept – which has been utilized since the first event in 1994, when NGOs attended a meeting in Geneva to discuss relevant issues with the Secretariat under the auspices of the Trade and Environment Division – has been expanded and repeated on an ad hoc basis with a growing number of NGOs and Member state delegates (Marceau and Pedersen 1999: 16–17; Scholte 2004: 153). The first symposium in 1994 was, according to Marceau and Pedersen (1999: 11), considered by the 'Members ... to be a useful, if arms-length, exercise in NGO-WTO relations, with the Secretariat serving as a "buffer" between Members and NGOs'.[13] The explicit reference to 'symposia' in the 1996 Guidelines was based on this 1994 symposium (Marceau and Pedersen 1999: 11), thereby suggesting that the first event would become the standard for all later symposia. The symposia offer more than an opportunity for Secretariat staff and NGOs to meet one another and any Member state delegates present, since they sometimes last for a couple of days and include speeches given not just by senior Secretariat staff but also seminars led by NGO representatives within the official programme.[14] Along with the NGO identity, individuals applying to attend symposia may include 'participants from governments, parliaments, civil society, the business sector, academia, and the media'.[15] Though the vast majority of these events take place in Geneva, since 2003 there have been symposia held in such locations as Cape Town, South Africa and São Paulo, Brazil (Scholte 2004: 153). Additionally, funding has been provided for around 40 persons from NGOs in developing countries to attend symposia in Geneva (Scholte 2004: 154).

Fourth, in addition to the symposia are the various other dialogues and briefing sessions mentioned above, some of which suggest another dimension to the WTO-NGO relationship where several events have been hosted by NGOs themselves. For example, rather than being held in the WTO head-quarters, briefings have sometimes been held within rooms provided by the Geneva-based International Centre for Trade and Sustainable Development (ICTSD) (Marceau and Pedersen 1999: 20, ft 34).[16] This suggests a more equal balance to the events, so that it is not always NGOs that must visit the WTO.

Fifth, the Secretariat receives documents from various parties outside the Member identity, which are framed as 'NGO Position Papers'. A list of these papers is disseminated to all Members as well as via the WTO Secretariat's e-mailed news bulletin service (Scholte 2004: 153). The Secretariat is active in selecting which papers are relevant, meaning that this channel of commu-nicating an NGO identity is limited by the criteria of relevance (Marceau and Pedersen 1999: 20). Within post-structuralist discourse theory, the WTO Secretariat can be understood as part of the discursive context framing the emergence of an NGO identity in the WTO, rather than exhibiting agency. This is because the WTO Secretariat cannot be distinguished from its subject position, which is discursive.

Beyond the formal NGO identity

As formalized in the WTO, the NGO identity has served to *include* some voices whilst *excluding* others, so that more critical demands have been mar-ginalized (Scholte 2004: 149; Wilkinson 2005: 156–57). Not only do many of those under the NGO identity carry dual identities as representatives of business, but the majority tend to be from the developed countries, are well-educated men and speak English (Scholte *et al.* 1999: 117).[17] As Wilkinson (2005: 171) writes, they tend to represent identities already well represented within global decision making.

In 2004, a consultation board commissioned by the Secretariat and chaired by the former GATT Director-General Peter Sutherland included a chapter titled 'Transparency and Dialogue with Civil Society' in their final report. Whilst having no legal bearing on the WTO institution itself, the term civil society rather than NGOs suggests acknowledgement of a potentially wider identity. However, whilst the chapter emphasizes the value of civil society to the WTO, it concludes with a recommendation that:

> [T]he Secretariat should be under no obligation to engage seriously with groups whose express objective is to undermine or destroy the WTO in its present form. The dialogue needs to be constructive on both sides and, given the expertise of non-governmental organizations in certain areas, it ought to be mutually reinforcing.[18]

This repeats the limitations found within the NGO identity, since 'present form' remains both ambiguous and therefore capable of grossly negating a large range of demands.

The derestriction of many formal WTO documents and the creation of a website through which these documents may be accessed, as well as forums in which the public may question Secretariat staff, can be seen as a response to demands from various groups for a democratization of the WTO (Scholte 2004: 150; Wilkinson 2005: 168). Additional accommodation of various demands include, Scholte argues, the expansion of global trade governance to include such areas as 'intellectual property', 'telecommunications' and 'financial services', made by 'business lobbies' (Scholte 2004: 153–54). However, despite high-profile campaigns demanding that development, labour rights and environmentalism be considered within the WTO, there has been little won except for a WTO Committee on Trade and Environment and a rebranding of the Millennium Round as the Development Agenda, both of which have since been argued as little more than publicity exercises (Scholte 2004: 154; Kwa and Jawara 2004: 237; Narlikar 2004).[19] However, these brief examples make clear that it is both impossible to say specifically where such demands have affected the WTO, as well as categorizing these demands within a single identity, such as NGO. To refer to those identities that have emerged to contest global trade governance but are not acknowledged within the WTO's formal NGO identity, one can refer to civil society.

Civil society

Within the literature, civil society reaction to the WTO is typically categorized into three categories, ranging from groups that make only minor demands, through to those that demand the abolition of the WTO. For example, the first category is described as either 'conformers' (Scholte *et al.* 1999: 112; Scholte 2004: 150) or 'supportive' (Wilkinson 2005: 162), and is said to include 'corporate business associations', 'commercial farmers' unions' and 'economic research institutes' (Scholte *et al.* 1999: 112). The middle category – the 'reformists' (Scholte *et al.* 1999: 113) or those who are 'critical ... but seek to engage' (Wilkinson 2005: 162), includes groups concerned with 'labour conditions', 'underdevelopment', 'environmental degradation', 'consumer protection' and 'gender inequalities', as well as 'democratisation' (Scholte *et al.* 1999: 113). Wilkinson's definition is perhaps more useful because there are many groups (such as Third World Network) which might otherwise be defined as 'reformist' and yet seek a reduction in the scope of global trade governance as embodied within the WTO.[20] The final category is less certain, with Scholte originally labelling it as the 'radicals' (Scholte *et al.* 1999: 115) with his co-authors, but then five years later changing it to 'rejectionists' (Scholte 2004: 152). By comparison, Wilkinson (2005: 162) labels this third category as those who are 'fundamentally opposed to the WTO and seek its abolition'.

For Wilkinson, the emergence of the NGO identity within the WTO has worked to quell some of the criticism from the first two categories, whilst marginalizing the third, which is evident in the above quotation taken from the report of the 2004 consultative board (Wilkinson 2005: 163).[21] Scholte lists a series of causal factors explaining what he describes as a 'shallowness' of relations between the WTO and civil society, including a resource deficit experienced by both the Secretariat's External Relations Division and 'civil society organizations' (Scholte 2004: 155–56). However, on top of these material problems, Scholte argues that there are structural conditions including: social hierarchies between countries, cultures, classes and genders; a remaining culture of secrecy; and a 'neoclassical economic orthodoxy ... [that acts as a] force against a more inclusive, deeper and more open dialogue between the WTO and civil society organizations' (Scholte 2004: 156–57).[22] Collectively, these factors serve to frame not only relations between such identities as the WTO and civil society/civil society organizations, but also the NGO identity. In other words, it is not possible to talk of an NGO identity, or even civil society, without consideration of a much wider network of societal relations that includes how the economy is understood and political action is legitimated.

Contesting NGOs in the WTO

The above section has traced the formalization of an NGO identity within the discursive formation of the WTO. Formal rules and events have given expression to a particular articulation of this identity, so that it has become increasingly sedimented. Equally, the physical presence of individuals categorized under an NGO identity has been part of this process. The WTO Secretariat has actively shaped the articulation, through interpreting formal agreements amongst the Member states in such a way that it has helped determine who/what may attend as an NGO at, for example, Ministerial Conferences. Earlier in the chapter, reference was made to the series of rulings in the dispute settlement process in which NGOs have been given the right to submit amicus briefs independently of a Member-state delegation (Marceau and Pedersen 1999: 34–42). Whilst the Secretariat can be said to be active within the articulation of a particular NGO identity, the emergence of new identities within global trade governance cannot be limited to the NGO identity. The inclusion of certain demands over others suggests a selection process in which the Secretariat has served as a significant part of the discursive context framing the shape of the NGO identity, excluding the 'rejectionists'. However, this does not explain why the Secretariat should need to acknowledge the 'reformists' or have made the overtures to the NGO identity that it has. As discussed above, the Uruguay Round that established the WTO signalled a vast expansion in global trade governance to incorporate many more areas of social activity than previously affected under the GATT. The NGO identity is not the product of the WTO Secretariat but is made possible through many other identities previously outside the global governance of trade.

Scholte *et al.* view the emergence of new identities in the WTO in the context of a wider process in which various UN bodies, the International Monetary Fund and the World Bank have all created a role for NGOs, so that the WTO was effectively forced to speak of greater NGO participation (Scholte *et al.* 1999: 116–17). A rise in meetings organized by environmental, gender, development and other identities to coincide with global summits of international regimes has made visible the inability of the nation-state, trade union and business identities to represent the individuals over whom the institutions of global governance claim jurisdiction (Wilkinson 2005: 156). Scholte *et al.* attribute the rise of these identities and their trade demands to the expansion in the authority of global trade law, or global trade governance, as embodied in the WTO (Scholte *et al.* 1999: 109). Thus, the formalization of an NGO identity underlines the discursive constitution of the WTO, subject to continual rearticulation. It is to the process through which these identities have emerged to contest the discursive formation of the WTO that the chapter now turns.

Politicization of global trade governance

This second section argues that the emergence of new identities to contest global trade governance – as embodied in the discursive formation of the WTO – has been dependent upon a formative process in which the articulation of earlier identities (e.g. environmentalist, labour), as well as that of global trade governance have changed. Whilst events tied specifically to the WTO institution, such as Seattle, have been part of this process, these new identities have been formed not in the context of WTO protests alone but through wider forms of protest, critical of other regimes that have come to be equivalentially linked with the WTO. To be discussed, these events include, but are not limited to, the campaigns around: the Canadian-United States Free Trade Agreement (CUSFTA), the North American Free Trade Agreement (NAFTA), and the Multilateral Agreement on Investment (MAI). The second half of the chapter is meant not as an evaluation of different political campaigns, but as an analysis of how new identities have emerged to contest global trade governance.

The links between these separate campaigns with activity contesting the shape of the WTO have been both physical through the shared presence of certain individuals and organizations, and the product of an articulatory strategy to draw an equivalential chain between these regimes as the 'other'. At the same time, equivalential links have been established amongst a wide series of identities/demands, e.g. consumer, environmental, labour, gender. The emergence of an NGO identity within the WTO can therefore be seen as both an effect and response to this wider social development. The NGO identity in the WTO is a product of articulation between the Secretariat and identities outside the WTO.

To construct this argument, consideration is given to a series of campaigning moments in which this formative process has taken place, tracing the emergence of demands rearticulating global trade governance from the GATT Uruguay Round through to the CUSFTA, the NAFTA, the MAI and the Third WTO Ministerial Conference.

The GATT Uruguay Round

Though various identities beyond the nation-states became interested in the Uruguay Round, visible protests came mainly from those easily identified as representing particular interests, for example, farmers (Croome 1995: 166). At the mid-term review held in 1988 at Montreal – which was to assess the progress of the round – a large demonstration was held by Canadian dairy farmers (Croome 1995: 169). With varying degrees of visibility, demonstrations were held under the 'farmer' identity in Europe, as well as East Asia, where the introduction of intellectual property (TRIPS) into the GATT system was seen as a threat to the right to re-plant crop seeds (Croome 1995: 169). TRIPS also became articulated as a threat to the provision of affordable pharmaceutical drugs in the low-income countries (Croome 1995: 169). An 'environmental' identity emerged with the articulation of the proposed Multilateral Trade Organization as a threat to nation-state jurisdiction over health, safety and the environment (Croome 1995: 337).

These various demands appear to have, at this stage, operated autonomously from one another. The notable exception would be those business demands which were equivalentially linked within the World Economic Forum, a business association, which had been a driving force in launching the Uruguay Round (Scholte *et al.* 1999: 110). There was network activity between other identities so that, for example, European groups took the lead in creating an NGO-GATT Steering Committee (Wilkinson 1996: 253–54). This Committee emerged out of a Shadow GATT Conference held in Montreal during the mid-term review and attended by various advocacy groups, and was established by 20 European development and environmental groups, as well as a series of NGO networks (Wilkinson 1996: 253–54). This left the Committee with a complex network of networks. It was chaired by the chief negotiator and trade programme coordinator (Myriam Vander Stichele) of the European ICDA (International Coalition for Development Action), which had existed since 1975 and was funded by development groups, church groups, governments and the European Commission (Wilkinson 1996: 252). The Committee was co-chaired by senior individuals from other European networks, including EUROSTEP (European Solidarity Towards Equal Participation of People) and the Liaison Committee for Non-Governmental Development Organizations to the European Communities.[23] The Steering Committee organized a second 'shadow conference' during the Brussels GATT Ministerial in 1990. The conference was co-funded between the Liaison Committee, the European Ecumenical Organization for Development (EECOD), various other 'development' groups and networks, as well as the World Council of Churches and the European Commission. The event was apparently attended by '28 NGOs from the North [developed countries], 27 from the South [developing countries]' (Wilkinson 1996: 253). In the wake of the conference, a 10-point declaration was published, titled 'A People's GATT for World Development'. This formed the basis for a series of public discussions organized under the title 'GATTastrophe'.[24] Other publications included: 'What Option for the Poor – Reflections on Agriculture and the Third World in the Uruguay Round' (published by EECOD in December 1990); and, 'Issues Left Out by the Uruguay Round: Environment, Social Rights and Democracy' (published by Stichele in September 1991).

EECOD also commissioned a paper presenting the GATT as a threat to democracy, as well as funding travel for individuals from the South to meet both MEPs in Brussels and members of the EC GATT negotiating team in Geneva. Information on the GATT negotiations was provided by seminars and regular updates distributed by the ICDA. Though the NGO-GATT Steering Committee was active in the preparation of the shadow conferences, it would appear that actions in between were orchestrated by individual groups and smaller networks. A series of global group petitions were produced to express transnational solidarity between groups based in different countries. For example, after a conference organized by groups to discuss the proposal for a Multilateral Trade Organization, a statement was signed by over 150 organizations, titled 'The US-EC Talks on the Uruguay Round: Developing Countries Suffer from the Democratic Deficit' (Wilkinson 1996: 254). Such petitions have become an established form of protest media utilized by transnational movement networks (Strange 2011a) and appear frequently within the politicization of global trade governance.

Despite these expressions of solidarity, the campaign was later to be considered a 'failure' amongst those involved. Little activity began prior to 1990, meaning that already much of the negotiations had been completed and, at least from the outside, the end of the round appeared imminent. Additionally, what solidarity there was rested much on specific individuals. For example, Wilkinson (1996: 259–60) refers to the difficulty the campaign faced when people left to take up positions elsewhere, such as one who departed to become a UK member of Parliament.

With respect to network activity, in January 1993 the Steering Committee was reformed into the Centre for European Networking on Trade, and in the United Kingdom the UK Trade Network was established by Christian Aid UK, Oxfam, Action Aid, the CIIR (Catholic Institute for International Relations), and the World Development Movement. However, this created problems of overlap, where networks came to act as an extension of their most dominant members and so ended up competing for overall dominance. This was particularly problematic where networks were heavily reliant upon funding from the European Commission.

Despite the formation and expansion of networks, as well as certain joint actions as the global group petitions, these groups lacked an overall unity. Decisions had to be taken by consensus, with the consequence that it was hard to respond rapidly to new developments, especially in respect of the late start of the initial campaign and the progress of the Uruguay Round post-1990 (Wilkinson 1996: 259). In comparison to business demands represented in such groups as the World Economic Forum, these groups lacked a specific set of terms around which their demands could be articulated – an empty signifier. 'Development' appears to have been repeated frequently, though it was not used to engage with a wider public, so that the audience of its demands was limited to those negotiating the Uruguay Round, who had already sedimented much of the agreement prior to when these groups launched their critique.

An 'environmental' identity with respect to global trade governance was made visible in January 1991, with a complaint brought by Mexico to the GATT dispute settlement mechanism against the USA (Danaher and Mark 2003: 111).[25] The complaint was against US restrictions on imported tuna caught with nets argued to be lethal to dolphins. The restrictions had come via campaigning by environmental groups and the threat of a consumer boycott of tuna that could not be guaranteed as 'dolphin-friendly'. After the leading US manufacturers announced that they would from then on only sell dolphin-friendly tuna, the US Congress passed legislation banning any other tuna from the US market. When a GATT dispute settlement panel declared in August 1991 that the restrictions were in violation of the GATT, the environmentalist identity suffered a dislocation and rearticulation that would now include demands related to global trade governance. A similar experience occurred for consumer groups such as the US-based Public Citizen, with lobbying on such matters as pesticide control and food labelling subject to the expanding GATT (Wallach and Woodall 2004: 3). Public Citizen established a research and campaigning unit called Global Trade Watch, which focused on the high-profile case of the tuna-dolphin dispute, articulating it as evidence of a GATT assault on the democratic process on the basis that an unelected panel were able to overturn publicly supported domestic legislation (Danaher and Mark 2003: 231). Publicly, this critique took the form of the slogan 'GATTzilla ate Flipper', accompanying a cartoon of a monster clasping a dolphin in one hand whilst trampling on the US Capitol (Danaher and Mark 2003: 244–46).

In the USA, a campaign against US ratification of the Uruguay Round text was launched that drew high-profile support from environmental groups as well as several leading Republican politicians, including the Senate Minority Leader. However, an internal divide within the leading trade unions made it difficult to develop a mass campaign, with some older labour officials having been active in supporting tariff reductions under the GATT and reluctant to change, whilst younger leaders were more critical (Danaher and Mark 2003: 247–48). A group representing small businesses opposed to the round was established – the US Business and Industrial Council (USBIC). By comparison, the round was strongly supported by 285 major US corporations, which expressed their support with a high-profile and well-funded advertising campaign that included the creation of a lobbying group titled Consumers for World Trade, and unified under the banner Alliance for GATT Now.

The emergence of new identities in the context of global trade governance was evident not only in these campaigns, but also in the language used in the preamble to the Marrakech Agreement establishing the WTO, which explicitly mentions 'sustainable development' (Qureshi 1996: 196). These identities did not emerge as a response to the WTO alone. For example, the campaign against US ratification was in the context of other campaigns that had taken place against the NAFTA, as well as Canadian activity around the CUSFTA, to which the chapter now turns.

Canadian-United States Free Trade Agreement (CUSFTA)

Activity around CUSFTA suggests how identities have been rearticulated to include a demand focused on global trade governance, as well as the role of equivalential chains in this process.

CUSFTA sparked little contestation in the USA, but was articulated into a public controversy within Canada (Danaher and Mark 2003: 229–30). Campaigning against CUSFTA left Canadian groups with a practice of organizing across otherwise quite diverse identities (e.g. 'labour' and 'gender'). This was because opponents of the agreement sought to frame it as not only relevant to Canada's economic position vis-à-vis the USA, but also in terms of its potential impact upon Canadian cultural and political sovereignty, as well as environmental and social policy (Huyer 2004: 49).[26] The Pro-Canada Network was formed to coordinate 'a coalition of popular-sector groups and social movements, including representatives from labour, the women's movement, churches, the environmental movement, and cultural and social justice groups' (Huyer 2004: 49). The coalition was facilitated via a series of cross-group meetings and conferences, as well as regional coalitions, which helped build working relationships between professional and volunteer campaigners from different backgrounds. Conferences in Canada critical of the then-proposed free trade agreement with the USA included the Free Trade Revues, Dialogue '86, and the Ecumenical Conference on Free Trade, Self-reliance and Economic Justice, and the Canada Summit (Huyer 2004: 50). The intention from the beginning appears to have been to create a very public campaign, with links to many different sectors of society, via the Canadian Labour Congress, National Action Committee on the Status of Women, the National Farmers Union, and the Ecumenical Coalition for Economic Justice, amongst others (Huyer

2004: 50). Though also involved within the wider network, Canadian environmentalists are said to have felt poorly 'integrated' within an analysis that came to reflect, principally, labour interests that approached CUSFTA as 'fundamentally left economists' and unable to appreciate an environmental analysis.[27] This appears to reflect wider tensions that occurred during the development of working relations between groups, Huyer's analysis of the Canadian anti-CUSFTA campaign revealing similar problems for women's groups, which felt all too often that they were being used to express the representativeness of the network rather than provide critical insight to a collective analysis overwhelmingly dominated by labour (Huyer 2004: 54–55). This is not to say that there were not strong women within the labour movement present, as there were, but that it was overly dominated by men, according to Huyer's (2004: 54–55) research.

Coalition-building efforts involved tensions between labour that saw itself as justifiably hegemonic because of its comparatively high membership and profile, and other groups, particularly social movement organizations, that worked via a more horizontal form of decision making, as opposed to the hierarchical approach of traditional trade unionism. Consequently, though representatives from many different sectors were present in the network's executive, many decisions are said to have taken place between a small group of individuals, the consensus then imposed on the rest of the network. Though perhaps an often-used technique of forming consensus amongst large numbers of parties, this particular technique for decision making created tensions because it contradicted many of the practices used by certain groups that considered themselves as 'horizontal' and, by their logic, 'democratic'.

Working with non-labour groups proved divisive for trade unions, which were split between adopting a wider social critique within their analysis, and those that are often termed 'business unionism'.[28] The involvement of labour with other groups within the Pro-Canada Network, though not without tension, does represent an important shift beyond these basic demands. Additionally, those sectors of labour that represented workers in export-dependent industries were much less hostile to CUSFTA, adding a further tension to labour unity and making the coalition with women's groups, amongst others, yet more significant (Huyer 2004: 52). The development of equivalential chains therefore does not necessarily have a multiplying effect on the size of a coalition but may in fact cause dissension where it also leads to certain tensions within the pre-existing equivalential logics, such as within the 'trade union' identity here.

Campaigning via the Pro-Canada Network took the form of seminars and speakers criticizing CUSFTA, but was most evident in an effort to force an election that might act as a referendum on the CUSFTA, removing the incumbent Conservative government, that was negotiating the agreement, out of office. This had the effect of focusing resources away from the critique of CUSFTA towards campaigning for the New Democratic Party (NDP), which was then critical of CUSFTA. When the Conservatives were re-elected in 1988, the loss provoked fierce tensions within the network. Many non-labour groups, which had been less supportive of the NDP, were critical of trade unions for having diverted resources away from the critique of CUSFTA and towards electioneering for the NDP. Though Huyer reports that some sectors of labour were critical of social movement organizations for not being sufficiently supportive of the NDP, there were also accusations that the party had not been attentive to labour, taking its support for granted (Huyer 2004: 52). Despite these tensions, however, CUSFTA proved an important learning curve for coalition building amongst those groups coming to incorporate demands related to global trade governance within their identities.

There appears to have been little activity from groups in the USA (Danaher and Mark 2003: 229). This seems to be reflected within the name of the Canadian anti-CUSFTA coalition – the Pro-Canada Network. To consider this point further, the chapter now turns to campaigning against the North American Free Trade Agreement which involved trinational cooperation between civil society groups in Mexico, the USA and Canada.

North American Free Trade Agreement (NAFTA)

As a consequence of the CUSFTA battle, Canadian groups were more experienced in contesting global trade governance, but defeat also created the belief that they could gain little by targeting their government alone, which was seen as too weak in comparison to the negotiating power of the USA (Hogenboom 1996: 996). This provided the grounds for cross-border collaboration between groups in the USA and Canada. Canadian groups not only worked to foster relations with anti-NAFTA groups in Mexico and the USA, but also helped to sponsor initiatives that made trinational cooperation between all three possible. They advised against criticizing NAFTA on 'nationalist' grounds so as to avoid alienating foreign groups who were needed to help contest the agreement (Stillerman 2003: 590).

Campaigning against the NAFTA provides an example of the growing importance of demands related to global trade governance within identities such as labour and environmentalism, as well as negation of the nation-state identity, though these demands were not necessarily opposed to NAFTA. Though it might be assumed that a global trade governance regime agreed between three nation-state governments might incite a transnational response from those identities with demands related to global trade governance, the uneven nature of such action suggests a much more nuanced picture. Campaigning activity began soon after the 1990 announcement that a trade pact would be established between Mexico, the USA and Canada, and continued through to the January 1994 formal establishment of the NAFTA.

As said, Canadian groups were active in facilitating trinational meetings between themselves and other groups in the USA and Mexico. Such action was made possible via the articulation of certain common concerns, such as the '*maquiladoras*'. The maquiladora sector consisted of US factories on the US–Mexican border, where labour and environmental conditions were poorly regulated, manufacturing cars and other goods for the US market. Pollution that crossed the border and the transference of US jobs to these export-processing plants undermined the 'national-level public interest lobbyist' identity of various environmental and labour groups in Mexico and the USA, which the Canadian groups were able to rearticulate into a trinational identity (Stillerman 2003: 585, 590–91).[29]

As a qualification to the previous paragraph, it should be said that Canadian and Mexican groups focused less on their national citizens and more on supporting campaigning in the USA. This is significant because the complexity it adds to the 'transnational' model of such mobilization. This can partially be seen as a consequence of national political differences, where Canadian groups viewed the US government as significantly more 'powerful' than their own, and Mexican groups found their own government comparatively closed. However, it also says much about how these groups viewed the NAFTA, and what they considered to be the central battleground. Nation-state territories provided a significant discursive context framing how different groups emerged to contest this particular trade regime.

In Mexico, the dominant labour organizations had traditionally held close affiliations with the government party, which had made the original formal proposition for a NAFTA (Cook 1995: 78). Those trade unions that were critical of the proposed NAFTA were relatively small and independent, unable to claim a high degree of official representation amongst the Mexican workforce. The most high-profile of these independent Mexican trade unions was the Frente Auténtico del Trabajo (FAT) (Stillerman 2003: 584–85), which was able to increase its role despite its comparatively poor resource base via actively seeking both cross-border and cross-issue linkages with environmental and human rights groups in Mexico, the USA and Canada (Cook 1995: 88).[30] The cross-border linkages were made evident in the role that Mexican groups played in directly lobbying the US Congress, where the NAFTA was seen to be decided (Hogenboom 1996: 995). Additionally, this increased the leverage of the Mexican groups within their own country, through being seen as important within the US debate as well as gaining information from US groups which was otherwise not forthcoming from the Mexican government (Hogenboom 1996: 995). The US linkages were particularly important for Mexican groups such as FAT because the well-resourced groups tended to be confined to Mexico City, with few domestic linkages to groups outside the capital, or social movements and intellectuals (Hogenboom 1996: 992).

Within the USA itself, a coalition was formed between labour, environmental, women's and consumer groups. The US anti-NAFTA campaign was a mix of unlikely comrades, including leading US nationalists such as Pat Buchanan and Ross Perot, as well as consumer-rights advocate Ralph Nader (Shoch 2000: 124). US President Bush presented an action plan claiming various protections that would prevent any detrimental impact upon US labour and environmental conditions, with the effect of weakening early criticism from environmentalist and labour identities (Shoch 2000: 123). This allowed the White House to gain the Congressional approval required for the NAFTA negotiations to begin.

Though the US Congress would eventually pass the final draft of the NAFTA, campaigning by those identities critical of the proposed regime was not necessarily a failure in that the final text did include certain side accords acknowledging labour (Shoch 2000: 123) and environmental (Grossman 2000: 62) concerns.[31] As with the NGO identity in the WTO, this suggests a rearticulation of global trade governance characterized as a negotiation in which no identity may fully dominate. As Grossman notes, in the case of environmentalism, any such demands were first fiercely rejected by business promoting NAFTA, with the phrase 'sustainable development' being accepted only towards the end (ibid.: 62).

However, as with the NGO identity in the WTO, the incorporation of some environmentalist demands had the effect of marginalizing certain environmentalist groups and creating a significant cleavage within the US environmental movement (Dreiling and Wolf 2001: 34). This process was supported by active engagement from business which sought to contribute funding and managerial expertise to certain groups (ibid.: 43). Dreiling and Wolf distinguish between the discourses used by pro-NAFTA and anti-NAFTA environmentalist groups (ibid.: 45–47), which may be re-modelled into equivalential sequences as in Figure 4.3.

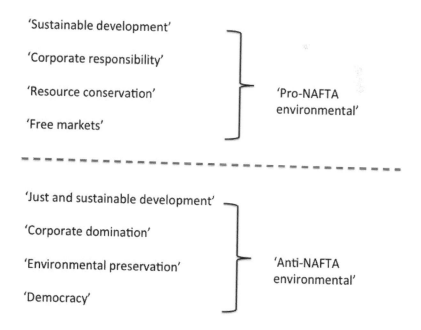

Figure 4.3 Competing equivalential sequences within the environmental movement during the NAFTA negotiations

Environmentalist groups such as the World Wide Fund for Nature (WWF) argued that NAFTA provided a means to force environmental regulations onto Mexico (Hogenboom 1996: 993). The 1990s had witnessed a series of international regimes either incorporating or specifically reflecting environmentalist demands, and it was in this context that NAFTA represented an opportunity to add environmentalist demands to global trade governance.

This polarized the environmentalist identity throughout North America, creating a cleavage between those who viewed their identity as lobbying Washington, and those who felt stronger empathy with the grassroots (Hogenboom 1996: 999). This is similar to the problem experienced by those European campaigners working on the GATT Uruguay Round, facing the same divisive question between working with the grassroots or lobbying government officials. For those environmental groups that rejected the Washington position – such as Friends of the Earth and Greenpeace – greater affiliation was found with Nader's Public Citizen, which focused on NAFTA as an enlargement of the power of the corporate sector (Hogenboom 1996: 993).

Coalition activity against the NAFTA was heavily weakened by the support given by part of the environmentalist identity in two ways: first, it removed important groups from the critical campaign; and second, it weakened attempts to articulate NAFTA as 'bad' for the environment in the context of US domestic politics where environmentalist demands carried a growing resonance. Originally appearing as a challenge, the environmentalist identity therefore came to help legitimate the proposed NAFTA. A further cleavage opened up between those who limited their critique of NAFTA as a threat to US jobs, and those who utilized wider demands concerning 'corporate power' and 'democracy' (Danaher and Mark 2003: 237). Additionally, the campaign was damaged by focusing on specific individual figures, such as Ross Perot, whose poor performance in a televised debate with the US Vice President was seen as 'the worst thing that ever happened to us' by campaigners (Danaher and Mark 2003: 239). Despite the problems faced in forming equivalential links between a vast spectrum of identities, the NAFTA campaign did provide the basis for rearticulating a larger number of identities towards incorporating demands related to global trade governance, as well as giving expression to an equivalential chain linking certain environmentalist identities with labour.

These identities were further sedimented and expanded in the campaigns against the OECD's attempt to create a Multilateral Agreement on Investment (MAI) (Danaher and Mark 2003: 260–67), and the WTO's Third Ministerial Conference, hosted in Seattle. Political movements critical of the MAI and the Seattle WTO Ministerial provide the focus of the next two sections, tracing out the equivalential chains through which they were made possible.

Multilateral Agreement on Investment (MAI)

The MAI was an agreement driven by representatives of the USA within the OECD, intended to liberalize regulations governing investment between member states. It was controversial because, its critics claimed, it threatened domestic control over regulations related to public safety, social provision, the environment and other such politically sensitive areas.[32]

According to Johnston and Laxer (2003: 52–53), initial mobilization against the MAI was provoked by a warning given from the director of the Malaysian-based Third World Network (TWN), Martin Khor. The TWN gained its information via close links with governments of economically weaker nation-states, which it aids in trade negotiations as well as receiving information from them (Johnston and Laxer 2003: 53). This information, as in the warning on the MAI, was passed on via TWN to groups in economically richer nation-states, through Khor speaking at an event of the International Forum on Globalization (IFG). IFG is a network of predominantly US-based non-governmental organizations researching and critiquing the hegemonic global political-economic order. Present at the meeting was Tony Clarke, a Canadian activist and veteran of both the anti-CUSFTA and anti-NAFTA campaigns, having been chair of the Pro-Canada Network that had been prominent in these campaigns.

The figure of Clarke was significant to the campaign considering the lack of anti-MAI activity amongst US-based groups despite their predominance within the IFG. Clarke was joined by Maude Barlow, a figurehead of the grassroots-based Council of Canadians. Together they analysed the draft MAI, obtained after extensive searching, via contacts with a member of the Canadian parliament who came across it by accident whilst in Europe – suggesting the importance of previous campaigns in positioning Clarke as an activist to whom the politician might turn. This was despite European groups having no such success, despite demands to the OECD for its release. Barlow and Clarke themselves did not release the draft in their possession until having analysed it as well as providing it to the US-based Public Citizen for separate analysis (Johnston and Laxer 2003: 53).

Barlow and Clarke eventually disseminated the MAI with their analysis via the Internet, presenting it as a Corporate Rules Treaty. This would become a master frame that would be utilized throughout national campaigns across North America, Australia and Europe (Johnston and Laxer 2003: 53). The critique generated front page news in Canada, tapping into a nationalism provoked by CUSFTA, NAFTA and a recent case in which a US corporation had successfully sued the Canadian government for banning an additive (ethyl) despite that additive being already banned in the USA. This ruling was made possible via NAFTA (Danaher and Mark 2003: 264; Johnston and Laxer 2003: 54–57).

The anti-MAI campaign was transnational in the sense that information was widely shared, the analysis disseminated so that it was used by groups far beyond Canadian borders. The master frame of the MAI as a 'corporate rules treaty' appeared within many of these campaigns. However, the campaigns remained national because activity was targeted at the nation-state. Egan (2001) has argued that though the MAI was pushed by capital, it was done via the nation-state. Consequently, the nation-state served as the site of contestation in the MAI fight. It would be misleading to suggest that contestation around the MAI was characterized by an anti-/pro-globalization fight. Instead it was more related to a contest around the power of capital within the state, utilizing transnational linkages for sharing in-depth critique and information vital to the advocacy.

Prior to the leak of the draft MAI, the OECD had denied NGO requests to engage in negotiations. These requests only received a positive response once the draft had been leaked. After the OECD finally met with NGO representatives, the proposed MAI began to include, however insubstantive, language adopting environmental and labour concerns. The effect was drastically to weaken support amongst capital (Egan 2001: 89–90).

The MAI was most weakened, however, by the nation-state-focused citizen campaigns, which led to many of the leading OECD member states putting forward a growing list of exemptions, including cultural protections and performance standards (Egan 2001: 88). These exemptions placed obstacles to agreement, with France to be the first member state to pull out of negotiations, motivated because of public concern regarding cultural protection voiced by its culture minister (Johnston and Laxer 2003: 58–59). This signalled the end of the MAI in 1998.

The anti-MAI campaign took place via nation-state-focused campaigns, and yet it was transnational in so far as it utilized transnational information exchange, and was articulated via certain master frames around the MAI as a 'corporate rules treaty' and as a 'threat to democracy'. This work helped to facilitate trust between activists across borders, requiring an acceptance of information provided in e-mails as well as conference telephone calls. The greatest level of coordination appears to have taken place in the international Joint-NGO statement to the OECD, which asserted the transnational nature of anti-MAI activity (Egan 2001: 88–89).

The campaign against the MAI was built upon a series of equivalential chains between otherwise divergent demands, as embodied in the Joint-NGO statement to the OECD.[33] Signed by 565 organizations in 68 countries, the statement was announced at the NGO/OECD Consultation on the MAI, held in October 1997.[34] The preamble to the statement presents it as the expression of:

> [A] coalition of *development*, *environment*, *human rights*, *labour*, and *consumer* and *women's* groups from around the world, with representation in nearly 70 countries, … [which] consider the draft Multilateral Agreement on Investment (MAI) to be a damaging agreement which should not proceed in its current form, if at all.[35]

This articulates an equivalential chain between a plurality of different demands with the critique of the MAI serving as the empty signifier through which their unity is established, as in Figure 4.4. A frontier is thus established against the MAI/OECD. This discursive formation is further developed

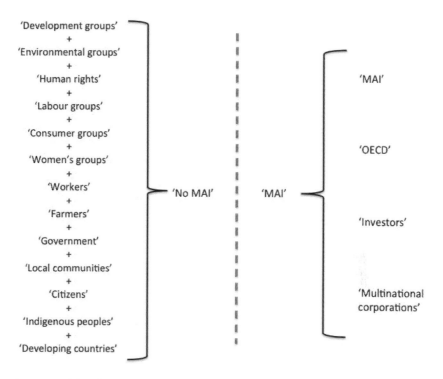

Figure 4.4 The discursive formation evident in the 'Joint NGO statement' to the OECD negotiations on the MAI

throughout the statement, so that workers, farmers, governments, local communities, citizens, indigenous peoples and developing countries are articulated into the equivalential chain with the other demands listed in the above quotation. In the model, all the demands appear equal, though it should be noted that in praxis certain demands would be more strongly articulated than others.

The statement does not reflect the full articulatory process because much will rely upon which groups are presenting it so that, for example, in certain articulations the empty signifier might have been 'No MAI as *pro-development*'. Added to the MAI/OECD as the 'other', are investors and multinational corporations. The statement concludes with a series of specific demands including: 'independent and comprehensive agreement', 'suspend the MAI negotiations', 'increase transparency', and 'broaden active participation of government departments'.[36]

The Third WTO Ministerial Conference and the emergence of 'Our World Is Not For Sale' – Seattle and OWINFS

The equivalential chains formed through the anti-MAI campaign led to the emergence of the relatively informal network Our World Is Not For Sale

(OWINFS), which bases its identity upon a global group petition[37] and an e-mail distribution list. OWINFS is a global network of groups that covers issues including gender equality, development, environment and human rights, which are aligned together to contest the WTO, as well as other multilateral trade agreements.[38] It was the series of personal contacts and information exchanges that facilitated the development of an overall network under the banner 'Our World Is Not For Sale'.[39] The network is informal, with no permanent staff. Work is carried out by volunteers from the member groups. Decision making is claimed to be by consensus, and coordination is made possible via conference calls, though in both cases it is hard to see how this might be feasible with hundreds of organizations. Instead, much relies on what it describes as 'movement leaders'. These individuals are the ones reaching consensus, telephoning each other, meeting and dominating e-mail listservs.[40]

The first global group petition was written prior to the Third WTO Ministerial Conference, and titled No New Round – Turn Around. This demanded that WTO member states reject expansion of the WTO, and attracted 1,500 signatory organizations.[41] The statement made specific reference to the collapse of the MAI, arguing that it 'demonstrates broad public opposition to the deregulation of the global economy, the increasing dominance of transnational corporations and escalating resource use and environmental degradation'.[42] Meant to have been signed by nearly 1,500 organizations prior to the Seattle WTO Ministerial,[43] the WTO serves as the 'other' and is equivalentially linked to: 'concentration of wealth in the hands of the rich few', 'increasing poverty for the majority of the world's population', 'unsustainable patterns of production and consumption', 'transnational corporations', 'undemocratic', 'untransparent', 'non-accountable', 'marginalise the majority of the world's people', 'global economic instability', 'collapse of national economies', 'increasing inequity both between and within nations', 'increasing environmental and social degradation' and 'globalisation'. On the opposite side of the frontier to this 'other', are 'international civil society', 'workers', 'farmers', 'other people', and 'the environment'.[44] The statement demands a halt to any expansion of the WTO, and a review to address 'the WTO's impact on marginalised communities, development, democracy, environment, health, human rights, labour rights and the rights of women and children. The review must be conducted with civil society's full participation'.[45]

To understand the events at Seattle, it is necessary to consider what happened in the aftermath of the GATT Uruguay Round.

The end of the Uruguay Round, Singapore, and new tensions leading up to Seattle

The Uruguay Round was viewed by labour, in particular, with disappointment because it lacked provisions originally included within the International Trade

Organization that recognized the role of the International Labour Organization within global trade governance (Wilkinson 2005: 160). Despite the inclusion of 'sustainable development' within the preamble to the Marrakech Agreement establishing the WTO, the lack of any legally binding acknowledgement of the environment meant that environmentalist groups also found their demands absent from the new body for global trade governance (Wilkinson 2005: 161).

The tensions present in this absence of labour within the global trade governance regime were underlined at the first WTO Ministerial Conference, in Singapore in 1996. The Uruguay Round was launched with a side statement acknowledging issues raised by some Contracting Parties but lacking consensus. One of these issues was workers' rights, which had been raised by the US delegation at the behest of the US Congress (Croome 1995: 35–36). Singapore represented an opportunity to resolve this disagreement. The International Confederation of Free Trade Unions (ICFTU) was present at the Ministerial and lobbied for consensus to bring a 'social clause' into the WTO, that would recognize basic rights on child labour and collective bargaining (O'Brien *et al.* 2000: 67–106). Those most openly opposed to such a clause included many developing countries and several development groups, including Martin Khor's Third World Network (TWN), which saw the clause as an attempt to close developed country markets to imports from low-wage countries (O'Brien *et al.* 2000: 87; Wilkinson 1999: 176). Whilst agreement was reached to expand the WTO to include work programmes to consider issues such as investment and government procurement, a proposal to launch a similar consideration of labour rights was abandoned. As a compromise, the Ministerial finished with a final declaration that stated commitment by Members to the observance of core labour standards, but that remained ambiguous beyond also stating that the setting and enforcement of those standards be the responsibility of the International Labour Organization (Wilkinson 2005: 161; Wilkinson 2002b: 216–17; O'Brien 2002: 224–25).[46]

Whereas the Marrakech Agreement formally states that relations with 'International Organizations' are to be left to the discretion of the WTO General Council (Article V:1),[47] Article III on the 'Functions of the WTO' specifically requires the WTO to cooperate with the IMF and the International Bank for Reconstruction and Development (the World Bank) in paragraph 5.[48] This formal requirement for cooperation with the IMF and the World Bank is legitimated as 'achieving greater coherence in global economic policy-making'.[49] Though Article V:1 means that the WTO is able to cooperate with the ILO, the imbalance between the ad hoc position of labour and the formal position of the IMF and the World Bank in the WTO means that, as Wilkinson argues, labour demands lack any 'comparable representation in the heartland of global economic decision making' (Wilkinson 2002b: 220). As such, the Marrakech Agreement sediments an articulation of global trade governance as weighted against labour demands.

At the second Ministerial Conference, in 1998, the US president made a suggestion at Geneva that a forum might be created to allow business, labour, environmental and consumer groups to advise the WTO (Wilkinson 1999: 180). At the Third Ministerial, in Seattle, a proposal was suggested by the US and EU Member state delegations for a joint WTO-ILO forum to explore labour issues (Wilkinson 2002b: 218). However, neither of these proposals has reached fruition.

The trade-labour debate is complicated and therefore cannot be discussed here beyond making the point that the tension it represents signals the emergence of new actors/identities within the WTO.[50] The same is apparent with respect to environmental demands. The dolphin-tuna case affecting the GATT in the early 1990s was repeated early on in the WTO, when a dispute was brought against the USA by India, Pakistan, Malaysia and Thailand. The dispute focused on a US ban on shrimp imports caught via fishing practices lethal to turtle populations (McGrew 1999: 201). When a WTO dispute settlement panel announced their decision that the ban constituted a violation of WTO rules, the case formed part of the folklore used during the Seattle street protests, with people dressed as turtles (Danaher and Mark 2003: 277). Most significantly, environmentalist and labour demands became equivalentially linked at Seattle, so that banners were carried stating: 'Turtles and Teamsters together at last' (Danaher and Mark 2003: 223).

Seattle

Hosted in Seattle, the Third WTO Ministerial Conference collapsed because of a failure to reach consensus amongst its Member states which fell into separate identities defined as North and South (or, alternatively, developed and developing). This polarization was made possible via campaigning activity that relied upon the equivalential chains that had been developed between campaigning groups in the above-mentioned activities. First, the MAI had involved joint activity between trade unions and civil society (including development groups and environmental organizations). The MAI collapsed because of inclusion of labour standards that were forced through via intense lobbying from the ICFTU. At Seattle, this would prove important once again. A key contributing factor to its collapse was pressure placed on the US president, who gave a seemingly insubstantial concession to the trade unions that the WTO might consider inclusion of labour standards within its trade agreements (O'Brien *et al.* 2000: 140). Though the suggestion was for nothing more than a working group to discuss such a possibility, it created dissensus from many countries which saw cheap labour as their 'comparative advantage' in international trade. Second, OWINFS made it possible for a certain degree of coordination between groups in Europe, Latin America, Asia and North America to play their governments off against one another, so as to force a collapse (Danaher and Mark 2003: 286).

This history had created an infrastructure of equivalential identities in the form of joint protest activities, global group petitions, and e-mail lists distributing critical analysis and news regarding ongoing developments. Collectively, such practices provided the backdrop against which the formalization of an NGO identity in the WTO took place.

Conclusion

The formalization of an NGO identity shows how a new identity has emerged and been sedimented within the WTO. This has been an historically contingent process, consisting of a contestation between alternate articulations. Tracing this process, as has been done here, is important because: 1 it indicates the articulatory process shaping the discursive formation of the WTO; 2 it highlights the part that a wider discursive context plays in affecting this process; and, 3 it shows that the WTO both shapes, and is shaped by, its historically contingent discursive context in a mutually constitutive relationship.

New identities have emerged via exposing the contingency of the then present discursive formation of global trade governance embodied in the WTO, introducing demands that exceed its discursive formation. This is a complex process in which both the WTO and those groups emerging to contest its global trade governance are rearticulated with new subject positions.

In respect to labour and environmental identities, the expansion of global trade governance facilitated within the discursive formation of the WTO has signalled a dislocation of those identities. For example, environmental groups as national-level public interest lobbyists find their identity destabilized by the intrusion of the WTO rulings on the dolphin and turtle cases. The group identity is shown to be contingent in two ways: 1 the inability to define the national level as an autonomous political sphere; and, 2 the inability to define the environment as a separate policy sphere. The environmental identity is shown to be overlapping with trade. The effect is that both environment and trade are rearticulated to include new demands. These identities are not pre-existent but require a formative process. Not only has an environmentalist identity come to be rearticulated through these campaigns to incorporate a concern with trade, but also global trade governance has been rearticulated to require acknowledgement of the environment. Though, for example, one might dismiss any reference to sustainable development within a WTO agreement as superficial, it remains significant, nonetheless, if understood as the early stage of sedimenting a new articulation of global trade governance.

Additionally, it should be noted that whilst the second half of the chapter has focused on campaigning moments where new identities have emerged to contest global trade governance, the articulatory process being discussed exceeds those campaigns to include their targets – the regimes of global trade governance. Each regime represents a moment in which global trade governance has been rearticulated. As already discussed throughout the book, and in Chapter 2 in particular, the Uruguay Round signalled a radical expansion of global trade governance. One effect of this expansion was to dislocate many identities previously operating with a much smaller remit so that they would be rearticulated to incorporate trade within their demands. In this sense, the campaigns and the regimes form part of the same articulatory process exhibiting the contingency of the WTO as a discursive formation. Whilst this may be read as a pessimistic statement on the transformative potential of global civil society – if its critical actions come to constitute that which it critiques – this is not the intent. Rather, as the broader literature has tried to demonstrate, the relationship between these groups and the stated targets of their critical actions is both complex and subject to contestation (Brassett and Smith 2010; Amoore and Langley 2004).

The findings show the role of equivalential chains, through which labour and environmentalist demands, for example, have been rearticulated to be equivalential in their incorporation of a larger demand directed at global trade governance. Thus, these identities do not exist in waiting, as such, but require a formative process through which they may emerge and come to contest the shape of global trade governance. Additionally, this formative process exceeds the WTO itself, to include other political moments, so that one is made aware of a much wider network of social practices in which the articulation of global trade governance is articulated.

In order that networks may be built, linkages at a more informal level need first to be established where divergent identities are able to operate equivalentially at certain moments of political action. The different campaigns discussed evidence an ongoing tension within this process, as in the case of gender and labour demands within the campaigning critical of the CUSFTA. An additional tension can be seen in the first half of the chapter, where the formalization of an NGO identity in the WTO is an ongoing contestation shaped by both identities external to the WTO and the discursive context of the WTO. It is in this sense that the WTO Secretariat is part of the discursive context framing the emergence of an NGO identity in the WTO, and yet is also subject to the rearticulatory process in which it is positioned.

The next chapter provides a case study of identity formation in the context of contestation critical of a specific WTO trade agreement – the General Agreement on Trade in Services (GATS). Though the chapter serves principally to provide more detail as to the process by which different identities are rearticulated to contest global trade governance, the above argumentation will apply – that the campaign is not a single political moment but should be seen as part of a much wider articulatory process which includes not only protests but the discursive formation of global trade governance embodied in the WTO.

Notes

1 This is based on the consensus principle that formally serves as the default mechanism for decision making in the WTO institution. According to the Marrakech Agreement, 'The body concerned shall be deemed to have decided by consensus on a matter submitted for its consideration, if no Member, present at the meeting when the decision is taken, formally objects to the proposed decision' (Footnote 1 to Article IX:1, *Marrakech Agreement Establishing the World Trade Organization*,

reprinted in Qureshi 1996: 201). Decisions are therefore articulated as being based upon the presence of the Members in a very literal sense.

2 Bronckers argues that this influence goes beyond just administrative or technical support, because the Secretariat also plays an 'important role ... in dispute settlement proceedings', in the judicial domain of the Appellate Body and the Dispute Settlement panels (Bronckers 2000: 297, ft 52).

3 Although the WTO formally has three languages – French, Spanish and English – it would appear that English is often treated as the primary language, with minutes of meetings being translated into French or Spanish only after their relevance within the negotiations has greatly decreased (Kwa and Jawara 2004: 220).

4 Article V:2 of the Marrakech Agreement Establishing the World Trade Organization. Quotation taken from a reprint in Qureshi 1996: 199.

5 As discussed in Chapter 3.

6 Based on Marceau and Pedersen's (1999: 46) data and categories, the NGO identity at the Singapore Ministerial Conference can be broken down as follows: environment 9 percent; development 25 percent; business 44 percent; consumers 2 percent; trade unions 9 percent; other 10 percent. No definitions of these categories are offered with the data, with definitional differences possibly explaining the disparity between Marceau and Pedersen's 44 percent figure for 'business', and O'Brien's 65 percent figure for 'business organizations'.

7 According to O'Brien *et al.*, in practice, access to the press room was limited by a requirement that NGO representatives be accompanied by a delegate from their national Member state, meaning that it was difficult for NGOs to 'press their government officials on particular issues' during media briefings, since they required the help of those officials to be physically present at those briefings (O'Brien *et al.* 2000: 93).

8 O'Brien *et al.* write that these Secretariat briefings provided minimal information to the extent that they appeared often 'surreal', serving to do no more than daily announce 'that nothing had yet been decided by member states' (O'Brien *et al.* 2000: 96).

9 The actions of those under the NGO identity at Singapore will be discussed in the second half of this chapter.

10 Although the General Agreement on Tariffs and Trade first appeared in 1947, it was not until 1948 and the failure to ratify the Havana Charter establishing the International Trade Organization that it came into effect.

11 WTO Secretariat Press Release (29th November 1999) *The WTO is not a World Government and No One has any Intention of Making it One, Moore tells NGOs*, emphasis added, www.wto.org/english/thewto_e/minist_e/min99_e/english/press_e/pres155_e.htm (accessed July 2006).

12 The formal publication of this decision does not detail the procedures for registration to which Wilkinson refers in this quotation, though the document does state that the procedures were at the time to be listed on the WTO website. The document itself merely states: 'NGOs that want to attend the Doha Ministerial Conference will be requested to supply, in detail, all the necessary information showing how they are concerned with matters related to those of the WTO.' WTO (10 May 2001) WT/MIN(01)/INF/3 *Procedures Regarding Registration and Attendance of Non-governmental Organizations at the Fourth Session of the Ministerial Conference*, available online at: www.wto.org (accessed July 2006).

13 See also Wilkinson 2005: 165.

14 For example, at the WTO public symposium organized to commemorate the tenth anniversary of the organization's creation, held at the Geneva headquarters from 20–22 April 2005, those organizing the seminars within the official three-day programme included groups categorized as NGOS, such as Third World Network, Friends of the Earth International, International Gender and Trade Network, and

Oxfam International. Individuals from many more groups such as War on Want and Christian Aid are listed as speakers within the seminars. The seminar programme is available online: www.wto.org/English/news_e/events_e/symp05_e/symp_devagenda_prog_05_e.htm (accessed July 2006).

15 Taken from WTO (May 2004) *WTO Hosts its Annual Public Symposium: 'Multilateralism at a Crossroads'*, www.wto.org/english/tratop_e/dda_e/symp_devagenda_04_e.htm (accessed July 2006).

16 See also Scholte 2004: 151.

17 The issue of who/what constitutes the NGO identity is sufficiently sensitive for Brown and Fox (1998: 440) to argue that there exists in the world a 'neo-colonization' of Northern NGOs (i.e. from developed countries) over Southern NGOs (i.e. from developing countries).

18 WTO (2004) *The Future of the WTO – Addressing Institutional Challenges in the New Millennium*, Report by the Consultative Board to the Director-General Supachai Panitchpakdi (Geneva: WTO Publications), 48.

19 As argued in Chapter 4, publicity exercises should not be dismissed as irrelevant because of what they suggest regarding the discursive context in which the WTO has being. In that respect, the Development Agenda is important because it points to the discursive potency of a development demand in global trade governance. The importance of development demands has been discussed in Chapters 2 and 3.

20 Indeed, the demand for contraction has been voiced by strong advocates of trade liberalization within the pages of the WTO's own academic journal, *World Trade Review* (Esty 2002: 17).

21 See also Scholte *et al.* 1999: 119.

22 Whilst providing useful insight here, Scholte's categorization of factors affecting relations between the WTO and civil society follows a material-ideational distinction, if one acknowledges what Scholte calls 'structural' to be 'ideational'. Such a distinction is naturally problematized in the book. This problematization is made apparent in the second section of this chapter, where emphasis is placed not on material or ideational factors, but on the articulatory process by which new actors have emerged to contest the shape of global trade governance. It is in the articulatory process that material and ideational factors effectively co-exist, as argued in Chapter 2.

23 Unless otherwise stated, discussion of the GATT-NGO Steering Committee is based on Wilkinson 1996.

24 See also Croome 1995: 276–77.

25 Except where otherwise stated, the account of the dolphin-tuna case and the campaign against US ratification of the Uruguay Round text is based on Danaher and Mark 2003.

26 Unless otherwise referenced, the account on the Canadian-USA Free Trade Agreement is based on Huyer 2004.

27 This was stated by Michelle Swenarchuk, of the Canadian Environmental Law Association that was part of the Pro-Canada Network (Huyer 2004: 55).

28 Business unionism refers to that sector of the labour movement that sees itself as a professional service improving its members' situation in their respective workplaces within a narrow remit of employment security, higher remuneration, and improved working conditions (Huyer 2004: 52). Wider social concerns are seen as a distraction from these basic demands and a misuse of their members' fees.

29 See also Bandy 2000: 232, 240–41.

30 See also Poitras and Robinson 1994; Babson 2000.

31 The question of how effective these side accords might be is the subject for another discussion. For discussion on this subject, see Grossman 2000: 76–77.

32 For a more detailed analysis of the MAI, see Egan 2001. Unless otherwise referenced, the account of contestation critical of the MAI is based on Johnston and Laxer 2003; and Egan 2001.

33 This statement can be viewed at www.twnside.org.sg/title/565-cn.htm (accessed February 2012).

34 Ibid.

35 Ibid.

36 Ibid.

37 A global group petition is a series of demands usually formed between a smaller set of campaigning groups, which is then formally endorsed by other campaigning groups. The value of such a petition is that it spreads awareness of an issue amongst groups, so that campaigning groups are effectively lobbying other campaigning groups to maximize their capacity. However, these petitions also help sediment relations into an equivalential chain, where often groups present the signature to such a joint statement as indicative of their identity. For more on these petitions, see Strange 2011a.

38 In addition to the trade agreements held within the WTO framework, OWINFS lists the Free Trade Area of the Americas (FTAA), the Africa Growth and Opportunity Act (AGOA), the Asian Pacific Economic Cooperation (APEC), and the Plan Puebla Panama (PPP). OWINFS sees these agreements as linked via all being part of the 'corporate-driven trade agenda'. This information was taken from their website, at www.ourworldisnotforsale.org (accessed July 2006).

39 On its website (www.ourworldisnotforsale.org), OWINFS describes itself as a 'loose grouping of organizations, activists and social movements worldwide fighting against the current model of corporate globalization embodied in global trading systems. OWINFS is committed to a sustainable, socially just, democratic and accountable multilateral trading system'.

40 E-mail listservs are e-mails distributed to a subscribed and typically private list of contacts. Usually, any subscribed member can contribute information, which includes a mixture of analysis of trade policy developments amongst member states, some relevant newspaper articles and strategy proposals, as well as general announcements relevant to meetings. The content of these e-mails tends to be informal, ad hoc, with little sense of hierarchical control, though key names dominate with particular individuals serving as information providers due to the research nature of their organization.

41 This is according to the OWINFS website: www.ourworldisnotforsale.org.

42 The statement was available at: www.twnside.org.sg/title/turn_cn.htm (accessed July 2006).

43 According to OWINFS website: www.ourworldisnotforsale.org.

44 The statement was available at: www.twnside.org.sg/title/turn_cn.htm (accessed July 2006).

45 Ibid.

46 The original text of the Singapore Ministerial declaration can be accessed online: www.wto.org/english/thewto_e/minist_e/min96_e/wtodec_e.htm (accessed December 2012).

47 Marrakech Agreement Establishing the World Trade Organization, reprinted in Qureshi 1996: 199.

48 Ibid., 197.

49 Ibid.

50 For discussion on the trade-labour debate in the WTO, see Wilkinson 1999.

5   The formation of new actors contesting the WTO

The example of anti-GATS campaigning

Introduction

When new actors appear in politics it may seem sudden but a lot has already taken place to make their political subjectivity possible. This was well demonstrated in the previous chapter. Certainly to be an actor in global trade governance, to contest its articulatory form, cannot be without a prior process. Relations must be formed between different political demands if activists are to be politicized around a new cause. Yet, to understand the emergence of collective action constitutive of new actors within the contestation of global trade governance, it is necessary to engage in the type of thicker analysis presented in this chapter. Drawing upon new research, this chapter tells the story of political activity targeting a specific WTO trade agreement – the General Agreement on Trade in Services (GATS). The discussion develops the account of new actors presented in the previous chapter, arguing that activity related to the GATS has been facilitated by earlier moments of collective action, including those around the MAI and the WTO Seattle Ministerial. This history had created an infrastructure of equivalential identities in the form of joint protest activities, global group petitions, and e-mail lists distributing critical analysis and news regarding ongoing developments in global trade governance. Analysing the formation of new actors within the contestation of global trade governance helps trace out the wider articulatory process in which the WTO is constituted, enabling appreciation of why/how identities are able to collectively form around an anti-GATS demand and provide a critical discursive context to the policy formation of GATS. The key point throughout is that 'actorness' – what it is to be an actor – is key to discourse and, in this book, the discursivity of global trade governance. It shows how disparate political demands and identities may be connected through an articulatory process of relation forming towards wider political phenomena.

Case study

The case study provides a detailed application of the same theoretical approach utilized to understand the more general emergence of the NGO identity with respect to the WTO, exhibiting its rearticulation. Therefore, a post-structuralist understanding of collective action as identity rearticulation modelled through Laclau and Mouffe's logics of equivalence and difference provides the basis for the analysis.[1] The analysis traces the emergence and sedimentation of a critical GATS identity.[2] Mobilization in response to the GATS 2000 negotiations has been 'global' in the sense that campaigning has formed and utilized coalition networks that exceed nation-state boundaries. However, the global identity of such activity is qualified by the empirical research,[3] which suggests the importance of the particular historical context local to different moments of critical GATS mobilization. To a large extent, much of the activity suggests more nationally or regionally focused identities (e.g. Austrian, European), though to deny the global construction of the mobilization would be to ignore the importance that this wider identity plays within the constitution of campaigning. Rather than arguing whether or not such collective action indicates the material existence of a 'global civil society', for example, this chapter – by focusing on the role of identity formation – considers how identities have come to be discursively linked to facilitate the collective action constitutive of new actors within the contestation of the WTO's management of trade. Whilst activity has differed widely, this does not mean that such alternate moments are not still part of a wider mobilization if understood from the perspective of their articulation. Information exchanges and joint demands have meant that identities in quite different geographical contexts have been positioned within the same critical articulatory process. It is the collective identities that emerge through this process that help facilitate the network linkages necessary to such contestation, and exhibit the articulatory process inherent to the WTO.

The task of translating a complex trade agreement into a critical mobilization has proven a challenge for campaigners, and by some has been seen as a serious impediment that has limited the scope and appeal of the campaign. That said, the chapter will argue that where activities have been apparently limited by this obstacle, it can best be partially explained as a consequence of the failure to form equivalential links. Where mobilization has taken place, the research shows that it is because campaigners have managed to form such links that activity has expanded to include a large number of political identities, including development organizations, trade unions, local government associations and environmental groups. An additional explanatory variable includes local historical conditions. As discussed in Chapter 1, discourse theory emphasizes the contextual dependence of political phenomena.

Emergence of a collective identity

Mobilization critical of the GATS has been chosen for the case study because it provides an empirical example of the emergence of a collective identity to contest global trade governance. It is not meant to suggest that such activity necessarily represents activity around other WTO regimes, such as that on

Trade-Related Aspects of Intellectual Property Rights (TRIPS), although many of the groups discussed have been active with respect to WTO policy formation agreements beyond just GATS. In this case study, the GATS provides the context for a detailed examination of how collective action constitutive of the emergence of new actors in the contestation of global trade governance is made possible. The emphasis is therefore upon the formation of equivalential links between political identities under a critical GATS demand rather offering an analysis of the policy agreement itself. Therefore, for example, where the chapter considers how groups critical of the GATS have tied their demands into a wider 'anti-privatization' demand, this is not to describe the character of the GATS but instead to map how a critique has been articulated. The distinction between the GATS and the GATS critique is central to the analysis. It is for this reason that the paper provides only an introduction to the GATS.

A very brief introduction to the GATS

Originally sedimented in 1994 as one of a series of formal trade agreements to be held within what would become the World Trade Organization (WTO), the GATS signalled the sedimentation of a new articulation of trade. Previously, tradable commodities had been defined as 'manufactured products, raw materials and agricultural products' (Krugman and Obstfield, in Sapir 1999: 51). Along with those WTO agreements that focused on such areas as 'investment measures' or 'intellectual property', the GATS was part of an attempt to redefine trade and, thus, governance.

The negotiations concluding in 1994 scheduled a second round of talks to begin on 1 January 2000. GATS 2000 – as it would be called – was to deal with the 'trickier issues' left unresolved in GATS 1994. Prior to the Uruguay Round, the management of trade was focused on tariffs placed by nation-states on foreign imports, though increasingly attention shifted to other barriers such as quotas used to limit such imports. In the case of services – which are non-physical – the idea of a trade barrier is more complex. Services are non-physical products – what are commonly described as 'something you can buy and sell but cannot drop on your foot' (Drake and Nicolaïdis 1992: 43, 43, ft 2), such as telecommunications, accountancy, broadcasting, construction, advertising, banking, health, education, transport, energy and water utilities.[4] Often the most important feature determining the shape of such activity is domestic regulation which, as Sapir says, 'almost always creates a powerful trade barrier', whether it is legitimated on health, cultural or other public good grounds (Sapir 1999: 53). The position of domestic regulation within the GATS is contested. Proponents of the GATS point to the preamble to the agreement, which states that the GATS recognizes 'the right of Members to regulate, and to introduce new regulations, on the supply of services within their territories in order to meet national policy objectives' (quoted in Sapir 1999: 55). However, the WTO Secretariat acknowledges that the GATS 'imposes constraints … on the use of unnecessarily restrictive or discriminatory requirements in scheduled sectors' (WTO Secretariat 2001: 6). It continues: 'Governments may thus be required to complement market-opening measures with a review of domestic regulation' (ibid.: 6). On the issue of domestic regulation, the GATS has been criticized on the grounds that the above-quoted preamble has questionable legal status, in the context of much more legally binding rules within the main body of the agreement (Sinclair and Grieshaber-Otto 2002: 44). It is the question of how to articulate and implement those rules that is at the heart of the debate over the GATS.

The GATS is a far-reaching agreement, exemplified in the attempt to categorize the four different ways in which a service may be supplied. These four 'modes of supply' are: 1 'cross-border', e.g. electricity sent from Turkey to Israel; 2 'consumption abroad', e.g. a Belgium cancer patient receiving chemotherapy in Germany; 3 the establishment of 'commercial presence', e.g. a French water company running a water treatment works in Bolivia; and, 4 'movement of natural persons', e.g. a South African physiotherapist working in a British hospital (Sapir 1999: 53). The issues left unresolved in GATS 1994 that would be passed on for further contestation in the GATS 2000 negotiations were, amongst others: movement of natural persons; subsidies; government procurement; and domestic regulation (Sauvé and Stern 2000: 9).

The critique of the GATS is complex, but it hinges upon two central issues: 1 liberalization of services such as finance is seen as principally benefiting the developed countries, because many so-called 'developing' countries have only weak industry in this sector; and, 2 the large scope of what constitutes a service means that politically sensitive sectors such as broadcasting, education, water and health potentially fall under its remit.[5]

Articulating the critique of GATS

GATS has been described as a 'sleeper issue'.[6] During the Uruguay Round, although there had been resistance against the GATS from certain Member-state delegations, there appears to have been little non-state contestation until at least several years after the formal creation of the agreement within the wider set of new rules that marked the birth of the WTO in January 1995. This lack of activity has been explained by Tony Clarke – already introduced in Chapter 4 as a veteran of campaigning critical of CUSFTA, NAFTA and the MAI, and later to be heavily involved within critical GATS campaigning – as a consequence of the high degree of ambiguity in the GATS at this stage, where the question of what would actually be covered by this new services agreement would not be the subject of negotiations until a second round of services talks set to begin in 2000. There appears to have been no non-state political mobilization critical of the GATS during the Uruguay Round. Despite the WTO appearing weaker after Seattle, the GATS emerged seemingly unscathed with the launch of the GATS 2000 negotiations on 1 January 2000.

Rearticulation of pre-existing equivalential chains

The political movement critical of the GATS would be made possible via a rearticulation of the chains of equivalence developed in the earlier campaigns against the MAI and the Seattle WTO Ministerial. However, this required a process in which GATS was articulated as a problem. This process consisted of a series of reports by different groups which connected a demand critical of the GATS to a wider series of demands. In effect, this worked to politicize GATS – rearticulating what was otherwise a seemingly abstract and highly technical international trade agreement. This took place through the infrastructure of contacts made possible by the equivalential chains formed in the MAI and Seattle campaigns. This is most evident in the role that members of the OWINFS network would play in GATS campaigning.

PSI and EI

In March 1999, the international trade union bodies Public Services International (PSI) and Education International (EI) co-published[7] *The WTO and the Millennium Round: What is at Stake for Public Education?*,[8] which articulated the GATS as a threat to publicly funded and regulated education. At the time, PSI was the only trade union body to be a member of OWINFS, acting as a bridge between the otherwise potentially distinct identities of trade union and NGO.[9]

The report warned that GATS risks increasing dependence on foreign education providers, a reduction in local culture, standardization, and a loss of sovereignty – all of which were argued to harm developing countries the most.[10] The winners in this hypothesis were 'a handful of large transnational corporations'.[11] GATS was argued to promote liberalization and thus create job insecurity.[12] Additionally, it was presented as creating a 'democratic deficit' by removing regulation of services from the domestic state to a 'world government'.[13] The conclusion stated:

> Major trade agreements, as should by now be apparent to all, have repercussions in every area of collective life and therefore there is no reason for them to remain the exclusive domain of technocrats, be they in the employ of the WTO, national governments or transnational companies. These plans concern all social players and must be debated openly and democratically.[14]

To evidence this 'threat', the report provides a case study of New Zealand's negotiating strategy on education in the GATS as an example of 'secrecy' in the process, as well as a 'risky gamble'.[15] This is supported by tracing the threat back to a similar critique produced in what the report describes as 'a study conducted by Jane Kelsey, a professor at Auckland University'.[16] A reference is given to a book chapter titled 'The Globalization of Tertiary Education:

Implications of GATS', which appeared in *Cultural Politics and the University,* in 1997.[17] Kelsey is the national president of New Zealand's Association of University Teachers (AUT NZ), and apart from being used to provide legitimacy to the PSI-EI report, her earlier work appears to have been important in shaping the problematization of GATS that appears in the PSI-EI publication.[18]

A second report co-published by EI and PSI followed in June 1999, this time focusing on health services.[19] The issues of concern raised are slightly expanded and include: 1 'loss of national sovereignty'; 2 prioritization of trade over 'health'; 3 'extended private influence on international health policies'; 4 'extended privatisation'; 5 'loss of job security'; 6 'reduction of democratic decision-making'; 7 'reduction of working conditions'; 8 unequal distribution of health services ('cream skimming').[20] This later report is more comprehensive than that on education, providing a chart detailing specific health-related GATS commitments made by different countries in the Uruguay Round. It also concludes with a list of suggested actions to trade unions affiliated to either PSI or EI, including supporting the International Confederation of Free Trade Unions (ICFTU) position at the then upcoming Third WTO Ministerial Conference to be hosted by Seattle, and lobbying domestic governments and engaging in network activity with health-related non-governmental organizations (NGOs).[21]

Despite this initial articulation of GATS as a problem, it did not feature in the protests against the Seattle WTO Ministerial Conference in November 1999. The slow development of mobilization critical of the GATS is perhaps not surprising considering the extent to which trade has – since 1934 and the USA's Reciprocal Trade Agreements Act – been increasingly sedimented as a 'legal-technical' issue.[22] This also illustrates the slow process of rearticulating the pre-existing chains of equivalence so as to adopt a critical GATS demand.

Though not forming part of the protests at Seattle, representatives from EI and PSI were actively contesting GATS during the Ministerial via organizing seminars and giving speeches repeating their joint research to individuals from other groups. In effect, this is where GATS was being articulated as a problem.

GATS as the 'next MAI'

GATS was articulated as the 'next MAI', deliberately tapping into the equivalential chains developed via the earlier campaign.[23] In 1999, Ellen Gould – a Canadian activist – wrote an article that was distributed to other groups, which began with the following paragraph:

> The lions are on the prowl, again. Just when victory over the Multilateral Agreement on Investment (MAI) had given us a chance to catch our breath, a new menace has been spotted in the tall grass of the World Trade Organization (WTO). The General Agreement on Trade in Services (GATS) may yet prove to be the way the world's corporate lions get their MAI.[24]

According to individuals from many of the groups that would become actively critical of the GATS, the MAI was more important than anything else in terms of creating the context in which GATS could become the focus of a critical political mobilization.[25] Mike Waghorne of PSI views the earlier campaign against the MAI as constituting the moment when much of what would facilitate critical GATS campaigning became possible, in terms of politicization as well as resources, stating:

> I think the MAI was quite similar in terms of both raising people's awareness about some of these international agreements – especially finance and investment agreements, and trade agreements – but also in raising people's awareness of the way in which you could use the internet in order to campaign globally. It put a very significant resource at people's fingertips that they've never had before.[26]

Whilst the Internet had pre-existed the MAI campaign, it was the linkages formed through that earlier mobilization that gave life to a community of websites and e-mail exchanges that would facilitate the dissemination of information constitutive of much of the collective action behind critical GATS campaigning. It is therefore important not to focus too much on the role of the Internet alone, but on the linkages through which it would achieve a central role. This role was developed in the MAI activity, and entered into a GATS critique via the electronic publication of such materials as were appearing from PSI-EI. Added to this was a rapidly growing body of critique from Canada.

The role of Canadian activists in early activity critical of the GATS is explained by Tony Clarke of Polaris as a consequence of contestation around CUSFTA and NAFTA,[27] stating that the 'experience that we went through ... had a real impact upon mindsets about trade, and what trade can do, and in terms of changing an awful lot, and the impact that can have on people's lives'.[28]

Ellen Gould was part of the Council of Canadians (CofC) – a formal network of local groups in Canada – which had been prominent within the MAI campaign and was an active member of OWINFS. She produced a substantial body of critical reports on the GATS, expanding on the education- and health-focused critiques of GATS. Gould articulated GATS as a threat to the power of local government. She argued that GATS threatened the ability of local government to regulate planning permission, for example, because it could be seen as a 'trade barrier' to foreign service providers such as supermarkets.[29] Other Canadian groups involved in the anti-MAI campaign and Seattle were also active in rearticulating a GATS critique along demands similar to those used against the MAI. The Canadian Centre for Policy Alternatives (CCPA) published *GATS: How the WTO New 'Services' Negotiations Threaten Democracy*.[30] Written by Scott Sinclair, the short book provided what was then the most comprehensive critique of the GATS, as well as prioritizing the 'democratic deficit' argument that had been present within the PSI-EI co-publications, and repeating the calls for 'assessment' and 'transparency' in the MAI campaign.

OWINFS

A critical GATS demand was further sedimented in the equivalential chains that had empowered the earlier campaigns when a new OWINFS global group petition appeared that included a specific GATS demand. This petition – titled 'Shrink or Sink!'[31] – was articulated to bridge an emerging cleavage between those groups that were critical of the WTO and those that advocated its abolition.[32] Being a signatory to this statement indicates OWINFS membership. It makes 11 key demands targeted at 'our governments', which include:

1 'No WTO expansion';
2 'WTO Hands off: Protect Basic Social Rights and environmental sustainability';
3 'Gut GATS: Protect Basic Social Services and public protections';
4 'Stop Corporate Patent Protectionism – Seeds & Medicine are Human Needs, not Commodities';
5 'No patents on life';
6 'Food is a Basic Human Right: Stop the Agriculture Agreement Fraud and Calamity';
7 'No Investment Liberalization';
8 'Fair Trade: Special and Differential Treatment';
9 'Prioritize Social Rights and the Environment';
10 'Democratize Decision-Making'; and
11 'Dispute the System'.[33]

The statement thus constructs a complex series of equivalential chains under the empty signifier 'Shrink or Sink!'. Each of these 11 demands includes a paragraph creating further equivalential chains so that, for example, in the agriculture demand (number six) a link is made between the different demands for reducing subsidies and ending 'import liberalization'.[34] The global group petition includes a series of general criticisms of the WTO regarding its 'democratic, transparency and accountability deficits', and a bias towards 'wealthy governments and the corporate lobbies'.[35] The equivalential chain of demands is therefore constructed against a frontier with the 'other' embodied by a shorter chain of equivalences between WTO, wealthy governments and corporate lobbies. The petition concludes with a pledge for each of the signatories, to mobilize people 'within our countries', and to 'support other people and countries who do so with international solidarity campaigns'.[36] This statement would be signed by 429 groups.[37]

Apparent campaigning success against the MAI and the Seattle WTO Ministerial had created a potential problem for those involved because a question remained as to how to continue activity whilst not adopting demands with any degree of specificity that might limit the equivalential chain. The 'Shrink or Sink!' statement was one answer, providing an equivalential link between two otherwise potentially contradictory demands. Clare Joy of the UK-based group World Development Movement (WDM), which was actively involved in this process, has argued that the 'victory' at Seattle created both confidence for further campaigns but also many questions regarding where to take future activity, stating:

> After Seattle, two things were clear. One was that the victory there gave people a lot of encouragement, it gave people a feeling that actually we can change things at this [global] level. We can influence things at this level. And, to empower people in that sense. But, I think on the other hand, it wasn't so clear about what to do next. We all went into Seattle with a general anti-WTO message, or a general reform the WTO message, wherever you were coming from. A lot of us came out of Seattle with an awareness that we need to be a bit more specific. We needed to develop our specific arguments about which bits of the WTO were wrong, and why.[38]

Another response to apparent success was the creation of a regional sub-body of OWINFS amongst groups in European Union member states. These groups operated in countries that were represented at the WTO via an aggregated negotiating position held by the European Commission. EU groups that had signed the 'Shrink or Sink!' statement formed a regional network called Seattle to Brussels (S2B).[39] One of its founders, Alexandra Wandel of Friends of the Earth Europe (FoEE), has described the network as:

> [F]ormed in the aftermath of the Seattle WTO Ministerial Conference because we felt the need for more European coordination, and we … unite … very diverse groups of people and organizations, coming from environmental groups, development groups, women's groups, farmers' groups, trade union-related groups, research groups, etc, so it's a broad range of groups coming together, and what really unites us is our jointly challenging … *Europe's corporate-led trade and investment liberalisation agenda*, but we also want to promote the alternative and to work towards the development of a *sustainable socially-accountable democratic trading system*.[40]

In this passage, there is evident use of an equivalential logic and the drawing of a frontier against the 'other', as illustrated in Figure 5.1.

To politicize trade, it was necessary to dislocate it from its abstraction as a technical issue, which meant confronting that technicalization. The GATS provided a means to do that, as a WTO agreement around which specific arguments could be articulated. Within European activity critical of GATS, one of the most prominent activists would be Clare Joy of WDM, who helped to co-found S2B. Despite being at the centre of much mobilization around GATS, she states:

I'm not actually that interested in GATS. What I'm interested in is the extent to which we can educate, empower and inform, and say that there are places where the market stops. And GATS is about that.[41]

It is in this context that campaigning around the GATS should be understood – not as focused specifically on one WTO agreement, but using it as a vehicle for wider demands. This fits within the model of such campaigning as formed via equivalential logics, where the central demand increasingly becomes emptied of specific content by its unifying role.

Activity in the United Kingdom

The development of activity within the United Kingdom formed an important part of wider European campaigning critical of the GATS. This was undertaken by WDM and People & Planet (P&P), a UK network based in sixth form colleges and university campuses consisting of students campaigning on the environment and development. P&P also attended meetings of the S2B network. There was close collaboration by WDM with smaller groups elsewhere in Europe, such as Corporate Europe Observatory in Amsterdam. According to Clare Joy, WDM were reluctant to launch a campaign until they were sure that a critique of GATS was being adopted by campaigning groups in what she identifies as the South.[42] This involved collaboration with Equations in

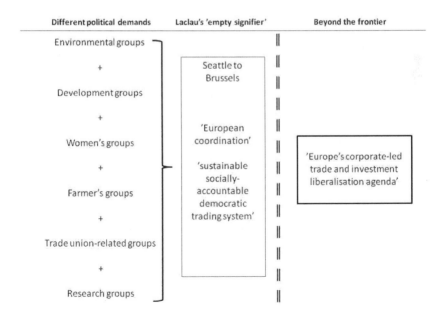

Figure 5.1 The articulation of the 'Seattle to Brussels' Network

India (working on improving labour conditions for Indian workers in tourism), Third World Network (TWN, based in Malaysia, acting as a bridge between Asian governments and Western NGOs), and Third World Network Africa (TWNA, the African branch of TWN, focusing on African governments). To increase global spread of its analysis, WDM published its GATS research in Spanish as well as English.[43] Jointly hosted with Friends of the Earth and P&P, WDM officially launched its campaign on GATS in November 2000, at an event in which talks were given by the high-profile social critics Naomi Klein and George Monbiot. The event would have taken place later but was brought forward to meet Naomi Klein's schedule, emphasizing the importance placed on attracting the attention of the journalists invited to attend the event.[44]

P&P did not launch its campaign until 2001, though its first piece of research was published in 2000 by its campaigns officer Jess Worth, titled *The Threat to Higher Education: A Briefing on Current World Trade Organization Negotiations*.[45] The report carried a quotation from EI on its front page which presented the GATS as a 'threat' to a 'quality public education system'.[46] Worth has said that she viewed 'education' as a means to engage in a wider critique, stating:

[O]ur thinking was ... how can we have the biggest impact, and that ... turned into a very UK-centric, very European campaign, specifically targeting higher education, and we were only partly doing that because ... the implications for higher education were very negative ... We were also doing it just to more generally make GATS controversial within the UK and within Europe, because once you open up that space, you can then start talking about developing countries' access to water and electricity and how negative GATS would be for other countries, but you can only do that if there's already that space to have those kind of discussions.[47]

The articulation of the GATS as anti-democratic and privatization that was present in the PSI-EI joint publications was repeated in P&P's first report on the GATS, illustrated in this passage from the document:

The GATS agreement could mark a dramatic step in the direction of a wholly *privatised HE* [Higher Education] sector. Surely such significant decisions should not be made behind the *closed doors* of the *controversial* WTO, but should be placed in the *public* domain, subject to *vigorous public debate*? This paper therefore calls for extensive research into the implications of GATS, and awareness raising within the government and the wider Higher Education sector.[48]

Other than the PSI-EI research, this report relied much on information obtained via contacts in the S2B network, as well as information provided by the Council of Canadians' Ellen Gould, as well as Scott Sinclair of CCPA.[49]

It also formed the basis of an alliance formed between not only P&P and WDM, but also with several trade unions representing higher education workers, including the National Union of Students (NUS), and the Association of University Teachers (AUT UK).

Clare Joy from WDM has commented that launching a GATS campaign was complicated because many potential partner organizations were initially uncomfortable to get involved. In the United Kingdom, the position of development organizations is represented to the government via the UK Trade Network (UKTN), which has traditionally been dominated by establishment groups including Oxfam, Christian Aid, and Catholic Agency for Overseas Development (CAFOD). Their reticence is explained by Joy as follows:

> I think, that a lot of UK groups weren't willing to accept that there was a problem with GATS. And, I think, [they] were nervous … [that], when you start to oppose the GATS, you're actually opposing quite a funda-mental ideology about how the market works, and where the market stops. And I think until that point, a lot of NGOs refused to take a position on actually [that] there are places where the market shouldn't go. Which is not that radical, but it was seen to be quite radical. And so, there was resistance, I think, from a lot of the mainstream NGOs.[50]

Evident here is the attempt to link two pre-existing equivalential chains – the UKTN, which had formed in the context of the GATT Uruguay Round, and the network formed through the MAI critique, and the difficulties experienced restricting the strength of the political movement.[51] Mobilization was slowed by this because each of these groups had access to a large mem-bership base of individuals identified as concerned about development, as well as status in lobbying the government on development-related trade matters, meaning that until these groups became active on GATS, it would be hard to articulate the agreement as a threat to development. This made the role of S2B particularly important for Clare Joy, stating:

> When you've got the dominant NGOs in the UK saying we're not sure this is a big issue, you really do need security, to say that we are right, and I think that's where Seattle to Brussels was really important. That we built our own confidence across Europe … And you can often under-estimate how important that is, just actually knowing that you're on the right track, and that your analysis is correct.[52]

The experience of WDM illustrates the importance of links between groups but also the role of those links in helping to shape the formation of demands and, thus, the identity and emergence of campaigning.

WDM worked within these conditions by trying to raise awareness of GATS within the UK parliament. This was achieved as early as January 2001, via an Early Day Motion (EDM 260) tabled by Dr Phyllis Starkey MP, which demanded 'assessment' of the impact of GATS prior to any expansion.[53] That EDM proved a success, which despite being no more than a petition of members of Parliament (MPs) because of it lacking any legal basis, it proved the third most popular EDM tabled that parliamentary session, signed by 262 MPs. Clare Joy and other campaigners at WDM encouraged Dr Starkey to write the EDM, providing guidance on its content, as well as contacting other MPs who were considered 'friendly' to the group.[54] These MPs were spread across the political parties, which was seen by Clare Joy as extremely important in giving legitimacy to any EDM.[55] Those MPs who were supportive went on to encourage fellow MPs to sign up. As well as this 'top-down' approach, WDM used what Joy calls a 'bottom-up' approach, explaining:

> [W]e did a campaigning action with our local members, who then informed their MPs about the EDM, and encouraged their MPs to sign up. So you've got it coming from two places. You've got the bottom-up, WDM Lough-borough writing to their MP, whoever it happens to be, saying 'sign up to this EDM'. At the same time you've got those MPs within the party who've signed up, that are sponsoring the EDM, getting their colleagues to sign up as well.[56]

As 2001 progressed, the GATS critique was mainstreamed, moving from the fringes to a more central place within activity by groups campaigning around the management of trade. The influence of the UKTN diminished with the emergence of the Trade Justice Movement (TJM), which was originally set up to help coordinate campaigning on trade amongst development groups but increasingly became representative of the groups.[57] The TJM included a critique of GATS within its founding set of demands that called for 'assessment' of the GATS prior to any expansion.[58] The TJM included P&P and WDM as founding members, as well as Oxfam, CAFOD and Christian Aid. Important to this shift of GATS into the mainstream of development politics was the role of Save the Children (StC) and John Hillary, who had previously worked on a freelance basis for WDM and had now moved over to StC. The emergence of the TJM was seen as a significant moment in the mainstreaming of a critical GATS demand.[59] The TJM ran a 'mass lobby' of the UK Parliament, where members of the constituent groups met their MPs at Westminster in June 2002 with a series of 'trade justice' demands, including a critique of the GATS. For Clare Joy of WDM, that was an important point for anti-GATS activity with regard to UK politicians.[60]

Mainstreaming a GATS critique

Then working for UK-based StC, Hillary produced the report *The Wrong Model: GATS, Trade Liberalisation and Children's Right to Health*, in 2001, which demanded assessment of the current impact of GATS as well as changes to the agreement text so that there was less ambiguity regarding the right of WTO Members to regulate and subsidize public services (Hillary 2001: 49–50). Much of the research within this early report was based on the material produced jointly by PSI and EI.[61] Whilst working within StC, Hillary was important in that his work helped to sediment the GATS as a campaigning problem. StC was a member of the UKTN as well as being an established organization, seen as mainstream. If StC could criticize the GATS, so could other mainstream groups. Although Oxfam, CAFOD and Christian Aid never placed much emphasis on GATS, all three adopted a demand critical of the GATS within their general position on development and trade. A critical GATS demand had by now picked up a significant degree of momentum, evidenced in its adoption by a growing number of groups. Rather than necessarily producing their own individual research, many groups became reliant upon material developed by groups such as WDM who had been amongst the first to produce critical analysis. Even in the case of large organizations with a large research capacity this was true, as in the case of Oxfam which, according to Hillary, began to include a critical GATS demand within their wider trade demands but, in so doing, relied much on the help of the smaller groups who had originally developed that critique.[62] Thus, the articulatory process in which equivalential links were formed occurred gradually.

The ecologist network group Friends of the Earth International (FOEI), and its regional and national offices, became involved through its own policy/ research personnel working on the WTO in Geneva who articulated GATS as presenting certain 'environmental challenges'.[63] In 2002 FOEI's report entitled *Primer on the General Agreement on Trade in Services*, pointing to the process by which governments were required to justify environmental regulations with respect to services, GATS was articulated as creating a 'regulatory hurdle [that] will likely place a chill on future efforts to protect the environment and may lead to environmental laws and regulations being overturned by WTO bodies'.[64] The report presents a series of examples to support this assertion, such as 'GATS rules will make it increasingly difficult to adopt and enforce environmental and natural resource protections'.[65] The general articulation of GATS as a threat to environmental protection was repeated in other reports within the Friends of the Earth network, such as in an FOE United States document where it was stated that 'Governments and citizens will be increasingly constrained in their efforts to protect the natural world from harmful service operations'.[66] More generally, this reiterated the articulation of GATS as an over-prioritization of trade over other issues, whether they be the environment, or education and health as in the PSI-EI perspective.

The articulation of GATS as perverting good governance provided a broad umbrella by which to incorporate other demands, including gender. According to Amandine Bach of Women in Development Europe (WIDE), a critical GATS demand proved useful for those groups already working on gender and trade.[67] Reports articulating this equivalential link were developed by groups such as the International Gender and Trade Network (IGTN) and some of its member groups, such as WIDE. IGTN was itself part of OWINFS, and its presence was reflected where a gender demand was incorporated within more general position papers such as the 'Shrink or Sink!' statement.[68] GATS provided a means to sediment the gender and trade link. The involvement of WIDE was made possible via a particular project already underway, which was intended to provide a gender perspective in debates around the privatization of public goods and services, and so in this sense a further equivalential link is represented here between GATS and privatization.[69]

A critical GATS demand can therefore be seen at the centre of a developing equivalential chain, with attempts to incorporate such other demands as anti-MAI, education, health, public services, democracy, anti-privatization, environment, gender, development and so on, within its discursive formation. With all of the demands, and well illustrated in the anti-MAI demand, is the role that these individual demands play at the centre of other equivalential chains. The next section will consider the sedimentation of this articulatory process.

The sedimentation of an anti-GATS equivalential chain

The articulation of a critical GATS demand from a particular demand to a unifying demand – the empty signifier – of an equivalential chain was a gradual process, but this articulation appeared increasingly sedimented where embodied within a series of devices, including: GATS-specific global group petitions; lobbying of government; e-mail lists; international and regional meetings; telephone conference calls; public protests; a website, and open debates with government officials supportive of the GATS. Each of these expressions of collective action critical of the GATS was facilitated via a particular equivalential chain, though it should not be assumed that there was simply one chain. In this respect, Peter Hardstaff of WDM has stated that whilst networks like Seattle to Brussels were important, and though there was often overlap with certain individuals or groups present in multiple networks, 'there's no kind of *one* network'.[70] This point is important in that when arguing the existence of equivalential chains constituting the collective action of critical GATS campaigning, the assertion is not that there was any one chain in particular. Instead, such collective action should be understood as a fluid process open to rearticulation, with the different moments of collective action (e.g. a joint statement, a protest, an e-mail distribution list) representative of certain moments of sedimentation. This is particularly important with respect to the process in which certain demands become the empty signifier of the wider equivalential sequence. In other words, GATS campaigning was responsive to hegemonic struggles where, for example, a development demand might be more dominant than an environmentalist demand, though both remain present. The different moments can be grouped together as constitutive of a wider mobilization to the extent that they repeat a certain sedimentation that might be labelled as critical of the GATS, as is done here.

Internet and e-mail lists

In January 2001, a website was created to provide access to the growing literature of critical reports on the GATS and ongoing developments in the negotiations. This was created as a collaboration between the Transnational Institute (TNI) and Corporate Europe Observatory (CEO), both based in Amsterdam, though in practice the website – GATSWatch.org – was the work of Erik Wesselius of CEO and Friends of the Earth Netherlands. According to Wesselius, his own perception at the time was that GATS had the potential to become the focus of a large campaign between many groups and so required its own critical website.[71] TNI were interested in being part of a project on the WTO and they had an already developed interest in public services, so that GATS became a means to combine the two areas.[72] Wesselius also set up an e-mail list (GATSCrit) for distributing news, which could be subscribed to by sending an e-mail to Wesselius via the GATSWatch website. He also set up a series of closed e-mail lists used for sharing strategy ideas, such as proposing joint protests, as well as distributing basic information such as mobile telephone numbers of other people working in groups critical of the GATS (e.g. GATS-Strat, GATS-Euro). The establishment of this GATS-specific communications infrastructure has been described as very important by those involved in the mobilization.[73] Wesselius himself has argued that whereas information on certain WTO issues is available through reading a daily newspaper, the media proved a relatively poor resource with respect to the GATS negotiations.[74] E-mail lists such as GATSCrit, he argues, have helped to bring together 'a community of ... people who work with different organizations who are pretty well-informed about what's going on with GATS'.[75] E-mail lists are also seen to overcome some of the problems encountered in physical meetings where there is a very limited amount of time in which to share information and discuss strategy.[76]

STOP the GATS Attack Now!

The first GATS-specific global group petition was launched in March 2001, under the name 'STOP the GATS Attack Now!' and with 596 signatory organizations from 63 countries.[77] The statement was presented as a collective project, though some leadership came from the Canadian-based Polaris Institute within the context of the OWINFS network.[78] Polaris argued the need for such a joint statement, producing the early drafts and coordinating suggested amendments, and helped to form the links necessary to get the group signatures.[79] Other OWINFS members, including PSI, fed into the re-drafting process as well as gathering signatures from other groups.[80]

The 'Stop the GATS Attack Now!' statement warns that the GATS negotiations threaten to:

> [R]adically restructure the role of government regarding public access to essential social services world wide to the detriment of the public interest and democracy itself.[81]

This general theme is maintained but expanded so as to claim that the GATS 2000 will impact on social rights, as well as sectors including the environment, culture, natural resources, drinking water, health care, education, transportation, social security, postal delivery and a variety of municipal services. The statement calls for a halt to the GATS negotiations until seven demands are met, which it lists as: 1 an assessment of the impact of GATS; 2 confirmation of 'the role and responsibility of governments to provide public services ensuring basic rights and needs of their citizens, based on UN Charters'; 3 to prevent pressure being applied against domestic regulation related to public interest laws and safety standards; 4 to 'guarantee the right of governments to require ironclad safeguards for public services that may be threatened by global trade and investment rules'; 5 to provide incentives and resources to ensure that all people receive public services 'based on peoples' needs rather than on ability to pay'; 6 to ensure citizen organizations can participate in the formation of government positions and negotiation of multilateral trade/investment rules; and, 7 to ensure 'rights and responsibilities of governments to enact and carry out laws' to protect environment, health, social well-being, and that such rules/regulations can be formed with participation of 'citizens' groups in all member countries'.[82]

The statement represents a complex equivalential chain between several hundred organizations, though based on the seven demands it is possible to represent, as in Figure 5.2.

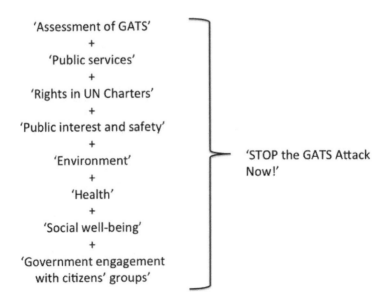

Figure 5.2 The equivalential sequence in the STOP the GATS Attack Now! global group petition

Mike Waghorne of PSI has said that the value of a global group petition is that it helps to raise awareness of an issue amongst groups as well as mainstreaming a demand so that governments are not able to dismiss it as on the margins.[83] However, he also argues that a potential problem is that activity for many groups stops at the level of adding their signature, with no following action.[84] Different groups that have signed a joint statement will clearly have quite different degrees of involvement with that process as well as any resulting activity. In this same respect, quite obviously not all the demands present under a critical GATS demand can be said to be equally active. When discussing the formation of an equivalential chain, the argument is not that the demands are equal, but that they are articulated as equivalential, meaning that they tendentially merge under the unifying demand – the empty signifier. Global group petitions serve various purposes, but the act of drafting the statement is, as Clare Joy of WDM has said:

> [An important and] painful political process [in its own right], where you're constantly vying over the messages that you want to get across. Trying to do that within a national context is hard enough. Trying to do it globally actually brings to the forefront some of the political disagreements in a coalition, and that's actually a really healthy process.[85]

The process of bringing political disagreements to the 'forefront' relates to the other side of the logic of equivalence – the logic of difference – without which the equivalential chain could not operate. Global group petitions thus serve the dual purpose of 'agreement' (the logic of equivalence) and 'disagreement' (the logic of difference).

In combination with the petition was a meeting and press conference held in Geneva, organized by the Polaris Institute and attended by groups from Africa, Asia, Europe, North and South America in March 2001. Other activities included joint publications such as the July 2001 report *GATS and Democracy*, produced through the S2B network and edited by John Hillary on behalf of WDM, which referred back to this action.[86] The document also offered readers the chance to learn more via subscribing to S2B's general e-mail list, sos-wto-eu.

In 2001 the WTO published *GATS – Fact and Fiction*, which argued that criticism of the GATS by civil society groups consisted of '[s]care stories [which] are invented and unquestioningly repeated, however implausible'.[87] This publication explicitly refers to WDM and PSI-EI. In part, this was seen to give WDM in particular, as a small organization, new status.[88] For PSI-EI the matter was more serious as both organizations had, since the publication of their initial concerns in 1999, been actively involved in dialogue with the WTO Secretariat.[89] The document made no reference to these discussions, for which PSI-EI threatened to sue the WTO. In response, the WTO withdrew its criticism of PSI-EI.[90] The value of GATSWatch and the e-mail lists (such as GATSCrit) also became evident in the context of *GATS – Fact and Fiction*, when they were used to facilitate a rapid counter-report. This was made possible after an urgent e-mail call was made on the GATSCrit list, distributing the WTO report prior to its public release. The report was first released to journalists before campaigners and so the matter of timing was highly significant. In response, a critique of the WTO document was produced by Friends of the Earth International, which was then published on GATSWatch.[91]

Polaris was actively engaged in forging links with groups outside Canada, where according to Tony Clarke:

> We ... programmatically worked at developing the capacities of our partner groups, and so forth, in both India and South Africa, [critically] to address [GATS] issues.[92]

This included organizing workshops criticizing GATS, as well as producing 'various types of tools to be used in those countries in collaboration with partner groups'.[93] In Korea, Polaris' Tony Clarke spoke on GATS as a threat to public services, at an event organized by the Korean Federation of Transportation, Public and Social Services Workers' Unions (KPSU).[94]

In 2002, the European Social Forum at Florence included several panels on GATS where European campaigners were able to meet and reaffirm their group identity.[95] Groups such as Friends of the Earth Europe collaborated with other groups, including PSI, to organize these public presentations critical of the GATS.[96] In the UK, WDM published *At Your Services: The Impact of the General Agreement on Trade in Services on Local Government*, which repeated the local-government critique developed in Canada. This critique was already active within France, via the Association for the Taxation of Financial Transaction for the Aid of Citizens (ATTAC France). ATTAC France is a network of local groups and so was well placed to articulate GATS as a threat to local municipalities. The campaign developed into a drive to create GATS-free zones, which signalled when the council of a local municipality had passed a motion to central government demanding an assessment of GATS as well as a greater say in negotiations.[97] ATTAC groups across Europe were active in similar campaigns in not only France, but also Switzerland, Austria and Belgium. The technique of creating motions for local councils to sign in opposition to GATS as a threat to the provision of public services had direct lineage back to the anti-MAI activity in the late 1990s, when many local councils were lobbied to sign resolutions critical of the MAI.[98]

One of the most significant events in the campaigning took place in April 2002, when WDM and CEO managed successfully to analyse and distribute a leaked document showing what requests the European Union had made of other WTO Member states in the GATS negotiations. Taken up by groups well beyond Europe, the leak was used to support them in lobbying their own governments.[99] This was a direct use of methods tried and tested in the anti-MAI campaign.

In October, the UK government's Department for Trade and Industry (DTI) began a public consultation on the GATS that was open for submissions through to January 2003. This was a key moment for Jess Worth of P&P, taking it as a sign that the campaigns were having an impact.[100] Clare Joy of WDM saw the process as relatively disappointing because the DTI followed the process by producing its own document stating how the critics were wrong.[101] Almost as soon as the DTI announced its own public consultation, the European Parliament launched its own public hearing, titled 'GATS: The Future of Services'. Whilst neither event met the frequently repeated call for an assessment of GATS, they made it clear that the campaigners had an impact upon policy makers. Despite the ability of the DTI to choose how it responded to its critics, Clare Joy does see the UK public consultation as useful in the sense that, she says:

> [I]n terms of being able to look at challenging something as mammoth as a trade agreement, and then have bite-size chunks that represent small victories, that was really important.[102]

In her perspective, Joy sees the consultation as something that the DTI were reluctant to do. Additionally, the UK consultation was seen to be a problem for the European Commission which, Joy claims on the basis of her own information, was concerned at the potential of a public consultation taking place in every one of the EU member states, particularly after Sweden followed the UK in hosting its own process. The European Commission's consultation was thus, for Joy, a stronger sign of her campaign having an impact.[103]

A further reason why the DTI consultation was important for groups like WDM was as a 'way of bringing in the trade unions ... [who] issued a response to that consultation. And it was a very practical way in which they could get involved in the campaign, and so the government, by issuing that public consultation, offered us a way of engaging the trade unions in a more solid way, in that they could actually do something'.[104] For Jess Worth, the consultation provided expression to the 'breadth of the opposition, the concern with GATS, within the UK', so that P&P were able to provide critique to be used by several of the education trade unions. This fitted into what Worth has described as a 'domino effect' strategy, of targeting the WTO via the UK government, stating:

> [W]e felt that was our best hope of having an impact. If we tried the European Union would we have any influence? Not necessarily. If we targeted [European Commissioner for Trade] Pascal Lamy, would we have any influence? Probably not. If we targeted the WTO, certainly we wouldn't have any influence. Because the UK government is such a key player, particularly in GATS, because it's the second largest services exporter in the world, so second only to the US ... Then we felt that

actually, if we could cause a controversy about the GATS within the UK government, then that would be much more powerful.[105]

For both Clare Joy and Jess Worth, the DTI consultation represented opening up a certain space for further contestation for a wider set of critical demands including trade unions and development organizations.[106]

In February 2003, the European Commission publicly announced that it would drop education, health and broadcasting from its GATS requests. This was seen by Jess Worth[107] as a victory and came on the day of a pre-planned mass protest in Brussels, organized by WDM and trade unions.[108] The protest represented an equivalential sequence between those groups active within S2B and trade unions, with the latter being responsible for mobilizing around 15,000 people in the protest. The involvement of the trade unions was particularly significant when comparing this 2003 demonstration with an earlier event organized by members of S2B in 2002 outside the Brussels venue for a meeting between EU member-state representatives from the trade committee and the European Services Forum representing EU service companies.[109]

Unequal mobilization

Analysing campaigning as a global mobilization is problematic because it risks suggesting a level of cohesiveness that is not necessarily present. Much of the activity critical of the GATS has taken place in Western Europe, despite it first emerging in Canada and New Zealand. What is more, despite the UK-based WDM being one of the most prominent groups in the campaigns, there remains little public awareness in the UK of either that campaign or the GATS. The question of the success, or not, of this mobilization will be discussed in the next section. Here, the chapter needs to consider *why* activity has taken quite different forms in different countries and regions.

Several of those involved with campaigning critical of the GATS have said that the movement had a largely European identity, as opposed to a more global one. The Europeanization of critical GATS campaigning is interesting particularly since much of the initial critique began in Canada and, to a lesser extent, New Zealand and that the target of the protests – a multilateral trade agreement – is ostensibly international. For several campaigners, this has been argued as a pragmatic response to the increasingly dominant position that the European Commission has taken during the GATS 2000 negotiations. For example, Alexandra Wandel of FOEE has commented that:

[T]here has been a European identity, in the terms of European groups feeling very responsible about what the European Commission and the EU in general is doing in the WTO ... I think there has been this identity of us Europeans basically having a responsibility to oppose this kind of agenda, and that is also something ... colleagues we work together with in Our World Is Not For Sale, from developing countries, are usually raising with us, as Europeans, that we all know ... which big role the European Union plays in the WTO.[110]

Despite this, however, Wandel does view GATS as the centre of a 'truly ... international campaign' on the basis that it has relied much on globally coordinated activities through such networks as OWINFS. Additionally, for Clare Joy, it was through discussions between WDM and developing country-based groups such as TWNA that the European focus developed, as a realization that rather than fight a campaign based upon the perceived impacts of GATS on other sectors such as retail and finance, articulating GATS as a 'threat to public services' in the EU was becoming the most effective means of affecting the wider GATS 2000 negotiations.[111] The developing European identity facilitated the necessary linkages by which to share information necessary to coordinate national-focused lobbying to contest the joint EU strategy, as were embodied in the various meetings and information/strategy exchanges in the S2B network.[112]

Although much of the initial substantial work critiquing the GATS was produced in Canada, Tony Clarke of Polaris has said that it was in Europe that the critique was further developed.[113] The increasing focus on the European Commission as the most active in the GATS 2000 negotiations appears to be a strong explanation for this geographical identity, as shaped by the political context.

To date, there have been three global group petitions targeting the GATS. The first – 'STOP the GATS Attack Now!' – has been discussed. The second was published in May 2003 and was much more modest in size, with only 25 signatory organizations.[114] It was agreed at a meeting in Nairobi, organized by WDM, and was consequently titled the *Nairobi Civil Society Declaration on the General Agreement on Trade in Services*, and claimed:

> The GATS represents a powerful and totally unacceptable instrument that limits policy space and restricts popular access to services which are essential to people's livelihoods and economic development.[115]

It ties GATS to economic liberalization forced through in developing countries by the 'IMF, World Bank, WTO, donor agencies and corporate interests', which have had 'negative impacts on people and communities'.[116] In other words, the statement shows an attempt to articulate a chain of equivalences by which to constitute the 'other' excluded from the campaign's identity, so that GATS is equivalent to forced liberalization, and negative understandings of IMF, World Bank, WTO, donor agencies and corporate interests.

The statement presents a set of demands specifically targeted at governments of developing countries. These are: 1 'share all necessary information and documents, and work with *their* civil society to develop policies that meet the needs of their citizens'; 2 'promote, protect and reclaim the *southern policy space*, to review, with a view to withdraw, current commitments and therefore not to make any new commitments in current GATS negotiations. There is no evidence to prove that GATS will attract productive investment. On the contrary, the developing countries lose whatever little share they currently have'; and, 3 'to share relevant information among *themselves* and to work *together* in order to increase their *negotiation capacity* to avoid being bullied in multilateral and bi-lateral forums'.[117] The only demand to Northern governments is to 'stop manipulating and abusing bilateral and multilateral processes'.[118]

The first interesting thing about this statement is the emphasis on the role of civil society within these countries in ensuring that policies 'meet the needs of their citizens'.[119] Second, GATS is articulated as the product of a development policy space perverted against developing countries.[120] The solution, presented here, is to empower developing country governments by encouraging them to work together and, overall, increase their negotiating capacity.[121] The vast majority of the signatory organizations are based in those developing countries, within only five of the groups based in the developed world.[122] The statement concludes with a statement of solidarity from the signatory organizations:

> We commit ourselves to continue building global solidarity in our common struggle against corporate-driven, northern imposed policy agendas. We also reaffirm our commitment to networking amongst ourselves in order to make sure that our governments protect the interests of their people.[123]

GATS is, therefore, seen as part of this 'corporate-driven, northern imposed policy' agenda.[124] Through articulating WTO Member states into distinct identities so that they are either developed/North or developing/South, the statement suggests an underdog narrative in which GATS is being imposed on the (temporarily disunited) South. As such, the statement attempts to argue the contingency of multilateralism or equality in the WTO.[125]

Campaigning as multi-pronged

GATS campaigning has had only a relatively low profile within these developing countries. John Kinuthia of the Kenya-based Consumer Information Network (CIN) sees the global campaign as multiple pronged, in that there are many different forms of activity that operate in parallel to slow down momentum towards the liberalization of services.[126] He sees public protest and international meetings as only part of what is a much wider process to derail the GATS and challenge services liberalization. The particular political regime within Kenya increases the costs incurred in a public protest, where past WTO-related protesters have suffered arrest and police imprisonment. The CIN has worked closely with the Kenyan government, advising caution in GATS negotiations, as well as holding a seat within a national think tank – the Kenya National Committee on the WTO – that provides the government with information on how to negotiate at the WTO. The CIN's interest in the

GATS stemmed from the Seattle Ministerial. However, importantly, it has received financial support from Dutch organizations, which have invited John Kinuthia to attend forums held by the Dutch GATS-Platform, and take part in a lobby of the Dutch government. These forums have brought CIN into contact with prominent figures in campaigning around the GATS, including the CCPA's Scott Sinclair, as well as Erik Wesselius of GATSWatch and CEO, exchanging information.

Groups from the so-called developing countries are said to have constituted the majority of those present at the 2004 Geneva meeting organized by Polaris, where campaigners shared strategy/critical research but also organized lobbying meetings with trade delegations representing developing countries.[127] Related actions have included workshops run by the Geneva-based South Centre – a group critiquing WTO policy from a development perspective – where representatives of developing countries attended a training week in which GATS was problematized.[128] Groups such as PSI used the Geneva meeting as a means to engage in further lobbying actions between several groups with whom they were able to form links.[129] OWINFS has provided the means by which groups based in developed countries have been able financially to support the involvement of those groups based in developing countries so that, for example, telephone conference calls are set up in such a way that the better-resourced groups cover the cost.[130]

Groups such as WDM have developed a double strategy when approaching governments of developing countries, whereby their representatives at the WTO have been invited to attend seminars in Geneva, as well as aiding groups within those countries that are able to lobby those governments directly. The same has been true with lobbying in countries such as India and South Africa where, respectively, Equations and the South African Municipal Workers Union (SAMWU) have developed critiques of the GATS.[131] SAMWU has had active involvement with groups in Canada,[132] organizing workshops at which individuals from Polaris have been present, as well as commissioning Scott Sinclair of CCPA to produce a report articulating GATS as a threat to public health in South Africa.[133]

Though most activity has taken place in Western Europe, there has been great variance in the character of that campaigning and the level of public participation. Mobilization has been concentrated within particular countries, organizations, and even within the hands of particular individuals such as Erik Wesselius. In the UK, P&P and WDM involved their members via running local workshops providing a critical education on the GATS as well as distributing postcards demanding that 'negotiations are conducted in a transparent and open manner' and 'essential services are removed from GATS altogether', which individuals were invited to sign and send to the Secretary of State at the DTI.[134] Other public involvement included WDM's call for its members to write to their local MPs to support the EDM. However, many members felt uncomfortable criticizing GATS in public because of problems understanding what remained a highly complex document.[135] P&P

experienced a similar problem, with many of its university campus and sixth form college groups uncomfortable with the critique, finding it difficult to argue against an agreement that they found extremely difficult to explain to fellow students.[136] There were exceptions to this, such as the P&P group based at Warwick University, the president of which was sufficiently politicized by the issue to become co-writer of the organization's second report on GATS and its submission to the DTI public consultation: *Trading it Away: How GATS Threatens UK Higher Education*.[137] However, after the announcement that the European Commission was removing education from its GATS requests, P&P shifted away from GATS. WDM continued, but much of its activity remained at the level of lobbying either the UK government or European Commission, as well as developing country WTO Member states directly or indirectly through their civil society.

The example of Austria

By comparison, campaigning constituted a mass movement in Austria.[138] The STOPP GATS campaign was a collaboration between ATTAC Austria, Greenpeace Austria, local trade unions, including a students' union, and an anti-poverty network representing many church groups.[139] These organizations operated as the driving body. Surrounding this core group were around 50 supportive organizations, including environmental groups, women's groups, a chamber of labour, church groups, some trade unions, development groups and youth groups. These supportive groups carried out strategies and helped to spread information. The organizers saw the campaign as being based upon three main instruments: information, lobbying and activism. Information was gained via connections with groups outside of Austria, via networks such as S2B and OWINFS, and their websites and e-mail distribution lists. Those involved cite Erik Wesselius of CEO as an important name within their campaign, despite never having met him in person during the campaign that came to a climax in 2003.[140] Within Austria, further information was collected via connections with groups in Germany (such as WEED), and disseminated through the organization of a regular series of workshops and special days for critical education on the GATS. The campaign began in 2002. In 2003, lectures and workshops criticizing GATS were taking place with a speaker somewhere in Austria every week. This allowed the campaign to reach an ever wider audience. Information was also provided to members of the Austrian parliament, as well as the media, all of which were previously uninformed on GATS.

Lobbying was targeted at the national and local levels. At the national level, political parties were contacted by letter, requesting their opinion on the GATS. The answers were then publicized. Apart from addressing the political parties as a unified campaign, the member organizations mobilized their memberships to write as individual citizens to each Austrian member of parliament, expressing their concern over GATS. In these letters, the demands were laid out clearly as follows: 1 halt the current negotiations; 2 evaluate the effects of earlier liberalization prior to further negotiations; and, 3 accountability of government for high-quality public services should be in the Austrian constitution. All towns and community councils were sent letters in which the STOPP GATS presented themselves as allies, warning local government against the potential centralizing powers of an expanded GATS. The effect was that nearly 300 local councils signed a resolution to the Austrian government to halt its GATS negotiations.

In terms of activism, there were two separate days of protest. The first took place outside the parliament building, in Vienna, in November 2002, when 188 activists each carried an information pack critical on the GATS, intended for each of the 188 parliamentary members. As each MP arrived to work, they were presented with a pack. This event was organized in agreement with the Socialist and Green parties, the MPs of which came out to meet the protesters and collect their packs. The effect of this day was to create a media presence, reaching the evening news and good press coverage, but also creating awareness within the parliament building, where it was said that the folders, in a bright colour, could be seen being carried throughout the parliamentary corridors. The second day of protest was on a more national scale, involving 200 towns and small communities, in Spring 2003, with activists publicly marking what they alleged to be threatened services, such as schools, hospitals and train stations. The activists stood outside the various buildings, providing information to people using the service within. This was helped by the municipal council of Vienna adopting, in March 2003, a resolution requesting further assessment of GATS, access to the Austrian negotiating position for local government, and rejecting any further liberalization of public services.[141]

For those involved, the campaign was a success for four reasons. First, it increased a critical awareness of the GATS amongst both members of parliament and the public. Second, it was seen as helping to force the Austrian government into providing more information on its requests and offers made within the GATS negotiations. Third, it created a wider debate around public services, with many politicians openly declaring themselves in favour of publicly funded services. Finally, despite the complexities of the GATS, the STOPP GATS campaign was seen as important for developing stronger civil society in Austria, opening up opportunities for further campaigns and actions.

A similar story was repeated in Belgium, led by a mixture of work in the French-speaking regions influenced by ATTAC France, and activity in Flanders made possible via the 11.11.11 network. By Autumn 2004, 55 percent of all Flemish communes had agreed motions against GATS and its implications for water services. Significantly, these signatories included Antwerp and Gent. Due to the work of ATTAC, even Belgium's capital signed an anti-GATS motion.[142] This campaign included radio commercials criticizing the GATS as a 'threat' to water provision.

The value of reports and analysis

Political mobilization critical of the GATS has been dependent upon the dissemination of reports and analysis. This helps to explain why certain groups such as WDM and CEO, and even individuals such as Erik Wesselius and Clare Joy, have become such significant figures, because they have been the ones either producing or disseminating these reports and analysis. This could partially explain why activity has not taken the form of a mass movement in the UK, whereas it has to a limited extent elsewhere. This would suggest that groups such as WDM and P&P were just less skilled as communicators to the public. However, both groups have access to local groups of members, and they produced materials that worked hard to communicate the GATS to an audience unfamiliar with trade semantics. An alternative explanation to be considered in the next section is the role of local historical conditions.

The end of political mobilization critical of the GATS?

At the time of writing, mobilization critical of the GATS has all but disappeared. Activists have moved onto other campaigns, many of which link to the global financial crisis of 2007. Whilst the negotiations are formally still active, delegates to the WTO are overwhelmingly occupied with other issues, the least of which are attempts to conclude the Doha Round. That said, the fact that the negotiations have not yet been completed has been seen as a sign of success by campaigners. The last global group petition to target the GATS was produced in June 2005, with the banner 'Stop the GATS power play against citizens of the world!'[143]

Stop the GATS power play against citizens of the world!

GATS was critiqued, once more, as an attempt by the North to bully the South into inappropriate policy parameters. GATS was argued to be the product of lobbying by US and EU service corporations to service their own expansionary interests. As with the earlier petitions, the statement warns that the GATS threatens to limit policy options open to governments. The primary demand made is for an 'independent assessment' of the GATS, prior to 'proceeding any further with the current round of GATS negotiations'. The statement demands a re-prioritization of other issues that affect 'people and environment' over trade, as well as greater domestic policy space within member states to discuss the implications of the agreement amongst all 'affected constituencies'. There is also a demand for the publication of all requests and offers, as well as greater clarification over issues like government procurement and domestic regulations before any negotiations are progressed. The statement demands that 'certain service sectors be explicitly excluded from multilateralised liberalisation', with reference to health, education, cultural/audio-visual, social assistance, water, postal services, energy services and new technologies.

Already containing a broad perspective, the final demand of the statement requests that the World Bank and International Monetary Fund cancel all 'odious and illegitimate Third World debts', and cease all pressure on developing countries to 'privatise their public services ... by placing such economic policy conditions on their loans'.

The statement includes 148 signatory organizations and is addressed to the heads of all WTO member state delegations, as well as the chair of the Services negotiations, the chair of the WTO General Council and the WTO's director-general.

Despite this statement, many of those groups formerly active on GATS have now moved away, deeming it necessary to shift their resources over to other issues. Many of those groups have moved to critique the involvement of Northern firms in the privatization of water services in the South, as in the case of WDM's 'Dirty Aid, Dirty Water' campaign, which focuses on the claimed role of the UK government's Department for International Development (DFID) in funding the work of groups such as the Adam Smith Institute in promoting neoliberal economics and the expansion of European water companies in Africa. Water has often featured in GATS campaigning and so this is not necessarily a different mobilization. Erik Wesselius has also taken up a brief critiquing the liberalization of water services, so that GATSWatch is now dormant.[144]

Difficulties for campaigning

The difficulties WDM and P&P faced in turning GATS into a mass mobilization in the UK can be explained because of an historical context in which governments have successively removed government ownership and regulation over key services. Whilst this could be seen as a cause for the emergence of political subjectivity, it could also be said that the logic of the market has become so firmly embedded within the UK as to be hegemonic. The postcard campaign by P&P and WDM was presented as a joint NGO/trade union GATS campaign, acknowledging the involvement of several trade unions in financing this activity.[145] However, trade union activity on the GATS remained minimal in the UK. According to Clare Joy, this was because trade unions were already busy fighting the UK government's private-public partnership schemes.[146] Where even minimal trade union involvement proved useful was in giving greater status to the campaign, which was apparently evident in meetings with civil servants in the UK government who responded much more positively to trade union representatives than WDM.[147] However, trade unions in the UK never perceived the GATS as requiring significant prioritization because, from the perspective of Clare Joy, they were already occupied with the fight to prevent the expansion of public-private partnerships within key public services such as health and education.

The difficulties of articulating a critique of GATS into a mass movement in the context of the logic of the market as an increasingly sedimented discourse was apparent at a meeting that potentially promised to expand GATS campaigning in February 2005. The event took place in Budapest and was hosted by a Hungarian member of the S2B network, Vedegylet. The first part of the meeting was a general conference with speakers discussing the role of the private and public sectors within service provision. This half was open to anyone interested in these debates, and was attended by academics, trade unions and civil society representatives, amongst others. The second part was intended to discuss what could actually be done to protect public services, with specific mention of the GATS, and took the form of an S2B strategy meeting, closed to all but those working for S2B members and civil society in Central and Eastern Europe who might cooperate with S2B, so that it was open only to those already articulated as activists within global trade governance rather than engage a wider set of identities.

'Public Services, Globalization and Sustainability in an Enlarged Europe'

Titled 'Public Services, Globalization and Sustainability in an Enlarged Europe', the conference was intended to explore the possibility of sharing tactical experience in affecting the European Commission's WTO negotiating position between civil society groups in the old and expanded EU. GATS was discussed as one of several issues including agriculture. Many of those groups from Central and Eastern Europe operated in a context in which the logic of the market had become sedimented as 'freedom', to the extent that several of those present were actively involved promoting links between foreign corporations and local municipalities in their own countries.

Though the meeting ended with a work plan for future activity on GATS, S2B members have had difficulty mobilizing to continue the campaign. WDM's own evaluation of its campaign suggests one possible reason for this, as it warns that a potential conflict emerged between the organization's remit to focus on issues affecting the South and campaigning against an agreement that also affected the North.[148] Many groups have moved away from actively working on the GATS to maintaining a formal monitoring role. E-mail listservers such as GATSCrit have quietened, though information on GATS negotiations is still distributed. Fewer groups are working on the GATS. A critical demand of GATS has dropped away from the high profile it once achieved.

The deadline for the GATS negotiations has been successively extended, with little positive response from developing countries. The negotiations have thus followed their articulation in the critical campaigns, where GATS has been presented as a product of the North imposed on the South. In leaked minutes of a meeting by the Liberalisation of Trade in Services (LOTIS) Committee, which included representatives of London financial and insurance firms as well as Reuters and UK civil servants, a plan was suggested to launch a counter-discourse to that constructed by the GATS critics that would get those identified as developing countries to criticize the campaign.[149] This never happened, but increasingly representatives of countries such as India and Brazil have accepted concessions in the GATS. Through articulating a divide between WTO Member states along the lines of North and South, campaigning has managed to obstruct consensus between the Members and thus slow the negotiations. In the process, the representatives of developing countries have been strengthened within their general WTO negotiating positions.

Conclusion: the elasticity of equivalential chains

The case study has illustrated the importance of equivalential chains in the formation of new actors contesting the shape of the WTO. Campaigners have stated the importance of coalitions as a means to strengthen their advocacy base. However, since this activity peaked in 2003, the equivalential chains have been weakened. This has implications for how one should understand the process of identity formation and political subjectivity within campaigns dominated by professional advocacy groups with paid activists. The rise and decline of campaigning around the GATS could be modelled as an elastic band, where the identity of groups has been stretched to form equivalential chains before a certain tension has caused those chains to weaken and, possibly, break. The logic of equivalence requires rearticulation of identities. If equivalences could be built between static subject positions, there would be no new group identity because there would be no process of identity formation. There would simply be a logic of difference. These subject positions are rearticulated via the construction of equivalential links. However, as the discussion of post-structuralist discourse theory showed, for identities to change it is necessary that there is a dislocation. The original identity must be dislocated in order to create the political subjectivity in which a new identity may emerge.

For example, an environmental group successfully lobbies its national government for increased regulations to protect dolphins at threat from tuna fishing. However, the subject position of environmental organization is threatened when a trade agreement defines the regulation as a trade barrier, causing the regulation to be removed from the statute books. This dislocates the identity of environmental organization as focused on protecting dolphins, showing the contingency of this identity. This creates political subjectivity, in which the groups of individuals formally concerned with protecting dolphins achieve the agency necessary to decide to include a demand critical of the trade agreement. Even where the group maintains its former nationally focused campaigns, the emergent identity is expanded and therefore altered. As similar subject positions such as development group or trade union are dislocated from their own particular fields, a series of equivalential chains develop around a central critique of the trade agreement.

The process of identity formation is complex: there are many different levels of identity within, for example, an environmental organization. Whilst one could point to its mission statement or the frequency with which certain demands appear within its campaigns – which could be used to claim that all of the professional activists exist under one identity – this is complicated by the series of executive committees, funding bodies and the wider membership. It cannot be assumed that each of the different layers of the group is equally subsumed within the same identity. This is particularly true of the funding bodies. Many groups are based on a relatively narrow remit of issues, which are used when gaining funding. Groups such as WDM are funded by members, but also various trusts as well as governmental bodies (e.g. the European Union). The expanding chain of equivalences involved in the GATS mobilizations meant that groups such as WDM gained rearticulated identities. If this chain of equivalences had become sedimented, so presumably the identities of the various funding bodies would have been rearticulated. Yet, without sufficient sedimentation, the former identity of WDM existed as a ghost within its formal remit, with the slogan 'Tackling the root causes of poverty'. This ghost is present within criticism against the GATS campaign voiced by a WDM member, who argued:

> I am not convinced that the GATS campaign is 'tackling the root causes of poverty'. It seems like a *political side-show* ... Debt, Aid and lifting Trade barriers on commodities seem much more directly linked to poverty.[150]

It is interesting that the current WDM campaign links the issue of privatization present within the GATS critique to aid,[151] which is a more traditional demand within the identity of development groups. This could then be seen as an attempt to compromise between the old and new identity of WDM. This same strategy has been adopted by CEO, though including emphasis on the influence of corporations in Brussels. Developing this point, the apparent decline in critical GATS campaigning does not necessarily indicate that the equivalential chains on which it was based are diminishing. Rather, it may be that they have been strengthened through the series of articulations that took place in the GATS campaign, and that just as much as these chains pre-dated activity focused on the GATS, they may well continue to facilitate future political movements. However, this cannot be taken as given and therefore requires further research into post-GATS activity involving such equivalential chains as embodied in the OWINFS and S2B networks.

This in-depth case study of identity formation in the contestation of a particular WTO policy does help to illustrate the immensely complex articulatory process shaping the wider discursive context in which the WTO – as a discursive formation – operates. This process cannot be fully mapped because: 1 it is simply too complex; and, 2 more importantly, it is constantly shifting. This fluidity is evident in the relatively small case evidenced in political campaigning critical of the GATS, where identities have become equivalentially linked and resources have been shared – showing that identity cannot be limited to the ideational but includes the material as a discursive social practice. In some cases, these links have become sedimented – often due to earlier articulatory moments, as in the case of semi-informal networks such as

OWINFS – but in other instances such links are only temporary, such as the global group petitions. Despite this evident uncertainty, however, much can be gained if one begins to see such activity not as external to the WTO but as part of the discursive context through which it is constituted. The growing force of identities equivalentially linked in criticism of the GATS articulated the GATS to be a problem, as evidenced where governmental trade departments and the WTO Secretariat have been forced to respond. Chapter 2 has evidenced the importance of such logics as multilateralism and equality to the political operation of trade management facilitating the WTO. Articulating GATS as supporting certain WTO Member states over others, for example, via publishing research and organizing conferences underlines the contingency of these constitutive logics. As will be discussed in Chapter 6, the complex nature of discourse precludes the possibility of causal explanation. Thus, it is ontologically impossible to determine accurately how critical campaigning has shaped the GATS 2000 negotiations.

The campaigning analysed in this chapter represents the wider discursive context of the WTO (and the GATS). However, such campaigning is also a product of the WTO through the series of mutually constitutive relationships embodied in discourse. Groups such as WDM and CEO experienced a rearticulation in which certain of those positioned under those identities became repositioned as 'critical experts' in the GATS, expressed in research publications and lobby meetings utilizing a technical vocabulary claiming knowledge of the various minutiae of the negotiations.[152] The tension present in this process, as former identities became challenged, is evident in the above quotation from a WDM member. Therefore, as argued throughout the book, articulation should not be seen as a strategic process subject to agency, but inherently complex, diffuse and uncertain where equivalential logics are dependent upon a much wider discursive context that exceeds any individual moment of collective action. This places political campaigning as subject to the same field as the WTO: discourse.

Notes

1 Understood as a social practice operating within discourse, *identity* is neither ideational nor material. Focusing on identity formation, therefore, does not negate disparities in the resource capabilities of different groups but, on the contrary, sees such material factors as part of the same discursive process. For example, the funding structure of a group is not an inevitable fact of reality but is discursively constructed in a particular fashion.

2 The research traces campaigning critical of the GATS from 2002 up to mid-2005. This cut-off point was chosen after receiving an overwhelming response from interviewees that campaigning had effectively come to an end, with activity becoming limited to a low-profile monitoring of negotiations. Since that time, recent developments in 2006 have seen a few groups returning to the production of critical reports and bringing GATS up in meetings with trade departments, according to feedback on an earlier draft of this chapter. However, such activity

remains at a low level compared to that discussed in what follows. As one commentator on the earlier draft suggested, campaigns flow in peaks and troughs of activity. The mid-2005 cut-off point is arguably no more than a trough rather than an end to critical GATS campaigning. A less disputable cut-off point might be whenever the GATS 2000 negotiations finally end, either in a formal agreement or abandonment of the process. However, as has been argued in Chapter 4, campaigns are not single events but often form part of a much longer narrative. Of interest to this book is not the single campaign, but what it suggests as regards the formation of identities critical of global trade governance.

3 As outlined in Chapter 1, the research on which this chapter is based includes interviews (face-to-face, telephone and e-mail) with participants in the campaigns, as well as first-person observation via attending a series of conferences and meetings that formed part of the campaign activity.

4 For a catalogue of these categorizations, see WTO Secretariat 2001.

5 For further background on the GATS, please see: Sapir 1999; Drake and Nicolaïdis 1992; WTO Secretariat 2001; Kelsey 1997; Sinclair and Grieshaber-Otto 2002.

6 This comment came from an interview with Tony Clarke (8 April 2005), director of Polaris, which is one of the civil society organizations that would become prominent within the critique of GATS.

7 The preamble to reports co-produced by Education International and Public Services International states: 'This is one in the series of *Common concerns for workers in education and the public sector*, produced jointly by PSI and EI. The papers in this series are meant to serve several purposes: to help trade unionists understand some of the issues; to enable trade union educators to run short sessions on education and public sector issues with their members; to provide material for union leaders writing speeches or informational material for wider audiences; and for distribution to a range of interested people.' Taken from EI and PSI (1999) *The WTO and the General Agreement on Trade-in-Services: What is at Stake for Public Health?* (Brussels: Educational International; Ferney-Voltaire: Public Services International).

8 EI and PSI (1999) *The WTO and the Millennium Round: What is at Stake for Public Education?* (Brussels: Educational International; Ferney-Voltaire: Public Services International).

9 Based on an interview with Mike Waghorne, Public Services International (16 June 2005).

10 'The massive import of higher education services by South-East Asia gives some idea of the harmful consequences which a hasty opening of the markets could have: increased *dependence* on *foreign* educational resources, *acculturation* – in many countries – caused by the use of a foreign language for teaching, a tendency to the *standardisation* of education and, lastly, a certain *curtailment of sovereignty*. In this connection, we can also ask ourselves what will be the impact of the liberalisation of international trade in education services on the quality and supply of these services in developing countries. Given the existence of huge disparities between countries, is the idea of placing national education systems in a competitive situation not tantamount to selling out the education systems in the weakest countries to a handful of large transnational corporations?' EI and PSI (1999) *The WTO and the Millennium Round: What is at Stake for Public Education?*, 20, emphasis added.

11 Ibid.

12 Ibid., 21.

13 Ibid.

14 Ibid., 22.

15 Ibid., 16–17, 23, ft 20.

16 Ibid., 16.

17 M. Peters (1997) *Cultural Politics and the University* (Wellington: Dunmore).

18 For example, evoking many of the same themes of democracy and collective life expressed in the PSI-EI 1999 report on GATS and education, in 1997 Kelsey wrote: 'New Zealanders can be forgiven their ignorance – successive governments and the media have decided that they don't really need to know. Yet the recent extension of the GATT to include services, intellectual property and investment measures has serious implications for the economic, social, cultural and political wellbeing of our society, and for the degree of control which present and future generations can exercise over their lives' (Kelsey 1997: 66). Her chapter presents GATS as a threat to the provision of public education, concluding that 'the GATS could produce a global education system run by trans-national education corporations ... based on one dominant value-structure' (ibid.: 87).

19 EI and PSI (1999) *The WTO and the General Agreement on Trade-in-Services: What is at Stake for Public Health?* (Brussels: Educational International; Ferney-Voltaire: Public Services International).

20 Ibid., 3.

21 Ibid., 17.

22 As discussed in Chapter 3.

23 E. Gould (1999) *The Next MAI – The Latest Threat to Medicare and Public Education has some Familiar Teeth and Claws* (Ottawa: Council of Canadians). This was available at: www.canadians.org (accessed July 2006).

24 Ibid.

25 Interview with Erik Wesselius of Corporate Europe Observatory (1 February 2005).

26 Interview (16 June 2005).

27 Discussed in Chapter 5.

28 Interview (8 April 2005)

29 E. Gould and M. Dobbin (n.d.) *'What is Currently at Stake for Local Governments at the WTO?* (Ottawa: Council of Canadians). This was available online at: www.canadians.org (accessed July 2006).

30 S. Sinclair (2000) *GATS: How the WTO New 'Services' Negotiations Threaten Democracy* (Ottawa: Canadian Centre for Policy Alternatives).

31 The 'Our World Is Not For Sale: WTO – Shrink or Sink!' global group petition is available at the OWINFS website, as well as being published on several member organization sites, including the Council of Canadians.

32 This was stressed by Nicola Bullard of *Focus on the Global South*. Interview (4 November 2004).

33 'Our World Is Not For Sale: WTO – Shrink or Sink!' global group petition.

34 Ibid. A general paragraph encompassing the principles behind these demands is included in the 'Shrink or Sink!' statement. It states: 'We need to protect cultural, biological, economic and social diversity; introduce progressive policies to prioritize local economies and trade; secure internationally recognized economic, cultural, social and labor rights; and reclaim the sovereignty of peoples and national and sub national democratic decision making processes. In order to do this, we need new rules based on the principles of democratic control of resources, ecological sustainability, equity, cooperation and precaution.'

35 Ibid.

36 Ibid.

37 This figure was taken from the Council of Canadians website and is said to be correct as of 8 August 2003, www.canadians.org (accessed July 2006).

38 Interview carried out 5 April 2005, shortly after Clare Joy had left the World Development Movement.

39 A complete list of S2B members is available online: www.s2bnetwork.org (accessed December 2012).

40 This was stated during a workshop organized by the Seattle to Brussels network at the Third European Social Forum, held in London, October 2003; emphasis added.
41 Interview (5 April 2005).
42 Ibid.
43 Ibid.
44 This is taken from WDM (2005) *WDM GATS Campaign 2000–2004: Evaluation* (unpublished).
45 P&P began its life as Third World First but changed its identity from a centralized organization disseminating campaigns to local groups based on university campuses, to become a more flexible network focused on environmentalism and trade justice under the leadership of a new director, Kevin Steele. Policy is decided at an annual general meeting, at which local groups are invited to represent themselves and put forward campaign ideas.
46 J. Worth (2000) *The Threat to Higher Education: A Briefing on Current World Trade Organization Negotiations* (Oxford: People & Planet).
47 Interview (8 November 2004).
48 Ibid., 3, emphasis added.
49 Interview with Jess Worth (8 November 2004).
50 Interview with Clare Joy (5 April 2005). This understanding of the UK Trade Network was supported by other interviewees.
51 In addition, this emphasizes the diffuse character of the discursive context in which the WTO operates, where the formation of actors contesting WTO policies is dependent upon such a gradual process of linking identities that have previously formed in earlier moments.
52 Interview (5 April 2005).
53 Full text: 'That this House welcomes the statement in the Government's recent Globalisation White Paper that recognises the role of government in ensuring that basic services are provided to all; notes that negotiations to expand the reach of the WTO's General Agreement on Trade in Services are underway; further notes that the GATS applies to all tradable services, including public services, if they are provided commercially or in competition with other suppliers; further notes that the GATS applies to all levels of government, including local authorities; is concerned over the lack of parliamentary and public debate on this agreement given its far-reaching implications; and calls on the Government to ensure that there is an independent and thorough assessment of the likely impact of the extension of the GATS on the provision of key services both in the UK and internationally, particularly on the poor in developing countries'. EDM 260, www.publications.parliament.uk (accessed February 2013).
54 Interview with Clare Joy (5 April 2005).
55 Ibid.
56 Ibid.
57 From interview with John Hillary (7 April 2005).
58 The founding statement of the Trade Justice Movement is available online: www.tjm.org.uk (accessed February 2013).
59 This was stressed in interviews with several campaigners.
60 Interview (5 April 2005).
61 Interview with John Hillary (7 April 2005).
62 Ibid.
63 Based on an interview with Alexander Wandel (14 June 2005), Friends of the Earth Europe.
64 Friends of the Earth International (31 July 2002) Primer on the General Agreement on Trade in Services (Geneva: FOEI).
65 Ibid.

66 David Waskow and Vicente Paolo B. Yu, III (n.d.) *A Disservice to the Earth: The Environmental Impact of the WTO General Agreement on Trade in Services* (FOE United States).
67 Interview (17 June 2005).
68 For example, the expansion of the WTO intended for the Doha Round is articulated as a 'risk' to 'national and local economies; workers, farmers, indigenous peoples, women and other social groups; health and safety, the environment, and animal welfare'. 'Our World Is Not For Sale: WTO – Shrink or Sink!' global group petition. Available at the OWINFS website.
69 Interview with Amandine Bach (17 June 2005). As stated in the Introduction, this chapter makes no claims towards any causal links between GATS and such issues as privatization, gender or development, for example. An equivalential link is concerned only with identity formation, which is understood here as the basis for collective action.
70 Interview (20 May 2005), emphasis added.
71 Interview (31 March 2005).
72 Ibid.
73 For example, this was stated in an interview with Marc Maes (13 February 2005) of the Belgium network 11.11.11.
74 Interview (1 February 2005).
75 Ibid.
76 Ibid.
77 The full statement was available online at: www.polarisinstitute.org (accessed July 2006).
78 According to an interview with Tony Clarke, Polaris Institute. The coordinating role of Polaris within OWINFS was also mentioned in an interview with Erik Wesselius (1 February 2005).
79 According to interview with Tony Clarke (8 April 2005), Polaris Institute.
80 Based on interview with Mike Waghorne, PSI (16 June 2005).
81 Available at website of the Polaris Institute, www.polarisinstitute.org.
82 Ibid.
83 Interview (16 June 2005).
84 Ibid.
85 Interview (5 April 2005).
86 S2B (2001) *GATS and Democracy*, Seattle to Brussels Network, is available online at www.gatswatch.org/GATSandDemocracy/index.html (accessed February 2013).
87 Available online at www.wto.org (accessed February 2013).
88 WDM (2005) *WDM GATS Campaign 2000–2004: Evaluation* (unpublished).
89 Based on interview with Mike Waghorne (16 June 2005), PSI.
90 This account is based on an interview with Mike Waghorne (16 June 2005) of PSI. According to the WTO website, the dispute between itself and PSI-EI concerned an allegation that GATS threatened public funding of national institutions. The WTO website account portrays that 'cooperation' between the WTO Secretariat and PSI led to this allegation being withdrawn by the trade union body. Though clearly open to alternative interpretations, what remains apparent is that specific mention by the WTO Secretariat of such groups gave them increased status within the developing equivalential chain critical of the GATS. For the WTO Secretariat's account, please see the WTO website: www.wto.org/english/tratop_e/ serv_e/
gats_factfiction7_e.htm (accessed February 2013).
91 Available online at: www.gatswatch.org (accessed February 2013).
92 Interview (8 April 2005).
93 Ibid.

94 The notes from this talk were available online at: www.polarisinstitute.org/polaris_project/public_service/articles_presentations/kpsu_pres_oct_04.pdf (accessed July 2006).

95 Information on the 2002 European Social Forum in Florence was available online at: www.florence2002.fse-esf.org (accessed July 2006).

96 Interview with Alexandra Wandel (14 June 2005). Interview with Mike Waghorne (16 June 2005), PSI.

97 Based on E. Sussex (2005) *Local and Regional Reaction to GATS and Similar Trade Rules* (unpublished).

98 This was noted in an interview with Erik Wesselius (1 February 2005), of CEO. This strategy also potentially relates back to much earlier moments of political contestation where, as suggested in an interview with Susan George (11 October 2004), of ATTAC France, a similar strategy of politicizing local councils was used during the protests against the US invasion of Vietnam.

99 One such example was Equations, India. According to WDM (2005) *WDM GATS Campaign 2000–2004: Evaluation* (unpublished).

100 Interview with Jess Worth (8 November 2004).

101 Interview with Clare Joy (5 April 2005).

102 Ibid.

103 Ibid.

104 Interview with Clare Joy (5 April 2005).

105 Interview with Jess Worth (8 November 2004).

106 This was noted in separate interviews.

107 Interview with Jess Worth (8 November 2004).

108 WDM (2005) *WDM GATS Campaign 2000–2004: Evaluation* (unpublished).

109 Account based on an interview with Erik Wesselius (1 February 2005).

110 Interview (14 June 2005).

111 Interview (5 April 2005).

112 As illustration of this process, Clare Joy provided the following anecdote: '[W]e were sitting in a meeting [with UK officials] and we were demanding documents, and the UK GATS negotiator … said, "Well, I'm surprised you're asking us for those. Can't you just get them from some of your European colleagues? I don't know why you come and bother us anymore". And that was a sign that they were watching the way in which we were working in Europe. And when we came back and said that we've heard that the Finnish government has raised concerns, and we've heard that the Italian government is saying this, the UK official were just like "How do you know this?" And, being able to generate within the UK officials of there being a European movement, I think is quite unnerving for them. And, I think there is one key political reason for that, is that we wanted to work across Europe. They actually don't want to work across Europe. You know, the UK government is still struggling with the fact that they have to reach a common European position on these issues. The French get on their nerves when it comes to agriculture. What we were able to do is to say "We're working across Europe effectively. You're still struggling to work across Europe effectively". And, I think that was a challenge for them. And, again, the European identity wasn't just about having a European identity in itself. It's about how you're able to use that in your national context'. Interview (5 April 2005).

113 Interview (8 April 2005).

114 This was available online at the WDM site: www.wdm.org.uk (accessed July 2006).

115 Ibid.

116 Ibid.

117 Ibid., emphasis added.

118 Ibid.

119 Ibid.
120 Ibid.
121 Ibid.
122 These five are: ARENA (New Zealand); Center for International Environmental Law (Swiss branch); 11.11.11 (Belgium); Polaris Institute (Canada); and World Development Movement (UK). The other 20, all from developing countries, are: Action Aid (Uganda); Alternative Information and Development Centre (South Africa); Business Watch (Indonesia); Consumer Information Network (Kenya); EcoNews Africa (Kenya); Equations (India); Food Rights Alliance (Uganda); Gender and Trade Network in Africa; Institute for Global Justice (Indonesia); Institute of Economic Affairs (Kenya); International Gender and Trade Network, Asia; Lawyers Environmental Action Team (Tanzania); MWENGO (Zimbabwe); REBRIP (Brazil); SEATINI (Uganda); SEATINI (Zimbabwe); SodNet (Kenya); Tanzania Gender and Networking Programme (Tanzania); Third World Network, Africa (Ghana); and Trade Watch (Kenya).
123 Ibid.
124 Ibid.
125 The importance of these logics to the operation of the WTO can be seen in the genealogy developed in Chapter 3.
126 Interview (29 March 2005).
127 Based on interview with Tony Clarke (8 April 2005).
128 Based on interview with John Hillary (7 April 2005).
129 Based on interview with Mike Waghorne (16 June 2005).
130 Ibid.
131 Based on an interview with Jeff Rudin of SAMWU (10 May 2005). Also, B. Kuruvilla (15/06/2005) 'Tourism: Sunset for Sustainable Policy?' *Financial Express* (India).
132 Based on an interview with Jeff Rudin of SAMWU (10 May 2005).
133 The report was titled *The GATS and South Africa's National Health Act – A Cautionary Tale*, www.policyalternatives.ca/documents/National_Office_Pubs/2005/South_Africa_and_GATS.pdf (accessed February 2013).
134 'Never heard of GATS? – That's the Way they Want it … ' postcard campaign, launched by ASLEF (Associated Society of Locomotive Steam Enginemen and Firemen), AUT UK (Association of University Teachers, UK), CSP (Chartered Society of Physiotherapists), CWU (Communication Workers Union), NASUWT (National Association of Schoolmasters Union of Women Teachers), NATFHE (University and College Lecturers' Union), NUJ (National Union of Journalists), NUS (National Union of Students), NUT (National Union of Teachers), PCS (Public and Commercial Services Union), People & Planet, RMT (National Union of Rail, Maritime and Transport Workers), UNISON (public services union), USDAW (Union of Shop, Distributive and Allied Workers), and World Development Movement.
135 WDM (2005) *WDM GATS Campaign 2000–2004: Evaluation* (unpublished).
136 Based on an informal interview with P&P activist formerly of Loughborough University P&P group.
137 Interview with Steven Kelk (6 February 2005).
138 The information on the STOPP GATS campaign comes from interviews with activists as well as a presentation given by members of ATTAC Austria at a conference on Public Services, held in Budapest in February 2005, called 'Public Services, Globalization and Sustainability in an Enlarged Europe'.
139 More information was available online via the STOPP GATS website, at: www.stoppgats.at (accessed July 2006).
140 Mentioned during the aforementioned ATTAC Austria 'Public Services, Globalization and Sustainability in an Enlarged Europe' conference.

141 Based on E. Sussex (2005) *Local and Regional Reaction to GATS and Similar Trade Rules* (unpublished).

142 Ibid. Also, interview with Marc Maes (13 February 2005), trade policy adviser for 11.11.11.

143 Available online via the PSI website, at: www.world-psi.org/powerplay (accessed July 2006).

144 Interview (1 February 2005; 31 March 2005).

145 The trade unions included ASLEF, AUT UK, CSP, CWU, NASUWT, NATFHE, NUJ, NUS, NUT, PCS, RMT, UNISON and USDAW.

146 Interview with Clare Joy (5 April 2005).

147 Ibid.

148 This conflict meant that WDM sought to avoid becoming too involved in articulating the potential impact of the GATS within developed countries, as is suggested in the internal evaluation of the campaign. WDM (2005) *WDM GATS Campaign 2000–2004: Evaluation* (unpublished).

149 The minutes of this meeting were leaked and are available online at the aforementioned WDM website.

150 Richard Martin, Medway WDM, quoted in: WDM (2005) *WDM GATS Campaign 2000–2004: Evaluation* (unpublished), emphasis added.

151 Called 'Dirty Aid, Dirty Water', the campaign criticizes the UK government's DFID for aid conditions which WDM argues promote water privatization in Africa.

152 The importance of utilizing such terminology as a means to gain credibility was acknowledged in an interview with John Hillary of War on Want, stating: 'I think it's much more about making the government officials aware that we knew at least as much about GATS as they did, because their standard response whenever anything came in was "You don't understand GATS", and they got very shirty about all the people who were writing them letters saying GATS is privatisation of health. And, they'd say "No, it's not". Or, "GATS is privatisation of water". And they'd go, "No, it's not". And they said "Nobody seems to understand GATS". And when we could go along to them and show them that we actually understood easily as much as they did, it meant they, for the first time, had to start taking some of the issues more seriously, and they realised that they actually had to address them, because it wasn't just lots of people writing in about it. It was, it was campaigners who could also take part in the lobby group meetings, who had the specialism on GATS, who could talk about what article 6.4 might or might not mean.' Interview (7 April 2005).

6 Conclusion

The discursivity of global trade governance

Introduction

The book's title – *Writing Global Trade Governance* – is a direct reference to David Campbell's now classic *Writing Security* (1992) in which he sought to expose the discursivity and social embeddedness of US foreign policy. As with that groundbreaking work, the term 'writing' exceeds the linguistic to include all forms of social interaction – discourse – through which the human world is constructed. The particular aspect of that world explored here has been the form of global trade governance embodied in the World Trade Organization (WTO). Yet, as the previous chapters have shown, treating the WTO discursively takes research far beyond its formal or informal institutional boundaries, to examine the wider series of social interactions through which it is made possible as a political entity with material effects. Like its near-namesake, this book seeks to expose the discursivity and social embeddedness of contemporary global trade governance. Post-structuralist discourse theory has provided the basis for a research strategy able to reconceptualize the WTO as to have *being* via a diffuse and complex series of mutually constitutive relationships in which the social practices comprising the WTO are inherently embedded within the wider discursive context. The value of this perspective is that it helps research better understand not only the WTO as it exists today, but also how change occurs, and political agency to bring about that change is made possible. These three aspects are core to a broader progressive project of reconnecting individuals with the forms of governance impacting their lives.

Summary

The analysis began by problematizing current attempts to understand the WTO within social science literature. The literature review identified two points: first, the WTO cannot be understood via a formal organization or regime alone but consists of a much more complex and diffuse political process; and second, current literature understands the WTO via an abstract interplay between material and ideational factors without concretely theorizing how

they effectively co-exist in the same practice constituting the WTO. Consequently, understanding how the historical context shapes the WTO appears
increasingly complex.

A complex and diffuse political process

First, it was shown how the literature contains *uncertainty* as to who/what
constitutes an 'actor' in the WTO. Gross heterogeneity amongst Member
states and overlap with other identities (e.g. business lobbyist, trade union)
indicates a much more complex and diffuse process than may be described if
viewing the WTO as the product of a static set of unitary actors. This challenges
those accounts (e.g. Hoekman and Kostecki 2009; Jackson 2009; Matsushita
et al. 2003) that have characterized the WTO as a product of rules and norms
formed between Member states acting as gatekeepers to political operation of
the WTO.

Ford (2003) has gone some way to theorize change in the WTO via applying a
social constructivist perspective. Her analysis argues that the WTO has facilitated
a collective identity – described as a 'Self of multilateral traders' (ibid.: 135) –
amongst its Member states. This 'Self of multilateral traders' has been actively
taught by so-called developing-country Member states in order to tie the
more materially capable developed-country Member states closer to a rule-
based system than they would otherwise accept (ibid.: 134–35). Ideational
construction (e.g. rules, norms, identities) is seen as a means to overcome the
inequalities of the material world (e.g. economic capabilities).[1] The book gives
two points of critique: 1 Ford's study lacks a sufficiently developed understanding of agency and, thus, risks relativism; and, more importantly, 2 Ford
repeats a similar mistake found throughout the literature, which is reliant upon a
false (and abstract) distinction between the material and the ideational.

An abstract distinction between the material and the ideational

Current literature theorizes the WTO as the product of interplay between
material and ideational factors where the latter serves to constrain the former
with varying degrees of effect. Ford's study may be placed towards the ideational
end of this spectrum, whilst those accounts (Hoekman and Kostecki 2001: 58;
Kwa 2003; and Dunkley 2000) emphasizing the explanatory value of, for
example, economic disparities between Member states in determining the
shape of the WTO can be placed at the material end of the spectrum.
Empirically, however, the material and ideational do not operate as separate
fields affecting one another, but in fact appear to co-exist in political process.
Acknowledging complexity and uncertainty within who/what constitutes an
actor in the WTO, for example, questions the distinction between ideational- and
material-based explanation. Identity constructions (e.g. developing-country WTO
Member state) are: 1 shaped within a world infused with material (e.g. distribution of economic wealth) and ideational (e.g. logic of multilateralism)

factors; and, 2 have material (e.g. exchange of butter for guns) and ideational (e.g. affirmation of a 'Self of multilateral traders') effects. Rather than remaining at the level of theorizing an abstract interplay between the material and ideational, the book has made the case for concretely theorizing how they effectively co-exist in the political operation of the WTO.

Post-structuralist discourse theory as a method

Outlining the key concepts, the book has shown how post-structuralist discourse theory underpins the relevance of the central hypothesis of the book – that the WTO should be understood as a product of the discursive interaction between both material and ideational factors. The material and ideational are understood to operate together within discursive practice. Arguing the materiality of discourse, the book has outlined the distinction between *existence* and *being*. Social practices (e.g. WTO, trade, nation-state) cannot have *being* as objects within the human world 'outside any discursive condition of emergence' (Laclau and Mouffe 2001: 108). This is not to say that the phenomenon of a set of individuals sat around a table uttering sounds to one another does not *exist*, but that they cannot constitute a particular form of global trade governance embodied as the WTO outside of discourse.[2] Consequently, nothing in the human world can be extra-discursive. Without an extra-discursive foundation, as has been argued, the concepts of agency and pre-given interests are problematized. The articulatory process and its conditions for stability and change – mapped as *sedimentation/hegemony* and *dislocation/rearticulation* – are seen to provide the conditions facilitating and constraining political action. The interplay of stability and change – understood to be discursive – creates a constantly shifting discursive context so that the only force shaping articulation is history itself – understood as previously sedimented discursive formations and dislocatory moments. The overlap of practices – understood as *overdetermination* – positions an entity such as the WTO firmly within its historically contingent discursive context. This context does not merely affect the WTO, but provides its constitutive foundations – the sedimented series of social practices facilitating its particular political operation.

Articulation and historical contingency

The Foucaultian genealogical analysis traced out the alternate logics through which global trade governance has been made possible since the 1934 US Reciprocal Trade Agreements Act, through to the GATT Uruguay Round that led to the emergence of the WTO in 1995. 'Trade' can be seen to have gone through multiple and overlapping rearticulations, facilitating quite alternate political projects. Practices exceeding the GATT regime have formed part of the discursive context through which it has been alternately constituted, as evidenced in the emergence of the developing-country identity. The crisis that conditioned the Uruguay Round and the formation of the

WTO organization – a largely unintended consequence – can be seen as a rearticulation in the wake of a series of dislocations in the shape of global politics that took place in the 1970s. Rather than just seeing alternate moments of global trade governance as shaped by their historical context, they can be seen as intimately constituted within the contingent series of social practices native to their temporal being which they, as social practices themselves, affect in a mutually constitutive relationship. These practices replace the pretence of agency.

Formal rules/procedures and informal norms provided a means by which to trace the discursive formation of the WTO that emerged in 1995. However, in so doing, they also made clear that the WTO cannot be limited to any set of finite practices but consists of a much less certain and diffuse process. The boundaries of the WTO are, as constituted within discourse, inherently uncertain. This uncertainty is evident in the rearticulation of the WTO post-1995, as reflected in rhetoric produced by the WTO Secretariat in response to a changing discursive context. These findings suggest that the WTO is far from a static entity, and therefore reading it within its historical context is essential to be able to appreciate its political operation.

A changing discursive context

Acknowledging (re)articulation in the historically contingent discursive context as a significant variable relevant to the research strategy, the formalization of NGOs in the WTO became an interesting example by which to map the relationship between the WTO and its historical context. An NGO identity has emerged in the WTO not as a result of individual/group agency, but through a series of dislocations in which a particular articulation of trade has been rearticulated to include many identities not previously connected to global trade governance. This has been a slow and gradual process in which equivalential links have been formed between identities, bringing more and more into the field of global trade governance, and eventually the WTO.

The in-depth case study of new identities forming to contest a particular WTO policy process – the GATS 2000 negotiations – helped to trace out part of the complexity characteristic of the relationship between the WTO and the historical context. The discursive context consists of an immense relational network of social practices, with different degrees of sedimentation and subject to constant rearticulation. As presented in the case study, these practices coalesce around certain nodal points, such as individual figures, groups and networks. It is at these points that collective action (e.g. critical research, lobbying government, global group petitions) takes place, leading to further sedimentation of identities around global trade governance (e.g. formalization of networks). Rather than viewing such campaign activity as on the periphery of research issues relevant to understanding the WTO, post-structuralist discourse theory makes it possible to see such practices as part of the discursive context constitutive of the WTO. However, adopting such a broad research remit for understanding the WTO is potentially problematic because it appears to make it very difficult to define what is and is *not* relevant to research. Thus, it is necessary now to consider the possible problems and implications that follow from adopting the research strategy developed here. This can be discussed by reconsidering the hypothesis driving this book.

So what if the WTO is understood discursively?

The hypothesis at the book's core – that *the WTO should be understood as a product of the discursive interaction between both material and ideational factors* – emerged through the problematization of current social scientific literature on the WTO. This problematization was provoked in response to an often under-acknowledged uncertainty as to how the WTO is defined as a research object in the literature, and the failure to theorize *how* the ideational and material interact to form the WTO. The hypothesis has motivated the enquiry, pointing to the utility of post-structuralist discourse theory, and demanding new questions relating to such fundamental components of the WTO as who/what constitutes an actor, through which to engage with the initial purpose of the project: to expose the discursivity or social embeddedness of the WTO.

The hypothesis is imbued with a certain set of ontological presuppositions – outlined through the discussion of post-structuralist discourse theory – that prevent the book from claiming any form of causal relationship between the material/ideational and the WTO. Consequently, it would be ontologically incorrect to demand verification of the hypothesis. Causality (and verifiability) is based on the assumption that ideational and material factors may be separated out into distinct variables. Some of these variables will be dependent, whilst others will be independent (or explanatory). On this basis, the claim may be made that changes in the WTO are caused by, for example, a change in the balance of (material) capabilities between Member states, or a new (ideational) rule. Post-structuralist discourse theory does not negate the value of studying such developments, but it opposes the suggestion that any relationship between social practices (e.g. trade capabilities of Member states and the shape of the WTO) is causal. This is because any such relationship is understood to be mutually constitutive within discursive practice (Hansen 2006: 25–28). As Hansen states:

> Causal epistemology cannot … establish its privilege through reference to any objective truth as its own criterion for truth is enshrined within a historically situated discourse of knowledge, not in a trans-historical, trans-discursive universal objectivity. Poststructuralism's break with causality is thus not a flaw within its research design but an ontological and epistemological choice.
>
> (Hansen 2006: 28)

The false pretence to causality is evident in Ford's (2003) social constructivist study, where – without asking how the actors emerged in the first place – she assumes the existence of a pre-constructed (material) foundation upon which the 'Self of multilateral traders' is constructed (ibid.: 135). In a rigorous critique of social constructivism, Zehfuss argues that 'the conviction that there is a reality which must be acknowledged as a baseline and an ultimate limit makes it possible to defer responsibility to "the circumstances"' (Zehfuss 2002: 255). Deeper-level questioning of how the material has come to *be* are deferred so as to claim a (false) credibility. Whilst justifying the need for post-structuralist discourse theoretical enquiry, however, the critique of causality and the material-ideational distinction creates potential problems for research. This problem is well summarized by Zehfuss, who states:

> Positions that assert the existence of a background [pre-discursive] reality validate themselves with appeals to that reality. Alternative positions that question the relevance of reality conceived of as separate from [discursive] representations fail to acquire the same authority. They are bound to look insecure, weak and unscientific.
>
> (Zehfuss 2002: 259)

Though standing on firm ontological groundings, post-structuralist discourse theory faces a challenge to state its credibility. In editing a collection of essays intended to represent the emergent nexus of post-structuralist engagement in the field of international political economy, de Goede (2006: 1) has noted that any perspective focused on discourse faces an up-hill struggle to show that it does not risk distraction away from the study of real material inequality. Its value is in de-naturalizing that which is otherwise taken as given – such as who/what constitutes an actor in the WTO – so as to be able to question the discursive formation of material inequality (de Goede 2006: 5–7). This is not a relativist position because of the emphasis on the (historically contingent) context (Zehfuss 2002: 255). The historical context – consisting of a particular relational series of (discursive) social practices – provides the boundaries to what is possible in discourse and, thus, politics. As demonstrated in the book, historically sensitive analysis of the articulation of the WTO provides the understanding necessary to research further the constitution of key aspects within the wider discursive context, such as the emergence of an NGO identity in the WTO. Whilst overdetermination means that articulation exceeds any finite political space, it is still possible to trace out part of this process through focusing on specific aspects. This means that it is impossible ever to produce a definitive text detailing the WTO in its entirety, not only because the articulatory process is diffuse, complex and unstable but also, more importantly, because knowledge production is an inherently discursive practice in itself and therefore objectivity becomes a misleading goal.[3]

Positivists such as Krasner (1999: 49) would reject the perspective advanced in the book on the basis that the propositions it presents cannot be tested against evidence. Though post-structuralist discourse theory rejects the possibility of an extra-discursive foundation from which we may objectively define 'truth' and 'knowledge', this by no means prevents the production of coherent knowledge. Simply put, asserting the discursive character of the material shifts the criteria for what constitutes knowledge to a deeper level of enquiry. The criteria justifying the research design adopted in this particular enquiry are laid out in the introductory chapter. More generally, however, the set of criteria for determining knowledge production in post-structuralist discourse theory is the same as that for qualitative research overall (Gaskell and Bauer 2000: 342–49), including methodological reflexivity, documentation of sources, and thick description (as in the use of in-depth case studies). Indeed, having shown the fallacy of positing testable causal relations, the ultimate criteria for any piece of social scientific research will be the judgement of peers who constitute the academic establishment. Producing credible social scientific knowledge about the human world that, as Zehfuss puts it, 'cannot be described or grasped other than through our interpretations and in relation to our [discursive] practices' (Zehfuss 2002: 255) is possible through methodological reflexivity, acknowledging the ontological presuppositions through which one works to produce knowledge. Post-structuralist discourse theory is able to constitute credible knowledge because it has a firm and rigorously theorized ontological basis that is at the same time constantly contested amongst individuals positioned as academics with long educations in the social sciences. To conclude this argument, it is necessary to return to the subject of this book's investigation: the WTO.

The WTO reconsidered

Theorizing the diffuse and mutually constitutive relationship between the WTO and its discursive context leads to a series of important implications for future study of the WTO.

First, it is important to problematize reflexively that which is otherwise taken to be given in the WTO, such as concepts like 'trade', or 'nation-state'. This facilitates a more nuanced understanding of how different practices constitutive of the WTO are formed. The book has shown the value of applying a deep-level enquiry to the concept of trade. This does not negate the utility of these concepts if social science is equipped to acknowledge them as practices operating within the discursive context rather than as pre-discursive objects. Rather than limiting trade to the technical-apolitical sphere, it becomes clear that it is subject to multiple articulations, each facilitating an alternative form of relational practices.

Second, the novelty of applying a post-structuralist discourse theoretical perspective to an entity such as the WTO has meant that the book has approached the WTO on a relatively general level, only becoming more specific after the enquiry pointed to the question of who/what constitutes an actor as a vehicle by which to study part of the discursive context through which the WTO is constituted. The thick description required of post-structuralist discourse theory empirical research means that it is necessary to work within relatively modest research parameters so as to make practical the complex articulatory process it studies. This leads into the third point.

Third, the uncertain character of the diffuse and shifting articulatory process means that it is ontologically impossible to produce a full understanding of the WTO. The problem is not one of scale, but a consequence of the historically contingent discursive character of knowledge, as discussed earlier. It is in this sense that the WTO has often been put into quotation marks during the book, where the question of what it *is* is most under question.

Instead of the claim to definitive knowledge, post-structuralist discourse theory requires research that traces the relationships between social practices. Such research produces credible knowledge to the extent that, along with meeting the criteria outlined above, it follows a coherent theoretical schema. In other words, the concepts through which these relationships are modelled need to be used in a consistent manner. In turn, this facilitates comparative research so that, for example, applying the logics of equivalence and difference to the formation of both the GATS and the TRIPS would provide useful knowledge on the articulation of trade agreements in the WTO. That research may be tested for its credibility to the extent that concepts are used with consistency, though it is also necessary that thick-descriptive research include extensive documentation of source materials by which others may critique and expand upon the analysis produced.

The account presented here has shown how, by theorizing the ideational and material as part of the same discursive practice through which the WTO is constituted, a new research strategy is opened up in which it is possible to theorize an infinitely complex series of mutually constitutive relationships between the WTO and its discursive context. New identities emerging to contest global trade governance have altered the discursive context and, consequently, led to a rearticulation of the WTO as 'development-friendly', but equally those identities are a product of the WTO itself, responding to a particular articulation of trade through which environmental groups have come to include a concern with global trade governance within their identities. The research into campaigning critical of the GATS showed that the WTO has a relationship with identities far exceeding its formal institutional structure, so that, for example, many individuals have been positioned within identities contesting the shape of global trade governance and the WTO.

Finally, it should be said that this book is indicative – but not exhaustive – of the potential that post-structuralist discourse theory has to understand the complex series of interactions constitutive of governance at the global level. The research strategy utilized here is not a universal model but should be readjusted according to the research subject. However, it is the ontological presuppositions theorizing the interaction of the material and the ideational that provide the basis for further enquiry in the same vein as conducted here.

Notes

1 As defined in Chapters 1 and 2.
2 As quoted in Chapter 2, Howarth (2000: 5) defines discourse as 'all the practices and meanings shaping a particular community of social actors'.
3 Implicit within the demand for causality is an assumption that the formation of accurate causal models will lead to greater success in the predictive capacity of political science. However, as Blyth (2006) has argued, the social sciences overall share an abysmal record when it comes to prediction. The value of post-structuralist discourse theory is apparent here, the diffuse and shifting character of the articulatory process representing why it is impossible to identify clear causal mechanisms. The failure to predict may be taken as either a weakness of the social sciences or the basis of a greater understanding of complexity in the human world. Post-structuralist discourse theory takes the latter option.

Bibliography

Adamantopoulos, K. (ed.) (1997) *An Anatomy of the World Trade Organization* (London: Kluwer Law International).

Allen, W. (1953) 'The International Trade Philosophy of Cordell Hull, 1907–33', *The American Economic Review* 43(1): 101–16.

Amoore, L. and Langley, P. (2004) 'Ambiguities of Global Civil Society', *Review of International Studies* 30(1): 89–110.

Antoniades, A. (2010) *Producing Globalisation – Politics of Discourse and Institutions in Greece and Ireland* (Manchester: Manchester University Press).

Babson, S. (2000) 'Cross-border Trade with Mexico and the Prospect for Worker Solidarity: The Case of Mexico', *Critical Sociology* 26(1/2): 13–35.

Bagwell, K. and Staiger, R. (2004) 'Multilateral Trade Negotiations, Bilateral Opportunism and the Rules of GATT/WTO', *Journal of International Economics* 63: 1–29.

Baldwin, R. (2000) 'Pragmatism Versus Principle in GATT Decision-making: A Brief Historical Perspective', in WTO Secretariat (ed.) *From GATT to the WTO: The Multilateral Trading System in the New Millennium* (The Hague: Kluwer Law International).

Ball, T., Farr, J. and Hanson, R.L. (1989) 'Introduction', in T. Ball, J. Farr and R.L. Hanson (eds) *Political Innovation and Conceptual Change* (Cambridge: Cambridge University Press), 1–5.

Bandy, J. (2000) 'Bordering the Future: Resisting Neoliberalism in the Borderlands', *Critical Sociology* 26(3): 232–67.

Barfield, C. (2001) *Free Trade, Sovereignty, Democracy – The Future of the World Trade Organization* (Washington, DC: The American Enterprise Institute Press).

Barnett, M.N. and Finnemore, M. (1999) 'The Politics, Power, and Pathologies of International Organisations', *International Organization* 53(4): 699–732.

Beane, D. (2000) *The United States and GATT – A Relational Study* (Oxford: Elsevier Science).

Bell, Duncan (2002) 'Anarchy, Power and Death: Contemporary Political Realism as Ideology', *Journal of Political Ideologies* 7(2): 221–39.

Blackhurst, R. (1998) 'The Capacity of the WTO to Fulfill its Mandate', in A. Krueger (ed.) *The WTO as an International Organization* (Chicago: The University of Chicago Press), 31–58.

Blackhurst, R., Lyakurwa, B. and Oyejide, A. (1999) 'Improving African Participation in the WTO', paper commissioned by the World Bank for a conference at the WTO, 20–21 September 1999 (Washington: World Bank).

Blyth, M. (1997) '"Any More Bright Ideas?" The Ideational Turn of Comparative Political Economy', *Comparative Politics* 29(2): 229–50.

——(2003) 'Structures do not Come with an Instruction Sheet', *Perspectives on Politics* 1(4): 695–703.

——(2006) 'Prediction, Probability, and Propensity in Political Science', paper presented to the *Centre for Business and Politics*, Copenhagen Business School, 29 May, forthcoming within *The American Political Science Review* (November 2006).

Boltho, A. (1996) 'The Return of Free Trade?' *International Affairs* 72(2): 247–59.

Brassett, J. and Smith, W. (2010) 'Deliberation and Global Civil Society: Agency, Arena, Affect', *Review of International Studies* (36): 413–30.

Bronckers, M. (2000) *A Cross-Section of WTO Law* (London: Cameron May).

Brown, L. and Fox, J. (1998) 'Accountability within Transnational Coalitions', in J. Fox and L. Brown (eds) *The Struggle for Accountability – The World Bank, NGOs, and Grassroots Movements* (Massachusetts: The MIT Press), 439–84.

Buzan, B. and Wæver, O. (2003) *Regions and Powers – the Structure of International Security* (Cambridge: Cambridge University Press).

Cable, V. (1996) 'The New Trade Agenda: Universal Rules Amid Cultural Diversity', *International Affairs* 72(2): 227–46.

Cameron, J. and Campbell, K. (eds) (1998) *Dispute Resolution in the World Trade Organisation* (London: Cameron May).

Campbell, D. (1992) *Writing Security – United States Foreign Policy and the Politics of Identity* (Manchester: Manchester University Press).

——(1998) *National Deconstruction – Violence, Identity, and Justice in Bosnia* (Minneapolis: University of Minnesota Press).

Campbell, J. (2004) *Institutional Change and Globalization* (Princeton: Princeton University Press).

Cass, D. (2005) *The Constitutionalization of the World Trade Organization: Legitimacy, Democracy, and Community in the International Trading System* (Oxford: Oxford University Press).

Cohn, T. (2002) *Governing Global Trade – International Institutions in Conflict and Convergence* (Aldershot: Ashgate).

——(2005) *Global Political Economy – Theory and Practice*, third edn (New York: Pearson Longman).

Cook, M. (1995) 'Mexican State-labor Relations and the Political Implications of Free Trade', *Latin American Perspectives* 22(1): 77–94.

Crandall, S. (1913) 'The American Construction of the Most-Favored-Nation Clause', *The American Journal of International Law* 7(4): 708–23.

Critchley, S. (1999) *The Ethics of Deconstruction – Derrida and Levinas* (Edinburgh: Edinburgh University Press).

Croome, J. (1995) *Reshaping the World Trading System – A History of the Uruguay Round* (Geneva: World Trade Organization).

Curzon, G. and Curzon, V. (1973) 'GATT: Traders' Club', in R. Cox and H. Jacobson (eds) *The Anatomy of Influence – Decision Making in International Organization* (New Haven: Yale University Press), 298–333.

Danaher, K. and Mark, J. (2003) *Insurrection – Citizen Challenges to Corporate Power* (London: Routledge).

Das, B.L. (1999) *The World Trade Organisation – A Guide to the Framework for International Trade* (London: Zed and Penang: Third World Network).

——(2003) *The WTO and the Multilateral Trading System: Past, Present and Future* (London: Zed and Penang: Third World Network).

Davis, J. and Daniels, J. (2001) 'Corporations and Structural Linkages in World Commerce', in A. Rugman and G. Boyd (eds) *The World Trade Organisation in the New Global Economy – Trade and Investment Issues in the New Millennium Round* (Cheltenham, UK: Edward Elgar), 70–94.

de Goede, M. (2005) *Virtue, Fortune, and Faith – A Genealogy of Finance* (Minneapolis: University of Minnesota Press).

——(2006) 'International Political Economy and the Promises of Poststructuralism', in M. de Goede (ed.) *International Political Economy and Poststructural Politics* (Basingstoke: Palgrave), 1–20.

Dobson, A. (1988) 'The Kennedy Administration and Economic Warfare Against Communism', *International Affairs* 64(4): 599–616.

Drake, W. and Nicolaïdis, K. (1992) 'Ideas, Interests and Institutionalization: "Trade-in-Services" and the Uruguay Round', *International Organization* 46(1): 39–100.

Dreiling, M. and Wolf, B. (2001) 'Environmental Movement Organizations and Political Strategy: Tactical Conflicts over NAFTA', *Organization & Environment* 14(1): 34–54.

Dreyfus, H. and Rabinow, P. (1983) *Michel Foucault – Beyond Structuralism and Hermeneutics*, second edn (Chicago: The University of Chicago Press).

Dunkley, G. (2000) *The Free Trade Adventure – The WTO, the Uruguay Round and Globalisation – A Critique* (London: Zed).

Dunn, K.C. (2009) 'Contested State Spaces: African National Parks and the State', *European Journal of International Relations* 15(3): 423–46.

Egan, D. (2001) 'The Limits of Internationalization: A Neo-Gramscian Analysis of the Multilateral Agreement on Investment', *Critical Sociology* 27(3): 74–97.

Endres, A. and Fleming, G. (2002) *International Organizations and the Analysis of Economic Policy, 1919–1950* (Cambridge: Cambridge University Press).

Epstein, C. (2009) *The Power of Words in International Relations: Birth of an Anti-whaling Discourse* (Cambridge, MA: MIT Press).

——(n.d., forthcoming) 'Who Speaks? Discourse, the Subject and the Study of Identity in International Politics', *European Journal of International Relations*.

Esty, D. (1994) *Greening the GATT: Trade, Environment, and the Future* (Washington: Institute for International Economics).

——(2002) 'The World Trade Organization's Legitimacy Crisis', *World Trade Review* 1(1), WTO Publications, 7–22.

Feagin, J., Orum, A. and Sjoberg, G. (1991) *A Case for the Case Study* (Chapel Hill: University of North Carolina Press).

Finlayson, J. and Zacher, M. (1983) 'The GATT and the Regulation of Trade Barriers: Regime Dynamics and Functions', in S.D. Krasner (ed.) *International Regimes* (Ithaca: Cornell University Press), 273–314.

Fisher, G. (1967) 'The "Most Favored Nation" Clause in GATT: A Need for Reevaluation?' *Stanford Law Review* 19: 841–55.

Flyvbjerg, B. (2001) *Making Social Science Matter – Why Social Inquiry Fails and How it can Succeed Again* (Cambridge: Cambridge University Press).

Footer, M. (1997) 'The Role of Consensus in GATT/WTO Decision-Making', *Northwestern Journal of International Law and Business* 17(2/3): 653–80.

Ford, J. (2003) *A Social Theory of the WTO – Trading Cultures* (Basingstoke: Palgrave Macmillan).

Foucault, M. (1980) *Power/Knowledge, Selected Interviews and Other Writings, 1972–1977*, first edn, ed. Colin Gordon (New York: Pantheon).

——(1983) *Discourse and Truth: The Problematization of Parrhesia – Six Lectures Given by Michel Foucault at Berkeley, Oct.–Nov. 1983*, foucault.info/documents/parrhesia/ (accessed February 2013).

——(1984a) 'The Subject and Power', Afterword in H. Dreyfus and P. Rabinow, *Michel Foucault: Beyond Structuralism and Hermeneutics* (Brighton: Harvester), 208–26.

——(1984b) *What is Enlightenment?* foucault.info/documents/whatIsEnlightenment/foucault.whatIsEnlightenment.en.html (accessed February 2013).

——(1984c) *Polemics, Politics, and Problematizations* (interview by Paul Rabinow), foucault.info/foucault/interview.html (accessed February 2013).

——(1991) 'Nietzche, Genealogy, History', in P. Rabinow (ed.) *The Foucault Reader* (London: Penguin), 76–100.

Freeden, M. (1996) *Ideologies and Political Theory: A Conceptual Approach* (Oxford: Clarendon Press).

——(2000) 'Practising Ideology and Ideological Practices', *Political Studies* 48: 302–22.

Gallin, D. (2002) 'Labour as a Global Social Force – Past Divisions and New Tasks', in J. Harrod and R. O'Brien (ed.) *Global Unions? – Theory and Strategies of Organized Labour in the Global Political Economy* (London: Routledge), 235–50.

Gammon, E. (2008) 'Affect and the Rise of the Self-regulating Market', *Millennium* 37(2): 251–78.

Gardner, R. (1964) 'GATT and the United Nations Conference on Trade and Development', *International Organization* 18(4): 685–704.

Gasché, R. (2004) 'How Empty can Empty be? – On the Place of the Universal', in S. Critchley and O. Marchart (eds) *Laclau – A Critical Reader* (London: Routledge), 17–34.

Gaskell, G. and Bauer, M. (2000) 'Towards Public Accountability: Beyond Sampling, Reliability and Validity', in M. Bauer and G. Gaskell (eds) *Qualitative Researching with Text, Image and Sound* (London: SAGE), 336–50.

Georgiev, D. (2003) 'The Decision-Making Process in the World Trade Organization', in K. van der Borght, E. Remacle and J. Wiener (eds) *Essays in the Future of the WTO: Finding a New Balance* (London: Cameron May), 25–46.

Gill, S. (1997) 'Global Structural Change and Multilateralism', in Stephen Gill (ed.) *Globalization, Democratisation and Multilateralism* (Tokyo: United Nations University Press), 1–17.

Gill, S. and Law, D. (1989) 'Global Hegemony and the Structural Power of Capital', *International Studies Quarterly* 33(4): 475–99.

Gilpin, R. (2001) *Global Political Economy – Understanding the International Economic Order* (Princeton: Princeton University Press).

Goldstein, J. (1989) 'The Impact of Ideas on Trade Policy: The Origins of US Agricultural and Manufacturing Policies', *International Organization* 43(1): 31–71.

——(1993) 'Creating the GATT Rules: Politics, Institutions, and American Policy', in J. Ruggie (ed.) *Multilateralism Matters – The Theory and Praxis of an Institutional Form* (New York: Columbia University Press), 201–32.

Goldstein, J. and Martin, L. (2000) 'Legalization, Trade Liberalization, and Domestic Politics: A Cautionary Note', *International Organization* 54(3): 603–32.

Gramsci, A. (1971) *Selections from the Prison Notebooks*, ed. and trans. Q. Hoare and G. Nowell Smith (London: Lawrence and Wishart).

Griggs, S. (2005) 'Problematizing the Mobilization of Hospital Directors', in D. Howarth and J. Torfing, *Discourse Theory in European Politics – Identity, Policy and Governance* (Basingstoke: Palgrave Macmillan), 117–38.

Griggs, Steven and Howarth, David (2000) 'New Environmental Movements and Direct Action Protest: The Campaign Against Manchester Airport's Second Runway', in D. Howarth, A. Norval and Y. Stavrakakis (eds) *Discourse Theory and Political Analysis: Identities, Hegemonies and Social Change* (Manchester: Manchester University Press), 52–69.

Grossman, P. (2000) 'Corporate Interest and Trade Liberalization – The North American Free Trade Agreement and Environmental Protection', *Organization & Environment* 13(1): 61–85.

Haggard, S. (1988) 'The Institutional Foundations of Hegemony: Explaining the Reciprocal Trade Agreements Act of 1934', *International Organization* 42(1): 91–119.

Hajer, M. (1993) 'Discourse Coalitions and the Institutionalization of Practice: The Case of Acid Rain in Britain', in F. Fisher and J. Forester (eds) *The Argumentative Turn in Policy Analysis and Planning* (Durham: Duke University Press), 43–76.

——(1995) *The Politics of Environmental Discourse – Ecological Modernization and the Policy Process* (Oxford: Clarendon Press).

——(2005) 'Coalitions, Practices, and Meaning in Environmental Politics: From Acid to BSE', in 'Discourse Theory: Achievements, Arguments, and Challenges', in D. Howarth and J. Torfing, *Discourse Theory in European Politics – Identity, Policy and Governance* (Basingstoke: Palgrave Macmillan), 297–315.

Hajer, M. and Versteeg, W. (2005) 'A Decade of Discourse Analysis of Environmental Politics: Achievements, Challenges, Perspectives', *Journal of Environmental Policy & Planning* 7(3): 175–84.

Hansen, A.D. and Sørensen, E. (2005) 'Polity as Politics: Studying the Shaping and Effects of Discursive Polities', in 'Discourse Theory: Achievements, Arguments, and Challenges', in D. Howarth and J. Torfing, *Discourse Theory in European Politics – Identity, Policy and Governance* (Basingstoke: Palgrave Macmillan), 93–116.

Hansen, L. (2006) *Security as Practice – Discourse Analysis and the Bosnian War* (London: Routledge).

Hart, M. (1995a) 'The 1947–48 United Nations Conference on Trade and Employment', in F. Hampson (with Michael Hart), *Multilateral Negotiations – Lessons from Arms Control, Trade, and the Environment* (Baltimore: The Johns Hopkins University Press), 125–67.

——(1995b) 'The GATT Uruguay Round – 1986–93: The Setting and the Players', in F. Hampson (with Michael Hart), *Multilateral Negotiations – Lessons from Arms Control, Trade, and the Environment* (Baltimore: The Johns Hopkins University Press), 168–201.

——(1995c) 'The GATT Uruguay Round, 1981–93: The Negotiations', in F. Hampson (with Michael Hart), *Multilateral Negotiations – Lessons from Arms Control, Trade, and the Environment* (Baltimore: The Johns Hopkins University Press), 202–52.

Hasenclever, A., Mayer, P. and Rittberger, V. (1997) *Theories of International Regimes* (Cambridge: Cambridge University Press).

Hettne, B., Inotai, A. and Sunkel, O. (eds) (1999) *Globalism and the New Regionalism* (Basingstoke: Macmillan Press).

Hillary, John (2001) *The Wrong Model: GATS, Trade Liberalisation and Children's Right to Health* (London: Save the Children).

Hiscox, M. (1999) 'The Magic Bullet? The RTAA, Institutional Reform, and Trade Liberalization', *International Organization* 53(4): 669–98.

Hobson, John and Seabrooke, Leonard (eds) (2007) *Everyday Politics of the World Economy* (Cambridge: Cambridge University Press).

Hoda, A. (2001) *Tariff Negotiations and Renegotiations under the GATT and the WTO: Procedures and Practices* (Cambridge: Cambridge University Press and WTO Publications).

Hoekman, B. and Kostecki, M. (2001) *The Political Economy of the World Trading System – The WTO and Beyond*, second edn (Oxford: Oxford University Press).

——(2009) *The Political Economy of the World Trading System – The WTO and Beyond*, third edn (Oxford: Oxford University Press).

Hoekman, B., Mattoo, H. and English, P. (eds) (2002) *Development, Trade and the WTO – A Handbook* (Washington, DC: The World Bank).

Hogenboom, B. (1996) 'Cooperation and Polarisation beyond Borders: The Transnationalisation of Mexican Environmental Issues during the NAFTA Negotiations', *Third World Quarterly* 17(5): 989–1005.

Hoogvelt, A. (2001) 'Globalisation and the Postcolonial World – The New Political Economy of Development', second edn (Basingstoke: Palgrave Macmillan).

Howarth, D. (2000) *Discourse* (Buckingham: Open University Press).

——(2005) 'Applying Discourse Theory: The Method of Articulation', in 'Discourse Theory: Achievements, Arguments, and Challenges', in D. Howarth and J. Torfing, *Discourse Theory in European Politics – Identity, Policy and Governance* (Basingstoke: Palgrave Macmillan), 316–50.

Howarth, D. and Stavrakakis, Y. (2000) 'Introducing Discourse Theory and Political Analysis', in D. Howarth, A. Norval and Y. Stavrakakis (eds) *Discourse Theory and Political Analysis – Identities, Hegemonies and Social Change* (Manchester: Manchester University Press), 1–23.

Howarth, D. and Torfing, J. (eds) (2005) *Discourse Theory in European Politics: Identity, Policy and Governance* (Basingstoke: Palgrave Macmillan).

Howse, R. and Nicolaïdis, K. (2001) 'Legitimacy and Global Governance: Why Constitutionalising the WTO is a Step too Far', in R. Porter, P. Sauvé, A. Subramanian and A. Beviglia Zampetti (eds) *Efficiency, Equity, and Legitimacy – The Multilateral Trading System at the Millennium* (Washington, DC: Brookings Institution Press), 227–52.

Huyer, S. (2004) 'Challenging Relations: A Labour-NGO Coalition to Oppose the Canada-US and North American Free Trade Agreements 1985–93', *Development in Practice* 14(1–2): 48–60.

Jackson, J. (1998a) *The World Trade Organization – Constitution and Jurisprudence* (London: Royal Institute of International Affairs).

——(1998b) *The World Trading System – Law and Policy of International Economic Relations*, second edn (Cambridge, MA: The MIT Press).

——(2000) *The Jurisprudence of GATT and the WTO – Insights on Treaty Law and Economic Relations* (Cambridge: Cambridge University Press).

——(2009) *Sovereignty, the WTO, and Changing Fundamentals of International Law* (Cambridge: Cambridge University Press).

Jameson, F. (1994) 'Postmodernism and the Market', in S. Žižek (ed.) *Mapping Ideology* (London: Verso), 278–95.

Johnston, J. and Laxer, G. (2003) 'Solidarity in the Age of Globalization: Lessons from the Anti-MAI and Zapatista Struggles', *Theory and Society* 32: 39–91.

Jones, K. (2010) *The Doha Blues: Institutional Crisis and Reform in the WTO* (Oxford: Oxford University Press).

Joseph, S. (2011) *Blame it on the WTO? A Human Rights Critique* (Oxford: Oxford University Press).

Karns, M. (1990) 'Multilateral Diplomacy and Trade Policy: The United States and the GATT', in M. Karns and K. Mingst (eds) *The United States and Multilateral Institutions – Patterns of Changing Instrumentality and Influence* (Boston: Unwin Hyman), 141–75.

Keeley, J. (1990) 'Toward a Foucauldian Analysis of International Regimes', *International Organization* 44(1): 83–105.

Kelsey, J. (1997) 'The Globalization of Tertiary Education: Implications of GATS', in M. Peters, *Cultural Politics and the University* (Wellington: Dunmore), 66–88.

Keohane, R. (1984) *After Hegemony – Cooperation and Discord in the World Political Economy* (Princeton, NJ: Princeton University Press).

——(1986) 'Reciprocity in International Relations', *International Organization* 40(1): 1–27.

Kim, S.Y. (2010) *Power and the Governance of Global Trade: From GATT to the WTO* (Ithaca: Cornell University Press).

Kingsnorth, P. (2003) *One No, Many Yeses – A Journey to the Heart of the Global Resistance Movement* (London: The Free Press).

Krasner, S. (ed.) (1983) *International Regimes* (Ithaca: Cornell University Press).

——(1999) *Sovereignty* (Princeton: Princeton University Press).

Kwa, A. (2003) *Power Politics in the WTO*, second edn (Bangkok: Focus on the Global South), www.aftinet.org.au/papers/kwa1.html (accessed February 2013).

Kwa, A. and Jawara, F. (2004) *Behind the Scenes at the WTO: The Real World of International Trade Negotiations – Lessons of Cancun*, second edn (London: Zed).

Laclau, E. (1990) *New Reflections on the Revolution of Our Time* (London: Verso).

——(1996) *Emancipation(s)* (London: Verso).

——(2004) 'Glimpsing the Future', in S. Critchley and O. Marchart (eds) *Laclau – A Critical Reader* (London: Routledge), 279–328.

Laclau, E. and Mouffe, C. (1990) 'Post-Marxism without Apologies', in E. Laclau, *New Reflections on the Revolution of Our Time* (London: Verso), 97–132.

——(2001) *Hegemony and Socialist Strategy – Towards a Radical Democratic Politics*, second edn (London: Verso).

Lake, D. (1983) 'International Economic Structures and American Foreign Economic Policy, 1887–1934', *World Politics* 35(4): 517–43.

Lancaster, C. (1992) 'Negotiations at UNCTAD 1', in A. Williams (ed.) *Many Voices – Multilateral Negotiations in the World Arena* (Boulder: Westview Press), 61–78.

Lanoszka, A. (2009) *The World Trade Organization: Changing Dynamics in the Global Political Economy* (Boulder: Lynne Rienner).

Larkin, J. (1937) 'The Trade Agreement Act in Court and in Congress', *The American Political Science Review* 31(3): 498–507.

Larsen, H. (2009) 'A Distinct FPA for Europe? Towards a Comprehensive Framework for Analysing the Foreign Policy of EU Member States', *European Journal of International Relations* 15(3): 537–66.

Lee, Donna (2004) 'Understanding the WTO Dispute Settlement Process', in B. Hocking and S. McGuire (eds) *Trade Politics*, second edn (London: Routledge), 120–32.

Lipson, C. (1983) 'The Transformation of Trade: The Sources and Effects of Regime Change', in S.D. Krasner (ed.) *International Regimes* (Ithaca: Cornell University Press), 233–71.

Little, R. (2005) 'International Regimes', in J. Baylis and S. Smith (eds) *The Globalization of World Politics*, third edn (Oxford: Oxford University Press), 369–86.

Maggi, G. (1999) 'The Role of the Multilateral Institutions in International Trade Cooperation', *The American Economic Review* 89(1) (March): 190–214.

Mahon, M. (1992) *Foucault's Nietzschean Genealogy – Truth, Power, and the Subject* (New York: State University of New York Press).

Marceau, G. and Pedersen, P. (1999) 'Is the WTO Open and Transparent? – A Discussion of the Relationship of the WTO with Non-governmental Organisations and Civil Society's Claims for more Transparency and Public Participation', *Journal of World Trade* 33(1): 5–49.

Matsushita, M., Schoenbaum, T. and Mavroidis, P. (2003) *The World Trade Organization – Law, Practice, and Policy* (Oxford: Oxford University Press).

McGrew, T. (1999) 'The World Trade Organization – Technocracy or Banana Republic?' in A. Taylor and C. Thomas (eds) *Global Trade and Global Social Issues* (London: Routledge), 197–216.

McRae, D. and Thomas, J. (1983) 'The GATT and Multilateral Treaty Making: The Tokyo Round', *The American Journal of International Law* 77(1): 51–83.

Meléndez-Ortiz, R. and Shaffer, G. (2010) *Dispute Settlement at the WTO: The Developing Country Experience* (Cambridge: Cambridge University Press).

Mendoza, M., Low, P. and Kotschwar, B. (eds) (1999) *Trade Rules in the Making – Challenges in Regional and Multilateral Negotiations* (Washington, DC: Brookings Institution Press).

Michalopoulos, C. (2001) *Developing Countries in the WTO* (Basingstoke: Palgrave).

Milliken, J. (1999) 'The Study of Discourse in International Relations: A Critique of Research and Methods', *European Journal of International Relations* 5(2): 225–54.

Moore, P.M. (1996) 'The Decision Bridging the GATT 1947 and the WTO Agreement', *The American Journal of International Law* 90(2): 317–28.

Mouffe, C. (2000) *The Democratic Paradox* (London: Verso).

Narlikar, A. (2001) 'WTO Decision-Making and Developing Countries', *South Centre TRADE Working Papers* 11, November, www.southcentre.org/publications/wtodecis/toc.htm (accessed July 2006).

——(2004) 'Developing Countries and the WTO', in B. Hocking and S. McGuire (eds) *Trade Politics*, second edn (London: Routledge), 133–45.

Nilson, H. (1998) *Michel Foucault and the Games of Truth*, trans. Rachel Clark (Basingstoke: Macmillan Press).

Nivola, P. (1986) 'The New Protectionism: US Trade Policy in Historical Perspective', *Political Science Quarterly* 101(4): 577–600.

Norval, A.J. (2000) 'Review Article: The Things We Do with Words – Contemporary Approaches to the Analysis of Ideology', *British Journal of Political Science* 30: 313–46.

Nye, J. and Keohane, R. (2001) 'The Club Model of Multilateral Cooperation and Problems of Democratic Legitimacy', in R. Porter, P. Sauvé, A. Subramanian and A. Beviglia Zampetti (eds) *Efficiency, Equity, and Legitimacy – The Multilateral Trading System at the Millennium* (Washington, DC: Brookings Institution Press), 264–94.

O'Brien, R. (2002) 'The Varied Paths to Minimum Global Labour Standards', in J. Harrod and R. O'Brien (ed.) *Global Unions? – Theory and Strategies of Organized Labour in the Global Political Economy* (London: Routledge), 221–34.

O'Brien, R., Goetz, A., Scholte, J. and Williams, M. (2000) *Contesting Global Governance – Multilateral Economic Institutions and Global Social Movements* (Cambridge: Cambridge University Press).

O'Brien, R. and Williams, M. (2004) *Global Political Economy – Evolution and Dynamics* (Basingstoke: Palgrave Macmillan).

Pahre, R. (1998) 'Reactions and Reciprocity: Tariffs and Trade Liberalisation from 1815 to 1914', *The Journal of Conflict Resolution* 42(4): 467–92.

——(2001) 'Most-Favored-Nation Clauses and Clustered Negotiations', *International Organization* 55(4): 859–90.

Patomäki, H. and Teivaninen, T. (2004) *A Possible World – Democratic Transformation of Global Institutions* (London: Zed).

Peet, R. (2003) *Unholy Trinity – The IMF, World Bank and WTO* (London: Zed Books).

Peters, B. (1999) *Institutional Theory in Political Science – The 'New Institutionalism'* (London: Continuum).

Poitras, G. and Robinson, R. (1994) 'The Politics of NAFTA in Mexico', *Journal of Interamerican Studies and World Affairs* 36(1): 1–35.

Porter, R. (2001) 'Efficiency, Equity and Legitimacy: The Global Trading System in the Twenty-first Century', in R. Porter, P. Sauvé, A. Subramanian and A. Beviglia Zampetti (eds) *Efficiency, Equity, and Legitimacy – The Multilateral Trading System at the Millennium* (Washington, DC: Brookings Institution Press), 3–15.

Potter, J. and Wetherell, M. (2001) 'Unfolding Discourse Analysis', in M. Wetherell, S. Taylor and S. Yates (eds) *Discourse Theory and Practice* (London: Sage).

Qureshi, A. (1996) *The World Trade Organization – Implementing International Trade Norms* (Manchester: Manchester University Press).

Rouse, J. (1994) 'Power/Knowledge', in G. Gutting (ed.) *The Cambridge Companion to Foucault* (Cambridge: Cambridge University Press), 92–114.

Ruggie, J. (1983) 'International Regimes, Transactions, and Change: Embedded Liberalism in the Postwar Economic Order', in S.D. Krasner (ed.) *International Regimes* (Ithaca: Cornell University Press), 195–231.

Rugman, A. (2001) 'The World Trade Organisation and the International Political Economy', in A. Rugman and G. Boyd (eds) *The World Trade Organisation in the New Global Economy – Trade and Investment Issues in the New Millennium Round* (Cheltenham, UK: Edward Elgar), 1–22.

Sally, R. (2004) 'The WTO in Perspective', in B. Hocking and S. McGuire (eds) *Trade Politics*, second edn (London: Routledge), 105–19.

Sampson, G. (ed.) (2001) *The Role of the World Trade Organization in Global Governance* (Tokyo: United Nations University Press).

Sapir, A. (1999) 'The General Agreement on Trade in Services – From 1994 to the Year 2000', *Journal of World Trade* 33(1): 51–66.

Sarup, M. (1993) *An Introductory Guide to Post-structuralism and Postmodernism*, second edn (Harlow: Harvester Wheatsheaf).

Sauvé, P. and Stern, R. (eds) (2000) *GATS 2000 – New Directions in Services Trade Liberalization* (Washington: Brookings Institution).

Sayre, F. (1939) 'The Most-Favored-Nation Policy in Relation to Trade Agreements', *The American Political Science Review* 33(3): 411–23.

Scholte, J.A. (2004) 'The WTO and Civil Society', in B. Hocking and S. McGuire (eds) *Trade Politics*, second edn (London: Routledge), 146–61.

Scholte, J.A., O'Brien, R. and Williams, M. (1999) 'The WTO and Civil Society', *Journal of World Trade* 33(1): 107–23.

Schott, J. and Watal, J. (2000) 'Decision-Making in the WTO', *International Economic Policy Brief* 2 March (Washington: Institute for International Economics), www.iie.com/publications/pb/pb.cfm?ResearchID=63 (accessed February 2013).

Schwartz, M. (1998) 'Critical Reproblematization – Foucault and the Task of Modern Philosophy', *Radical Philosophy* 91: 19–29.

Sen, Gautam (2003) 'The United States and the GATT/WTO System', in R. Foot, S. MacFarhane and M. Mastanduno (eds) *US Hegemony and International Organisations – The United States and Multilateral Institutions* (Oxford: Oxford University Press), 115–38.

Setser, V. (1933) 'Did Americans Originate the Conditional Most-Favored-Nation Clause?' *The Journal of Modern History* 5(3): 319–23.

Shoch, J. (2000) 'Contesting Globalization: Organized Labor, NAFTA, and the 1997 and 1998 Fast-Track Fights', *Politics & Society* 28(1): 119–50.

Silverman, D. (2001) *Interpreting Qualitative Data – Methods for Analysing Talk, Text and Interaction*, second edn (London: Sage).

Sinclair, S. and Grieshaber-Otto, J. (2002) *Facing the Facts: A Guide to the GATS Debate* (Ottawa: Canadian Centre for Policy Alternatives).

Skinner, Q. (1989) 'Language and Political Change', in T. Ball, J. Farr and R.L. Hanson (eds) *Political Innovation and Conceptual Change* (Cambridge: Cambridge University Press), 6–23.

——(1998) *Liberty Before Liberalism* (Cambridge: Cambridge University Press).

Smith, A.M. (1998) *Laclau and Mouffe – The Radical Democratic Imaginary* (London: Routledge).

Snyder, R. (1940) 'The Most Favored Nation Clause and Recent Trade Practices', *Political Science Quarterly* 55(1): 77–97.

Soloway, J. and Anishchenko, A. (2001) 'Agenda Setting for a Millennial Round: Challenges and Opportunities', in A. Rugman and G. Boyd (eds) *The World Trade Organisation in the New Global Economy – Trade and Investment Issues in the New Millennium Round* (Cheltenham, UK: Edward Elgar), 46–69.

Sørensen, E. and Torfing, J. (2002) 'Network Politics, Political Capital, and Democracy', *International Journal of Public Administration* 26(6): 609–34.

Srinivasan, T. (1998) *Developing Countries and the Multilateral Trading System – From the GATT to the Uruguay Round and the Future* (Oxford: Westview Press).

Stavrakakis, Y. (1999) *Lacan and the Political* (London: Routledge).

Stein, E. (2001) 'International Integration and Democracy: No Love at First Sight', *The American Journal of International Law* 95(3): 489–534.

Steinberg, R. (2002) 'In the Shadow of Law or Power? Consensus-Based Bargaining and Outcomes in the GATT/WTO', *International Organization* 56(2): 339–74.

Stillerman, J. (2003) 'Transnational Activist Networks and the Emergence of Labor Internationalism in the NAFTA Countries', *Social Science History* 27(4): 577–601.

Strange, M. (2011a) '"Act Now and Sign Our Joint Statement!" – What Role do Online Global Group Petitions Play in Transnational Movement Networks?' *Media, Culture & Society* 33(8): 1236–53.

——(2011b) 'Discursivity of Global Governance: Vestiges of "Democracy" in the World Trade Organization', *Alternatives* 36(3): 240–56.

Strange, R. and Katrak, H. (eds) (2004) *The WTO and Developing Countries* (Basingstoke: Palgrave Macmillan).

Strange, S. (1983) '*Cave! Hic dragones*: A Critique of Regime Analysis', in S.D. Krasner (ed.) *International Regimes* (Ithaca: Cornell University Press), 337–54.

——(1996) *The Retreat of the State – The Diffusion of Power in the World Economy* (Cambridge: Cambridge University Press).

Sykes, A. (2001) '"Efficient Protection" Through WTO Rulemaking', in R. Porter, P. Sauvé, A. Subramanian and A. Beviglia Zampetti (eds) *Efficiency, Equity, and Legitimacy – The Multilateral Trading System at the Millennium* (Washington, DC: Brookings Institution Press), 114–41.

Tabb, W. (2001) *The Amoral Elephant – Globalization and the Struggle for Social Justice in the Twenty-first Century* (New York: Monthly Review Press)

Thaddeus Jackson, P. and Nexon, D.H. (1999) 'Relations before States: Substance, Process and the Study of World Politics', *European Journal of International Relations* 5(3): 291–332.

Thies, C. (2001) 'A Historical Institutionalist Approach to the Uruguay Round Agricultural Negotiations', *Comparative Political Studies* 34(4): 400–28.

Thomassen, L. (2005) 'Antagonism, Hegemony and Ideology after Heterogeneity', *Journal of Political Ideologies* 10(3): 289–309.

Torfing, J. (1999) *New Theories of Discourse – Laclau, Mouffe and Žižek* (Oxford: Blackwell).

——(2005) 'Discourse Theory: Achievements, Arguments, and Challenges', in D. Howarth and J. Torfing, *Discourse Theory in European Politics – Identity, Policy and Governance* (Basingstoke: Palgrave Macmillan), 1–32.

Trebilcock, M. and Howse, R. (1999) *The Regulation of International Trade*, second edn (London: Routledge).

TWN (2003) 'Analysis of the Collapse of the Cancun Ministerial', *TWN Info Service on WTO Issues (Sept 03/14)*, 16 March, www.twnside.org.sg/title/twninfo76.htm (accessed February 2013).

van Apeldoorn, B. (2002) *Transnational Capitalism and the Struggle Over European Integration* (London: Routledge).

van der Borght, K., Remacle, E. and Wiener, J. (eds) (2003) *Essays on the Future of the WTO: Finding a New Balance* (London: Cameron May).

Veltmeyer, H., Petras, J. and Vieux, S. (1997) *Neoliberalism and Class Conflict in Latin America – A Comparative Perspective on the Political Economy of Structural Adjustment* (Basingstoke: Macmillan).

Verdier, D. (1998) 'Democratic Convergence and Free Trade', *International Studies Quarterly* 41(1): 1–24.

Wallach, L. and Woodall, P. (2004) *Whose Trade Organization? – A Comprehensive Guide to the WTO* (New York: The New Press).

Waterman, P. (2001) *Globalization, Social Movements and the New Internationalisms* (London: Continuum).

Watson, M. (2005) *Foundations of International Political Economy* (Basingstoke: Palgrave Macmillan).

Weale, A. (1999) *Democracy* (Basingstoke: Macmillan).

Weiss, T. (1986) *Multilateral Development Diplomacy in UNCTAD – The Lessons of Group Negotiations, 1964–84* (Basingstoke: Macmillan).

Wilkinson, M. (1996) 'Lobbying for Fair Trade: Northern NGDOs, the European Community and the GATT Uruguay Round', *Third World Quarterly* 17(2): 251–67.

Wilkinson, R. (1999) 'Labour and Trade-related Regulation: Beyond the Trade-labour Standards Debate?' *British Journal of Politics and International Relations* 1(2): 165–91.

——(2002a) 'The World Trade Organization', *New Political Economy* 7(1): 129–41.

——(2002b) 'Peripheralizing Labour – The ILO, WTO and the Completion of the Bretton Woods Project', in J. Harrod and R. O'Brien (ed.) *Global Unions? – Theory and Strategies of Organized Labour in the Global Political Economy* (London: Routledge), 204–20.

——(2005) 'Managing Global Civil Society – The WTO's Engagement with NGOs', in R. Germain and M. Kenny (eds) *The Idea of Global Civil Society – Politics and Ethics in a Globalizing Era* (London: Routledge), 156–99.

——(2006) *The WTO – Crisis and the Governance of Global Trade* (London: Routledge).

Williams, M. (1999) 'The World Trade Organisation, Social Movements and "Democracy"', in A. Taylor and C. Thomas (eds) *Global Trade and Global Social Issues* (London: Routledge), 151–69.

Winham, G. and Lanoszka, A. (2000) 'Institutional Development of the WTO', in A. Rugman and G. Boyd (eds) *The World Trade Organization in the New Global Economy* (Cheltenham: Edward Elgar), 23–45.

Winters, L. (1990) 'The Road to Uruguay', *The Economic Journal* 100(403): 1288–303.

Wolman, P. (1992) *Most Favored Nation – The Republican Revisionists and US Tariff Policy, 1897–1912* (Chapel Hill: The University of North Carolina Press).

Woods, N. (2002) 'Global Governance and the Role of Institutions', in D. Held and A. McGrew (eds) *Governing Globalisation – Power, Authority and Global Governance* (Cambridge: Polity Press), 25–45.

WTO Secretariat (1999) *High Level Symposium on Trade and Development – Geneva, 17–18 March 1999* (WTO Publications: Geneva), 12, www.wto.org/english/tratop_e/devel_e/tr_dvbadoc_e.doc (accessed February 2013).

——(2001) *Guide to the GATS – An Overview of Issues for Further Liberalization of Trade-in-Services* (Geneva: World Trade Organization; London: Kluwer Law International).

——(2002) 'Democracy, Development and the WTO – Speech by Director-General Mike Moore', 26 March, www.wto.org/english/news_e/spmm_e/spmm82_e.htm (accessed February 2013).

——(2003) *10 Common Misunderstandings about the WTO* (Geneva: WTO Publications), April, www.wto.org/english/thewto_e/whatis_e/10mis_e/10m00_e.htm (accessed February 2013).

——(2004) *The Future of the WTO – Addressing Institutional Challenges in the New Millennium*, report by the Consultative Board to the Director-General Supachai Panitchpakdi (Geneva: WTO Publications), www.wto.org/english/thewto_e/10anniv_e/future_wto_e.htm (accessed February 2013).

——(2008) *10 Common Misunderstandings about the WTO*, fourth edn (Geneva: WTO Publications), www.wto.org/English/thewto_e/whatis_e/tif_e/tif_e.htm (accessed February 2013).

Young, O. (1986) 'International Regimes: Toward a New Theory of Institutions', *World Politics* 39(1): 104–22.

Zehfuss, M. (2002) *Constructivism in International Relations: The Politics of Reality* (Cambridge: Cambridge University Press).

Zeiler, T. (1999) *Free Trade – Free World: The Advent of GATT* (Chapel Hill: University of North Carolina Press).

Žižek, S. (1989) *The Sublime Object of Ideology* (London: Verso).

Index

Action Aid 119, 175
actor/agency 2, 3, 4–7, 23, 138, 178;
    business 4–7; discourse theory 17, 19,
    101, 138 (subject positioning 26–27;
    subject positions/political subjectivity
    distinction 16); globalization 6–7, 103;
    Member state 4, 5–6, 102, 177; NGO
    4–7, 103, 105; trade union 5–6; Venn
    diagram 4, 5; WTO Secretariat 4, 5, 6;
    see also Member state; NGO
agreements, conventions, treaties 19, 28,
    66; Atlantic Charter 37; Cobden-
    Chevalier treaty 31; Creation of an
    International Union for the Publication
    of Customs Tariffs 66; Geneva
    Convention on Import and Export
    Prohibitions and Restrictions 32;
    Long-Term Agreement on Common
    Textiles 46; Multifibre Agreement 51,
    55, 61; 'single undertaking'/'single
    package' approach 7; see also GATS;
    GATT; Marrakech Agreement
agriculture 34, 55, 61, 89, 145;
    protectionism 17, 58, 91
American Express 6, 103
anti-GATS campaigning 21, 138–76;
    democracy 142, 143, 153, 171;
    developing country 142, 159, 160, 161,
    166; EU/European Commission 156,
    157, 158–59, 162; GATS, critique of
    22, 141–52, 171 (domestic regulation
    142, 144, 170; liberalization of services
    141, 142, 159, 166, 170; mainstreaming
    a GATS critique 150–52); health 143,
    150–51, 154; MAI 138, 141, 142,
    143–45, 149, 156; 'Public Services,
    Globalization and Sustainability in an
    Enlarged Europe' 166–67; Seattle
    Ministerial Conference 138, 141, 142,
    143, 144, 145, 146, 147, 149, 152, 161;
    water services 140, 141, 163, 164, 165,
    176; WTO: *GATS–Fact and Fiction*
    155–56, 173; *see also* anti-GATS
    campaigning/mobilization
anti-GATS campaigning/mobilization
    139, 144, 158–60, 164, 180, 184;
    Austria 162–63; campaigning as
    multi-pronged 160–64; Canada 144,
    156, 158, 159, 161; collective action 22,
    139, 140, 144, 152, 169, 173, 180;
    collective identity, emergence of 22,
    139–40; difficulties for campaigning
    165–66; education 142–43, 148–49,
    162, 170, 171; end of political
    mobilization 164–67 (mid-2005 cut-off
    point 169–70); equivalential chain 140,
    142, 143, 145–46, 149, 152, 154, 159
    (elasticity of equivalential chains
    167–69; sedimentation of anti-GATS
    equivalential chain 152–58); European
    identity 158–59, 174; New Zealand
    142, 143, 158; reports and analysis 142,
    143, 144, 148, 150, 151, 155–56, 164,
    169, 176, 180; trade union 143, 149,
    156, 157, 158, 161, 165, 175, 176; *see
    also* CEO; EI; FoE; global group
    petition; Internet/e-mail list;
    NGO/WTO interaction; OWINFS;
    P&P; Polaris Institute; PSI; S2B; trade
    union; UK
articulation 14, 19, 20, 22; articulation
    process 19, 21, 22, 92, 94, 169, 179,
    185; non-static nature 27; rearticulation
    19, 20, 29, 65, 179, 180 (global trade
    governance 25–26, 32, 56–61, 64, 65,
    77, 125, 133, 179–80); trade in services
    57–61; WTO 21, 92, 94, 168, 179–80,
    184 (rearticulation 21, 69, 77–78, 84,
    92, 94, 112, 117, 180, 184); *see also*
    discourse theory